TV Drama in China

Hong Kong University Press thanks Xu Bing for writing the Press's name in his Square Word Calligraphy for the covers of its books. For further information, see p. iv.

TransAsia: Screen Cultures

Edited by Koichi IWABUCHI and Chris BERRY

What is Asia? What does it mean to be Asian? Who thinks they are Asian? How is "Asian-ness" produced? In Asia's transnational public space, many kinds of cross-border connections proliferate, from corporate activities to citizen-to-citizen linkages, all shaped by media — from television series to action films, video piracy, and a variety of subcultures facilitated by internet sites and other computer-based cultures. Films are packaged at international film festivals and marketed by DVD companies as "Asian," while the descendents of migrants increasingly identify themselves as "Asian," then turn to "Asian" screen cultures to find themselves and their roots. As reliance on national frameworks becomes obsolete in many traditional disciplines, this series spotlights groundbreaking research on trans-border, screen-based cultures in Asia.

Other titles in the series:

The Chinese Exotic: Modern Diasporic Femininity, by Olivia Khoo

East Asian Pop Culture: Analysing the Korean Wave, edited by Chua Beng Huat and Koichi Iwabuchi

TV Drama in China

Edited by

Ying Zhu, Michael Keane, and Ruoyun Bai

香港大學出版社

HONG KONG UNIVERSITY PRESS

Hong Kong University Press
14/F Hing Wai Centre
7 Tin Wan Praya Road
Aberdeen
Hong Kong

Hardback   ISBN 978-962-209-940-1
Paperback   ISBN 978-962-209-941-8

British Library Cataloguing-in-Publication Data
A catalogue record for this book is available from the British Library.

Secure On-line Ordering
http://www.hkupress.org

Printed and bound by Kings Time Printing Press Ltd., Hong Kong, China.

Hong Kong University Press is honoured that Xu Bing, whose art explores the complex themes of language across cultures, has written the Press's name in his Square Word Calligraphy. This signals our commitment to cross-cultural thinking and the distinctive nature of our English-language books published in China.

"At first glance, Square Word Calligraphy appears to be nothing more unusual than Chinese characters, but in fact it is a new way of rendering English words in the format of a square so they resemble Chinese characters. Chinese viewers expect to be able to read Square Word Calligraphy but cannot. Western viewers, however are surprised to find they can read it. Delight erupts when meaning is unexpectedly revealed."

— Britta Erickson, *The Art of Xu Bing*

Contents

Notes on Contributors

Ruoyun BAI is an assistant professor in the Department of Humanities (Scarborough) and the Centre for Comparative Literature at the University of Toronto. Her research interests include television criticism, television drama in the global context, media institutions and practices in East Asia, and digital media. She has published in the *Global Media Journal* and *Studies in Symbolic Interaction*. She is completing a book on Chinese anti-corruption television dramas. She was assistant professor of Media, Culture, and Communication of New York University from 2007 to 2008.

Rong CAI is an associate professor of Chinese at Emory University, Atlanta, USA. Her recent publications include *The Subject in Crisis in Contemporary Chinese Literature* (2004) and "Gender imaginations in *Crouching Tiger, Hidden Dragon* and the *Wuxia* World," *positions* (2005) 13(2).

Yi-Hsiang CHEN is an associate professor in the Department of Public Relations and Advertising at Shih Hsin University, Taiwan. She has received grants from Taiwan's National Science Council for a research project in media diversity. Her current research interests include diversity studies in television programming, prime-time TV dramas, and language variety in Taiwan TV programs. Her English-language publications include a chapter co-authored with Liu Yu-Li in *Television Across Asia: Television Industries, Programme Formats and Globalization,* edited by Albert Moran and Michael Keane (2004).

Carol CHOW is a doctoral student in communication at the Chinese University of Hong Kong.

Ya-chien HUANG is currently a researcher at National Centre for Social Research in London and a PhD candidate at the Communication Research Centre of Loughborough University. While finishing her thesis on the processes of cultural globalization and regionalization in Asian popular culture through detailed studies of young (female) audiences and consumers, she has published in *Asian Women* and has contributed to *Media Consumption and Everyday Life in Asia* (2008), edited by Youna Kim.

Michael KEANE is an associate professor and senior research fellow at the Australian Research Council Centre of Excellence for Creative Industries and Innovation at Queensland University of Technology. His research interests are creative industries and urban regeneration policy in China, media industry development in China, South Korea, and Taiwan; and television formats in Asia. His most recent book is *Created in China: The Great New Leap Forward* (2007).

Shuyu KONG teaches at Simon Fraser University, Canada. Her research interests include modern Chinese literature, film, and popular culture. Her most recent publication is *Consuming Literature: Best Sellers and the Commercialization of Literary Production in Contemporary China* (2005). She is currently working in the areas of genre film and television drama.

Dong-Hoo LEE is an associate professor in the Department of Mass Communication at the University of Incheon, Korea. She obtained her PhD degree from New York University. After moving back to Korea, she briefly worked with the Seoul Broadcasting System, and has written several articles on the hybrid nature of media culture in Korea. Her research interests include medium theory and local media culture. Her English-language publications include a chapter in *Television Across Asia: Television Industries, Programme Formats and Globalization,* edited by Albert Moran and Michael Keane (2004).

Eric MA is a professor at the School of Journalism and Communication at the Chinese University of Hong Kong. He is the author of *Culture, Politics and Television in Hong Kong* (1997) and the co-author of *Hong Kong, China: Learning to Belong to a Nation* (2008). He has written 15 books in Chinese on the popular culture of Hong Kong and South China. His articles have appeared in journals including the *China Review, Visual Anthropology, Cultural Studies, International Journal of Cultural Studies, Asian Journal of Communication, Social Text, Positions, Gazette,* and *Inter-Asia Cultural Studies.*

Di MIAO currently serves as dean of the Literature School at the Communication University of China, and is vice chairman of the *Contemporary Film Magazine* editing committee, Plurality Professor of Beijing Pedagogic University and Capital Pedagogic University, adviser to Hubei Television Station and Dalian Television Station, and committee representative for the National Golden Eagle Awards and Starlight Awards for Chinese Television. His books include *Study on Comparison Between the Art of Chinese Television and that of American Television* (2005); *Reading Television* (2004); *American TV Dramas, On Popular Culture: Analysis of Genre of American TV Dramas* (2004), and *Television: A Media Students' Guide* (2003).

Gong QIAN is an associate lecturer in the Department of Languages and Intercultural Education at Curtin University of Technology. She is also a doctoral candidate in the Faculty of Media, Society and Culture at Curtin. Her research interest is in Chinese media and popular culture.

Wanning SUN is an associate professor at Curtin University, Australia. She was a visiting professor at State University of New York, Binghamton (2005–06). She researches on media, migration, and gendered mobility. Her works include *Leaving China* (2002), *Media and the Chinese Diaspora: Communication, Commerce and Commerce* (2006) and *Maid in China: Media, Morality and the Cultural Politics of Boundaries* (forthcoming).

Janice Hua XU is an assistant professor in the Department of Communication at Cabrini College, Pennsylvania. Her research interests include cultural studies, media globalization, and gender and communication. She has published in *Journalism Studies, Outlook,* and *Media, Culture, and Society,* and contributed chapters to several books on Chinese mass media. Her current research project focuses on consumer culture and television in China.

Li ZENG is an assistant professor of film studies in the School of Theater at Illinois State University. She received her PhD in screen culture from the Department of Radio, Television, and Film at Northwestern University, US. She has published articles in China on literary theory and media studies. Her research interests include popular culture, the representation of history in contemporary visual culture, feminist theory, and film and television history.

Ying ZHU is an associate professor of Media Culture and Co-coordinator of Modern China Program at the College of Staten Island, the City University of New York. A recipient of the American Research in the Humanities in China Fellowship (2007–08) and the 2006 Fellow of National Endowment for the Humanities, she has written extensively on Chinese film and television. Her publications have appeared in leading media journals such as *Cinema Journal, Quarterly Review of Film and Video, Journal of Communication* and various edited volumes. She is the author of *Chinese Cinema during the Era of Reform: The Ingenuity of the System* (2003) and *Television in Post-Reform China: Dynasty Drama, Confucian Leadership and Global Television Market* (2008). Her co-edited books, *TV China* (with Chris Berry) and *Chinese Cinema after a Century: The Interplay of Art, Politics and Commerce* (with Stanley Rosen), are forthcoming. She serves as a Chinese media expert and contributor for *New York Times'* "China Studies" website.

Introduction

Ying Zhu, Michael Keane, and Ruoyun Bai

In the decade prior to China joining the World Trade Organization in December 2001, Chinese television producers began to measure success and failure, not so much from a political yardstick, but in comparison to market expectations. Foreign programs were feeding into the system, finding enthusiastic audiences, and challenging the style of local production. By 2001, moreover, the technological possibilities of the medium were becoming increasingly evident. Digital channels, multi-platform programming, new formats, niche channels and short message service (SMS) interactivity were creating new demands for more programming and greater variety. However, despite an increase in formats and genres — including reality TV, quiz, and game shows — drama has retained pre-eminence in viewing schedules. Research estimates that the "Chinese viewer" watches an average of fifty-two minutes of television drama per day — a diet constituting more than 30 percent of overall television consumption. The status of television drama is reflected in advertising: in 2002, 90 percent of all revenue from television advertising came from television drama.[1] Although drama's domination of advertising is now challenged by reality and "factual" television formats, drama production remains central to the viability of China's large but fragmented television industry.

Chinese Television Drama as a Research Topic

The pre-eminence of TV drama consumption in China contrasts sharply with the scant academic attention accorded Chinese TV drama. Aside from a few studies of the distribution of Chinese videos in diaspora markets, and occasional book chapters and journal articles — many of which refer to television serial drama either within the context of social reforms or as cultural discourse and anthropological text — we know very little about Chinese television drama as a distinctive narrative form within the parameters of political economy and its role in sustaining Chinese television as a cultural institution.[2]

Some recent scholarship has begun the task of providing formal analysis — in this instance, the historical dramatic text — both from a comparative perspective and by examining this genre's role in cultivating Chinese prime-time drama as an economically viable and culturally significant enterprise.[3] Overall, though, the production and consumption of television drama in China has received only passing attention in the English-speaking academy.

The institutional and cultural contexts of television dramas, their narrative and stylistic intricacies, and the complex relationships between popular dramatic programs and their viewers have been at the center of television research in the West since the mid-1970s. Ethnographic studies have chronicled the different receptions of *Dallas* and *Dynasty* in Europe and the Middle East.[4] Television serials from the United States, United Kingdom, Australia, Brazil, Mexico, and Venezuela have likewise attracted academic scrutiny.[5] Writers have further redefined drama within the hybrid forms of docu-soap, factual television, and *téléroman*.[6] In the past few years, however, the focus of attention has begun to recognize the importance of TV drama in East Asia. In 2004, the first critical anthology concerning Japanese drama appeared; this contribution to the field examined "trendy dramas," arguing that they extended the nature of Japanese cultural power and influence in the East Asian region.[7]

The first international publication dedicated to Chinese television drama was an edited volume, *Television Drama: Chinese and US Perspectives* by Chunjin Qu and Ying Zhu.[8] Published in Chinese in 2005, with contributions from leading television scholars in China and the United States, this collection of essays approached television drama as a narrative form, as social discourse and as a tradeable cultural commodity. In addition, the volume adopted a comparative framework that foregrounded similarities and differences between both TV drama, and the study of TV drama, in the People's Republic of China (PRC) and the United States. The limited scope of this volume, however, left little room for the discussion of the circulation of East Asia trans-border dramas from Japan, Hong Kong, Korea, and Taiwan; fashion and fads of particular genres against the backdrop of a Chinese television industry in transition; and the continued exploration of TV drama's story-telling and discourse-generating functions during an era of unprecedented social, cultural, and economic reform.[9]

Chinese TV Drama as a Narrative Form

The lack of research on Chinese television serial drama is even more conspicuous considering the extensive literature on Chinese cinema. Writers have examined its ontology, the nature of authorship, generic conventions, and expectations in relation to Hollywood films, its particular stylistic traits, and ideological interpretations of texts. Such issues also pertain to our study of Chinese television drama as a distinctive narrative form, especially since Chinese TV drama has replaced Chinese cinema as the number one myth-making engine in popular culture. Despite this repositioning, Chinese television drama draws many of its codes, conventions, and narrative strategies from cinema. Indeed, many popular prime-time dramas are being made by prominent film directors and feature well-known movie stars. The cross-fertilization between Chinese film and television practitioners and critics/scholars is unprecedented due to reforms in media production that allow filmmakers to moonlight in TV and vice versa.

The close relationship between Chinese film and television, however, should not elide the specificity of television as a powerful story-telling medium and mode of address. Film criticism took the individual, autonomous cinematic text as its primary object of study — a practice that conforms to the economic logic of commercial cinema, wherein each individual pays to see a given feature film at a particular time and place. Yet the mode of viewer engagement with television and the economic logic of commercial broadcasting are different. In the West since the 1960s, and in China since the early 1990s, television has rarely organized dramatic programming in terms of a series of anthology dramas. Rather, the emblematic narrative form of television drama has been the episodic series of hour-long or half-hour programs featuring the same cast, setting, and dramatic tension; or the serial form, which develops multiple narrative lines across multiple episodes that might be broadcast over a period of time — long or short.

In both variations, however, the fundamental plan is to establish continuity. In the television series, continuity is maintained through building familiarity with characters and their relationship to the environment, sometimes a domestic setting, at other times a hospital or a police station. In the second context — and this is more relevant to China — there is a strong sense of seriality that resonates with popular story-telling traditions, great tales of adventure and intrigue such as *The Dream of the Red Chamber* (*Honglou meng*, 1986), *The Water Margin* (*Shuihu zhuan*, 1998), and *The Romance of the Three Kingdoms* (*Sanguo yanyi*, 1994), to name a few. This organization of television drama as a recurrent set of multiple "moments" of textual presentation and audience engagement over periods of time has challenged television scholars to develop new analytical strategies for dealing with the unique textuality of television.

Television drama in China has developed in tandem with social reforms, embracing international ideas as well as celebrating tradition. In May 1958, Beijing Television broadcast the first Chinese television drama, a single-act play transposed to the small screen. *A Mouthful of Vegetable Pancake* (*Yikou caibingzi*) symbolized the television's role as a new technology of political education.[10] While television was initially a curiosity confined to the larger cities, the Chinese TV audience immediately saw itself reflected as the new subject of TV drama; its members constituted an imagined community seemingly on the verge of creating the great society; their story was now available for domestic consumption. Compared with today's multi-vocal dramas, this first teleplay was basic propaganda. At the time, however, it was a narrative close to people's lives. The elder sister of a peasant family chides her younger sister for sharing food with a dog, telling her of an earlier time when they were younger, before the Communist triumph of 1949. The second daughter had asked a landlord for help, only to be set upon by his dogs. Returning home, the only food available was a single vegetable pancake, which the girls' widowed mother refused to eat, insisting that the younger sister should have it. In keeping with the Communist Party's development goals at the time, this was a lesson about frugality and class struggle.

From 1958 until 1966, Beijing Television and newly established stations in Shanghai, Guangzhou, Tianjin, Xi'an, Wuhan, and Changchun broadcast almost two hundred television dramas. Beijing Television alone originated ninety of these dramas.[11] Writers moved from stage plays to television plays. The first serial drama (*lianxuju*) appeared on Chinese television screens in February 1981, a time when overseas serials were finding their way into viewing schedules in China. *Eighteen Years in the Enemy Camp* (*Diying shiba nian*) was a nine-episode action-thriller serial produced by the national broadcaster. It failed to win over the local audience. According to critics, this failure was not due to audience unfamiliarity with the serial form —

viewers already had tasted overseas dramas — but its rather clumsy attempt to imitate the overseas action genre. The stimulation for the TV serial format in Mainland China needs to be understood therefore in the context of successful imported dramas, such as *A Doubtful Blood Type* (*Xueyi*: Japan 1980), *Huo Yuanjia* (Hong Kong 1982), *Stars Know My Heart* (*Xingxing zhi woxin*, Taiwan 1988), *Last Night's Stars* (*Zuoye xingchen*, Taiwan 1988), *Isaura the Slave* (*Nünu*, Brazil 1984), *Slander* (*Feibang*, Mexico 1985) and *Frustration* (*Kanke*, Mexico 1986).

Sensing a need to reward local quality, the National Association of Television Drama, in conjunction with the Ministry of Radio and Television (hereafter, MRFT, predecessor of the State Administration of Radio, Film and Television, or SARFT), instituted an annual award ceremony for outstanding television drama in 1982. By the third award ceremony, this had been proclaimed as the Feitian award. Nevertheless, there were already some indications of China's competitive advantage within Asia. In 1982, Shandong Television produced a highly acclaimed adaptation of the popular classic *The Water Margin* (*Shuihu zhuan*), stimulating television dramas based on popular legends. In 1986, a rendition of the Qing classic *The Dream of the Red Chamber* (*Hongloumeng*) was followed a year later by a dramatization of the popular tale *Journey to the West* (*Xiyouji*, 1987).

During the 1980s, narratives of social change were the dominant themes.[12] By the turn of the decade, however, the focus had turned from social injustices toward the more secular concerns of living in an increasingly competitive and less egalitarian society. Unsurprisingly, in the context of China's political struggles, there was a steady supply of historical dramas (*lishi ticai*), dealing with epic themes and the lives of great leaders and patriots. During the 1980s and 1990s, such depictions were required to maintain an adherence to official historiography. However, other genres emerged as a result of social and economic reforms, expressing social conflicts. This social commentary category bore the weight of China's social reform agenda. An important and well-documented example of this category was the 1986 serial *New Star* (*Xin xing*), about cadre politics.[13]

These kinds of productions are sometimes referred to as realist drama. In the sense that they reflect social change in the tradition of socialist realism, Chinese television critics have made use of a musical term, the "main melody" (*zhuxuanlü*). The main melody is a synthesis of theme and CCP ideology. The official slogan, "propagate the main melody and uphold diversity," was formulated at the 1987 National Conference for Cinematic Production and promptly taken up by propaganda and cultural departments, as well as by the literary establishment and television producers.[14] In the 1980s and 1990s, those serials that "upheld" the main melody had more success in winning the coveted *feitian* award.

The early 1990s witnessed a short-lived period of innovation. The commercial impetus that coincided with the reduction of state funds for the media unleashed a wave of new money in television and film, often from multiple sources: non-media organizations, advertising companies, personal loans, and *guanxi* networks (personal contacts and favors). Themes of authority emerged, highlighting class reversals in the new society in which people could prosper. The power of the home-grown television serial to stop a nation was demonstrated in 1990. Guangdong Television's *Public Relations Girls* (*Gongguan xiaojie*) beat out even its Hong Kong competitors, peaking with a market share of 90 percent.[15] In the same year, the Beijing Television Arts Center's *Yearning* (*Kewang*) created an unprecedented response (see Chapter 5, this volume). This fifty-episode serial was conceived by a group of writers including novelists Zheng Wanlong and Wang Shuo, script editor Li Xiaoming and Beijing Television Arts Center director Chen Changben.[16] The impetus for this production reportedly came from the success in China of the Japanese drama *Oshin*.

Following the broadcast of *Yearning*, Li Ruihuan, the Politburo member responsible for culture and ideology, praised the serial for providing a new model of social relations which represented "socialist ethics and morals." Li's commendation was subsequently taken up by Ai Zhisheng, the Minister for Radio, Film and Television at the time, who asserted that the success was due to the producers having an awareness of the needs of Chinese viewers.[17] With *Yearning* receiving official endorsement and attention from overseas Chinese, television drama began to attract a new kind of critical attention. In 1991, *The Enlightenment Daily* (*Guangming Ribao*), China's "intellectual" newspaper, published *The Shock Wave of Yearning* (*Kewang chongjibo*), which contained forty-seven articles about the serial as well as interviews with the producers and writers, letters from viewers, and comments from officials.[18] In a forum held in 1993 to discuss the effect of the new popular dramas on the established morality of audiences, Lu Xiaowei, the director of *Yearning*, was direct about the educative role of television drama:

> What kind of thing is it that can put bums on seats? It's something that doesn't need a lot of effort or attention, something not too dense. But does this necessarily lack intellectualism, taste or a pedagogical component? I don't see it this way. We tend to look at things too seriously. If you think you could include everything from the dawn of time to now in a television serial, you're full of yourself! You think yourself so elegant, so good, but nobody watches. This is just bullshit![19]

The following years saw a change in direction and the emergence of several new genres.[20] The dominant genre was undoubtedly costume drama: in which characters are dressed in pre-modern costumes and tell stories that purportedly occurred in pre-1911 China. Although historical drama was produced as early as the 1980s, in keeping with the need for educational propaganda, the costume drama rapidly gained momentum after 1993. In this year a Hong Kong-produced drama *Tales About Qian Long* (*Xishuo qianlong*: Hong Kong, 1991) was broadcast. This serial depicted Emperor Qianlong's encounters with several beautiful courtesans during his "undercover" royal visits to South China. In the eyes of historians it was scandalous, a perverse distortion of history. However, its enormous popularity indicated to Mainland drama producers that there was a market in the Chinese past. In 1996, another costume drama followed, set in the same Qing Court of Qianlong. *Hunchback Liu, the Prime Minister* (*Zaixiang Liu Luoguo*), seized the popular imagination with tales of the valiant prime minister of the day cleverly fighting against court corruption. In 1998, *Princess Huanzhu* (*Huanzhu gege*), a co-production between Hunan TV (the provincial television station of Hunan Province) and Zhongjie Cultural Communication Co., a Taiwan-based talent agency, became the hit of the year. The story concerns the identities of a real and a fake princess. The fake princess named Huanzhu, played by Zhao Wei whose popularity soared following the broadcast, is a pretty, free-spirited girl with no formal education, and her clumsy encounters with the imperial family provide an unfailing source of entertainment for many viewers. The following years witnessed a steady stream of both costume and historical dramas. In 1999, historical dramas (all stories set in pre-1911 China) accounted for 10.7 percent of all productions. In 2000 this had risen to 21.6 percent; the following year it was 24.8 percent.[21] In the broadcast schedules, historical dramas made up the largest proportion of content between 7.00 pm to 9.30 pm. Provincial and city stations, seemingly unrestrained by quota regulations, broadcast considerably more historical dramas than the national broadcaster, CCTV.[22]

The pre-eminence of historical content on Chinese television can be attributed to several factors. First, official censors apply different standards to these dramas, in comparison with contemporary stories. As their narratives are ostensibly distanced from the modern history of the Chinese Communist Party, they are inclined to use comedy and satire to expose bureaucratic absurdities in the imperial government. Viewers are quick to see the resemblance between the realities of the twenty-first century and times past. Some historical dramas play on nationalism: connecting the grandeur and glory of ancient China to current-day fascinations with China's emergence.

Importantly however, historical dramas are usually laced with conspiracies and power struggles, themes that hold strong appeal for a large segment of viewers. Historical dramas interweave the past with the present; in the process they create complex scenarios that produce multiple levels of identification. Their role in the innovation of Chinese television content should not be underestimated: they have absorbed and nurtured creative and critical talent. In this sense, it can be argued that they have acted as a buffer zone for Chinese television, a kind of an incubator of critical discourse.

The only development comparable to costume drama was a surge of interest in tales of corruption and crime. Since the late 1970s, the Chinese government has worked to build a legal system to meet the needs of reform. Television, by then the dominant media, became the means of promoting the powerful image of law enforcement institutions, together with promoting legal consciousness among the audience. Dramas about public security officers pursuing criminals began to appear in the 1980s. During the 1990s these stories took a back seat to historical dramas. After 2000, however, crime dramas rocketed. Some crime dramas blended detective elements with sentimental love stories in order to attract more female and young viewers. The writer Hai Yan was instrumental in creating this subgenre of crime drama. His work includes *A Romantic Story* (*Yichang fenghua xueyue de shi*, 1997), *I'll Never Close My Eyes* (*Yongbu mingmu*, 2000), *How Can I Save You, My Love* (*Na shenme zhengjiu ni, wode airen*, 2003), *Jade Budda* (*Yu guanyin*, 2003). Other crime dramas are more conventional detective stories. The theme of corruption was also linked to the surge of crime drama. In 1995, CCTV broadcast *Heavens Above* (*Cangtian zaishang*) during its prime-time evening slots. This drama was purportedly the first television drama about high-level official corruption to appear in China. The political imperative of fighting corruption provided the backdrop for huge audience appeal. The so-called "anti-corruption drama" genre established its credibility. Anti-corruption dramas and crime dramas forged ahead, arm in arm as it were, although the former never became an official category.

A penchant by producers to feature gory and violent crime scenes eventually forced the SARFT in 2004 to adopt a radical measure. It removed the entire crime drama genre from prime-time television. The ban aroused a great deal of criticism and resistance. Several months later, however, the SARFT adopted a more conciliatory approach, arguing that the ban was targeted at dramas that contained "violence, sex, gore and horror." By this time, crime dramas were making a comeback, albeit disguised under different designations such as "suspense drama" and "anti-espionage drama."

Aside from these two dominant drama genres, there are a number of other noteworthy developments. Since the late 1990s, dramas about everyday life have gained enormous followings. While small in number, these dramas are very influential. The most successful have been *Holding Hands* (*Qianshou*, 1999), *Garrulous Zhang Damin's Happy Life* (*Pinzui Zhang Damin de xingfu shenghuo*, 2000), *Mirror* (*Kong jingzi*, 2002), *Elder Brother* (*Dage*, 2002) and *Love Tree* (*Qinqing shu*, 2003). Evoking a melodramatic turn, these are tales of ordinary people braving life's vicissitudes. A dominant motif is that life is hard, but with love, patience and perseverance, there will be a better tomorrow.

In 2001, *Those Days of Passion* (*jiqing ranshao de suiyue*), a story about a retired army officer and his family life spanning more than three decades was a smash hit. This was quickly followed by several other popular dramas about army officers of the People's Liberation Army: *Soldiers' Secrets* (*Junren jimi*, 2004), *Brothers* (*Lishi de tiankong*, 2004) and *Draw Your Sword* (*Liang jian*, 2005). Of all the dramas on CCTV in 2005, *Draw Your Sword* was the most popular, with an average audience share of 10.3 percent.[23] Compared with earlier conventional military-theme dramas, this subgenre strives for entertainment value, breaking away from conventional images and storylines about military heroes by combining spectacles of war with the hero's personal life and interpersonal relationships.

Despite the persistent push of the government for more portrayal of rural life on Chinese television, drama producers and television stations (excepting CCTV) have generally avoided dramas in rural settings. These are considered ratings-killers. This presents an enduring problem for a government that regards television as a crucial means of reaching farmers, the majority of the Chinese population. Despite audience aversion to peasant stories, a series of rural drama serials attracted hundreds of millions of viewers across the nation between 2002 and 2006. The creative force was Zhao Benshan, a leading Chinese comedian who produced, directed, and acted in these dramas: *Liu Laogen* (2003) and *Ma Dashuai* (2004). Both of these had sequels. *Liu Laogen* is about a retired party secretary of a rural village who has started a tourism business that transforms the poverty-stricken but beautiful village into a money-spinning tourist spot. *Ma Dashuai* is about a former village head and his adventures in a city where his daughter, who escaped from an arranged marriage on the wedding day, works as a waitress at a hotel. The stories are ultimately about encounters between rural backwardness and urban modernity. By cleverly incorporating humour, narratives about farmers become acceptable to the urban market.

Regulatory Issues, Uncertain Development, and Internationalization

In the latter half of the 1990s and beyond, Chinese television drama production has been subjected to an increasingly intense control by the market and by the government. Intensified commercialization is driven by two related factors: first, private capital now dominates television drama production by accounting for 80 percent of the total annual investment in drama production nationwide; second, television stations primarily — if not entirely — depend on their drama programs for advertising revenue, which in turn accounts for about 90 percent of the total annual revenues for the stations. Therefore advertisers, television stations, production companies, and to some extent the SARFT share common ground in television drama commercialization.

The expanded role for the market by no means leads to a reduced regulatory power of the state. In fact, what we have witnessed in the last few years has been the reassertion of content control by a combination of legal and administrative means supplemented now and then by personal intervention from the top leadership. The current regulatory regimes are largely defined by the Broadcast Regulations (*Guangbo dianshi guanli tiaoli*), enacted in 1997, the Provisional Regulations on Television Drama Censorship (*Dianshiju shencha zanxing guiding*) of 1999, and the Television Drama Regulations (*Dianshiju guanli guiding*) of 2000.

The net effect of these regulations is that the state maximizes control over television drama production from the initial stage of conception to screening. Very briefly, a television drama script has to pass an initial proposal review by SARFT, be produced by a licensed television drama unit, pass the end-product censorship by SARFT or its local affiliated bureau, and receive a distribution licence. Licences to produce television drama have only in the past few years been granted to private companies. However, initial screening does not necessarily guarantee that a drama will continue — if it incurs the displeasure of the party leadership, it runs a real risk of being taken off the air or at least being subject to major revisions.

Since the mid-1990s, within the terms set by the state and the market, Chinese television drama has experienced strong growth and great transformations. Annual drama production steadily grew and genre dramas flourished. The following categorization of genres adopted by industry analysts provides evidence of how much Chinese television drama has diversified in this period. CSM, a CCTV audience research joint venture with the French company SOFRES, has identified three major categories of television dramas: pre-modern, modern, and the Republican era. Pre-modern dramas include "legendary tales," "martial arts," "historical events," "law and justice," and "gods and ghosts." Modern dramas encompass "urban life," "crime," "ordinary folks," "reform," "military revolutions," "trendy drama," "sitcoms and dramas in local dialects," and "children's drama." Finally, in the category of Republican dramas there are "sentimental love drama," "action drama" and "drama that reflects the vicissitude of the Republican period."

These are useful industrial classifications that capture the evolution of drama since the mid-1990s. However, we are not endorsing or adopting any specific methodology of genre classification in this study; when individual contributors discuss genre dramas, they will establish rationales for naming such genres. Therefore, instead of dwelling on individual genres in this introduction, we highlight several major drama events of the past ten years. In addition, we have chosen to provide readers with a broad range of perspectives, including essays by scholars working on East Asian drama. For this reason, the contributions are concise and linked by thematic commonalities.

Tradition, History, and Politics

The chapters in this book are arranged into four sections. Part I looks at dramas that reflect ideology and continuity with the past. Ying Zhu's chapter examines history retold in revisionist Qing drama. This genre has dominated dramatic programming in prime time since the mid-1990s. Zhu examines factors conducive to the rise of the revisionist Qing drama and the ideological positioning of such dramas. She argues that the revisionist Qing drama is informed by post-1989 Tiananmen Square intellectual debates concerning the current state and future direction of China's march toward modernization and the ramifications of the march. Zhu uses the popular serial *Yongzheng Dynasty* (*Yongzheng wangchao*, 1999) as a case in point to illustrate how dynasty dramas have responded to the political and cultural ethos of the time.

Janice Hua Xu's chapter looks at popular "big family" serial dramas, analysing their themes and cultural significance in the context of China's modernization drive. Xu identifies several major lines of conflict in these dramas — between individual desire and family interest, between modernity and tradition, and between family life and national political turmoil. In these conflicts, the pursuit of romance and maintenance of family social status are often polarized and intertwined in the story development. Xu argues that such stories, situated in early twentieth-century China, actually address the concerns of contemporary viewers.

In the third chapter Ruoyun Bai examines a more contemporary canvas, anti-corruption dramas (*fanfu ju*). Through a context-sensitive textual analysis of an anti-corruption drama, *Pure as Snow* (*Daxue wuhen*, 2001), she demonstrates how a traditional Chinese cultural icon, Judge Bao (a fearless judge who pits himself against politically powerful criminals), is reinvigorated in contemporary dramatization of corruption scandals to create an emotional moral community. The emotion of anger is the hallmark of this fictional community. By appropriating the ownership of this community, the Party (represented by upright Party cadres and officials in the drama) attempts to reconstitute its moral leadership. In the meantime, as anger of the upright challenges the status quo, the text of the anti-corruption drama is not without tension. This chapter draws attention to the complexity of Chinese political dramas that can be easily dismissed as too propagandistic to be interesting.

Li Zeng then describes a "transnational period" in the 1990s. Several dramas captured popular attention by featuring either Chinese in a foreign country or foreigners in China. This chapter examines the emergence of this particular television program and its unique way of representing cultural encounters and foreign images. Li Zeng argues that the genre is the outcome of the Chinese media's adjustment to competition from the global television market, to the Chinese audience's desire to know the world beyond the national territory, to a new sense of gender and sexuality, and to the state's shifting ideology and concerns under the influence of globalization.

Gender and Domestic Sphere

In their pioneering 1978 book on television criticism, John Fiske and John Hartley refer to television as a medium for consensus-building.[24] They argue that television communicates "a confirming, reinforcing version" of a national culture. This notion of television as a vehicle through which a culture's collective values and concerns are reprocessed and reproduced through narrative depends on the centripetal force of a highly centralized national system of broadcasting bringing individuals together as "the" television audience. Echoing Raymond Williams' important legacy in television studies, Fiske and Hartley argue that television has become one of the central institutions of modern society — not only due to commercial monopoly or government control, but also because television has responded to a cultural need for a common center. In Williams' terms, television was a medium that brokered and maintained "structures of feelings." Its portrayal of social reality showed how aesthetic standards were influenced by political realities as well as by the mores, values, and rituals of everyday life.[25]

The explosion in channel capacity, however, has effectively decentralized the experience of television. Particularly in the mature media markets of the West, cable channel economics are frequently predicated upon social fractions and audience fragmentations. Entire channels can be organized around appeals to particular demographic groups, taste cultures, or other sub-audiences constructed around religion, ethnicity, or language groups. VCR and DVD players further inhibit the centripetal pull of television by separating the moment of broadcast from the moment of reception. In this new technological environment, TV drama presents a multiplicity of meanings, responding to real social events and shifts in cultural attitudes and values. Television drama in China functions as a "cultural forum," to adopt Newcomb and Hirsch's term, for millions of Chinese viewers to make sense of the rapid evolving culture.[26] As Newcomb and Hirsch put it, "contemporary cultures examine themselves through their arts": television drama in contemporary China provides a space for the society to engage in cultural debates about its citizens' most prevalent concerns and deepest dilemmas.[27]

The essays in Part II examine clashes of values in Chinese society. Shuyu Kong examines prime-time series that deal with love and marriage in the contemporary urban middle class family. She argues that family life and sexual relationships represented in these family dramas usually adopt narratives of mid-life crisis, extramarital affairs and marriage break-ups, and mirror a reality of moral collapse and unstable human relationships in a rapidly changing and morally ambivalent Chinese society. The chapter illustrates how gender relations and women's issues are expressed in popular culture via such family dramas. Wanning Sun's chapter gives us a different image of contemporary reality. She is concerned with public representations of private lives as they unfold in the urban family. Using the maid — a ubiquitous yet "invisible" figure in many television dramas — as a point of entry to modern family life in the city, Sun argues that, although peripheral in most narratives of urban life, the figure of the maid offers important clues to unravelling the dark side of the modern city in China.

Following this theme of gender, Ya-chien Huang looks at "pink dramas," a new subgenre reflecting the social empowerment of single women in modern Confucian societies. Huang explores elements of post-feminist irony in perplexing modern relationships, representations of the changing politics of femininity, as well as tensions between modern and traditional gender values faced by young single women. One style of pink drama in China and Taiwan closely follows the *Sex and the City* format (Home Box Office), portraying the friendships and relationships experienced by four single young female professionals. These programs are *Falling in Love* (*Haoxiang haoxiang tan lian'ai*)

(Beijing, 2003), *Mature Women's Diary* (*Shunü riji*) (Taipei, 2003), and *Pink Ladies* (*Fenhong nülang*) (Shanghai, 2003; Taipei, 2002). The discussion also follows the reception of *Sex and the City* in China and Taiwan.

Overall, textual analysis of a particular drama or a group of dramas in this section points to the density and complexity of contemporary Chinese television drama in its active engagement with pressing cultural and political issues. The dramas covered in this section are by no means a comprehensive collection, but the examples used offer glimpses of the significant role Chinese TV drama assumes in social and cultural debates in contemporary China.

Production, Reception, and Distribution

Part III examines how international genres and styles have exerted influence on the production of local content and export markets; the essays in this section also investigate how audiences have chosen to consume TV drama. Di Miao looks at the development of the Chinese sitcom from the highly satirical *Stories from an Editorial Office* (*Bianjibu de gushi*, 1992) in the early 1990s. Miao looks closely at two sitcoms, *I Love my Family* (*Wo ai wo jia*, 1993) and *Chinese Restaurant* (*Zhongguo canguan*, 1998) produced by Ying Da, who came into contact with the sitcom format while studying in the United States during the early 1990s. Miao argues that low-cost situation comedies have potential to be prime-time programs yet regulatory restrictions and quality issues associated with low budgets have prevented the sitcom from gaining a prime-time slot.

Rong Cai's chapter poses the timely question of what happens when TV dramas are consumed on DVD, tackling both the ideological and commercial significance of the DVD market of TV drama for contemporary society. Her chapter focuses on the DVD market for TV drama in China since the mid-1990s from the perspective of political economy. While TV drama remains the most popular item in contemporary Chinese television programming, another well-spread venue of its consumption is the multimedia market. According to official estimates, sales of VCDs and DVDs of TV drama generated approximately RMB 2.7 billion (US$346.2 million) annually in recent years, not including those of pirated versions estimated at ten times the volume of legal sales. Cai's chapter canvasses issues relating to state regulations and censorship, and in particular how these impact upon publication of multimedia versions of TV drama. She also addresses TV drama in VCD and DVD formats as commercial ventures, including DVD sales of domestically produced TV drama versus imported drama.

Apart from well-made classic tales, what has stopped Chinese drama from achieving international success? This important question needs to be considered in the context of what is now being termed China's "cultural trade deficit."[28] Since 1996, China's copyright imports have increased 57 percent annually, while cultural exports have struggled to make their mark even in culturally proximate regions such as Taiwan, South Korea, and Singapore. China's television dramas are illustrative of this trade deficit, a point taken up by Michael Keane, who argues that the deficit in terms of trade in television drama rights is symptomatic of a larger problem: how to produce "good content." China's domestic market is both large and fragmented, and this had led to an over-reliance on a supply model of production, in which cultural producers seek to replicate genres and formats rather than target lucrative export markets with imaginative content. Prior to China's accession to the World Trade Organization in 2001, critics of cultural globalization joined with cultural nationalist voices to express concerns about an impending "cultural invasion," arguing that market opening would seriously weaken China's audio-visual industries.[29] While openness to "foreign" content is more of a concern in cinema than in television, nevertheless this watershed event helped to focus attention on deficiencies in television market structure and the lack of outward sales of television content.

The final chapter in this section looks at how nostalgia for the revolutionary past functions to provide ideas for the contemporary TV drama market. The term *Red Classics* (*hong se jing dian*) has appeared with regularity in Chinese media. These "classics" were created in the modern era, a conscious endeavor by the Chinese State to promote a revolutionary culture which would mold the socialist subject. Gong Qian's chapter looks at this re-versioning of socialist history — from film, literature, and operatic traditions to television drama. Invariably, the austere socialist role model characters receive a makeover in order to appeal to a new generation raised on a diet of popular television, and more recently reality shows. Villains and tyrants likewise appear more human. Well-known stories receive injections of new life and more modern fashionable settings, in the process drawing criticism from traditionalists and those who "lived" the past.

Co-productions and Pan-Asian Markets

Television drama worldwide has shown a propensity to move within and across national boundaries, a process of cultural exchange made even more profitable during the past decade by globalization, technology, market liberalization, normalization of trade in culture, and commonalities of tradition. Part IV turns to the East Asian marketplace and its relationship to the future of Mainland Chinese TV drama. In a discussion of Taiwan's terms of TV drama trade with China, Yi-Hsiang Chen examines the background to the Taiwanese TV drama industry, including historical and cultural perspectives, political and policy concerns, and economic inducements. She discusses changes in audience tastes and the search for new markets, illustrated by profitable dramas that have utilized linguistic and cultural affinities. The chapter also looks at recent co-productions in China and the interaction among TV professionals from related audio-visual industries.

In Chapter 13, Dong-Hoo Lee examines the very important topic of South Korean drama and its rapid penetration into regional markets. Since the late 1990s, Korean popular culture has established a presence in Mainland China, Hong Kong SAR, Taiwan, Vietnam, and Japan. Korean television dramas have been at the forefront of the so-called Korean Wave, or *hanliu*, which has diversified the media and cultural landscape in Asia, in turn challenging the unilateral, top-down flow of globalization.

The somewhat unexpected popularity of Korean TV drama in Asian countries in recent years has impelled producers to re-examine the kinds of appeal that their cultural products have for transnational audiences. The Korean Wave also allowed them to reflect on the "transnational cultural identity" of their cultural products. Lee examines the impact of the Korean Wave on Korean domestic drama productions, and how Korean producers have responded to the popularity of Korean culture in China, Taiwan, and Hong Kong. The kinds of efforts which the Korean producers have made to meet both their local and international audiences are also discussed.

The final chapter looks at a different kind of co-production, which Carol Chow and Eric Ma call "trans-border production." The border between the Mainland and the "special administrative region" (SAR) of Hong Kong is less rigid than before 1997. However, Hong Kong has been outsourcing its production in more cost-efficient locations. Chow and Ma examine how, when, and why Hong Kong producers have moved their TV drama production to the Mainland, and discuss the impact of the "trans-border production" on the rescaling of Hong Kong, particularly TVB's output. They also look at the mutual exchanges of knowledge and creative ideas that have serendipitously taken place in the process of co-producing drama.

All the essays in this volume reinforce the impression that a high level of uncertainty exists in the production of television drama. Of course, some might say nothing is ever certain in China. The consumers of television are given more choices. Is television drama therefore losing its appeal to younger audiences? Will genres splinter and target niches, as has been the case internationally to varying degrees? Will Chinese television drama embrace the challenges of the multi-platform media era and the fragmenting mediascape of abundance? Can Chinese drama seek out international markets? In the discussions that follow, we hope to offer a better understanding of the future of Chinese television drama, first by examining its past and then by observing its present. We cover a great deal of territory, and in doing so hope to set out an agenda for further research in this important topic.

I

Tradition, History, and Politics

1

Yongzheng Dynasty and Totalitarian Nostalgia

Ying Zhu

During the mid-1990s, a new wave of serial dramas emerged to dominate dramatic programming in Chinese prime-time television. The trend climaxed in the late 1990s and the early 2000s with saturation scheduling of palace dramas set in the Qing dynasty (1644–1911). Chinese critics were quick to coin the term "Qing drama." Dynasty dramas set in the Qing palace were not new, however. They had previously appeared in the late 1980s — productions such as *The Last Emperor* (*Modai huangdi*, 1988) and *Kang-Liang Reformation* (*Kangliang bianfa*, 1989) garnered popular as well as critical acclaim. Interestingly though, while the Qing dramas of the 1980s focused on the political and cultural decline of the late Qing, the Qing dramas of the 1990s and the early 2000s — the revisionist Qing dramas — shifted gears, paying tribute to the sage leaders of the early Qing who oversaw a period of prosperity and national unity.

   Yongzheng Dynasty (*Yongzheng wangchao*, 1999), *Kangxi Dynasty* (*Kangxi wangchao*, 2001), and *Qianlong Dynasty* (*Qianlong wangchao*, 2003) are the best illustrations of the revisionist genre. They feature emperors and patriots who

A different version of this chapter was published as "Yongzheng dynasty and Chinese primetime television drama," *Cinema Journal* 44.4 (2005): 3–17. Thorough analyses of dynasty dramas and Chinese serial dramas can be found in my book, *Television in Post-Reform China: Serial Dramas, Confucian Leadership and Global Television Market* (London: Routledge, 2008).

struggle against internal corruption and social injustice as well as external threats, depicting a fictional time of heroic figures and events. Subjects and themes that might invite censorship in contemporary settings — government corruption, political infighting and power struggles, moral cynicism, public unrest, and so on — receive prime-time exposure in revisionist Qing dramas.[1] Fascinated by the palace politics and nostalgic for an era of upright rule that perhaps never was, the Chinese public has genuinely welcomed these dramas, delighting in their contemporary relevance.

Two major factors contributed to the rise of dynasty dramas: ideologically, the treatment of contemporary social and political issues wrapped in historical fabric allows for otherwise sensitive issues to pass the censorship review committees; creatively, the constructed nature of "history" allows room for artistic interventions, particularly in areas of historical "uncertainty" — where memory is fuzzy and where improvisation unearths previously obscured events. The politically charged, revisionist Qing drama thus becomes a public forum for debates on contemporary social and political issues previously segregated within the domain of elite intellectuals and policy-makers.

Leading the charge of the revisionist Qing drama was the forty-four-episode prime-time blockbuster *Yongzheng Dynasty* (*YD*), a show featuring one of the most controversial Qing dynasty emperors. In this adaptation of the epic novel of the same name,[2] a cast of 100 characters depicts the political struggles of the period from Kangxi (1662–1722) to Yongzheng (1722–36). With over 600 scenes, the production is epic in scale. The Qing's first three emperors, Kangxi, Yongzheng, and Qianlong (1736–96) provided strong leadership and a period of peace and prosperity for China. Yet, contrary to the benevolent image of his predecessor Kangxi, Yongzheng is remembered as a cold-faced, indeed, cruel and ferocious man, with no interest in literature or art, and no patience with Confucian scholars and bureaucrats. In an effort to eradicate a corrupt bureaucratic system ruled by Confucian principles, Yongzheng burned books and executed Confucian scholars. Yongzheng's transitional role linking the peace and prosperity of his father's dynasty to the tremendous expansion and growth of his son Qianlong's empire is historically downplayed in the official Chinese annals. The deftly touched-up television version shows us a new side of Yongzheng, a leader of great integrity and inner strength. Yongzheng's hard-line rule has considerable appeal in the current era of rampant political corruption and moral cynicism. Nor is this fascination confined to the Mainland. *YD* has been popular among overseas Chinese too, helping to make the revisionist Qing drama one of the most exportable Chinese television genres.

This chapter examines the ideological positioning of the revisionist Qing drama. I argue that the revisionist Qing drama is informed by post-1989 Tiananmen Square intellectual debates concerning the current state and future direction of China's march toward modernization and the ramifications of the march. *YD* serves as a case in point to illustrate how dynasty dramas have responded to the political and cultural ethos of the time.

Yongzheng Dynasty within the Context of China's Political and Cultural Landscape during the Post Tiananmen Era

One of the unique aspects of *Yongzheng Dynasty* lies in its radical representation of the historically notorious Yongzheng. A wave of revisionist historiography of the Qing dynasty had begun to emerge from the mid-1980s, challenging the accepted version of the Qing dynasty. Long the target of denunciation due to its non-Han origin, the Qing dynasty was re-evaluated favorably by revisionist historians for its consolidation of China's borders and the phenomenal increases in wealth and population. The great emperors of Qing dynasty subsequently became hot subjects of literary and art treatments. *Yongzheng Dynasty*'s take on Yongzheng was very much informed by the revisionist historiography of Qing dynasty advocated by the leading figures of neo-conservatism, a pro-centralization political camp that came to prominence in the early to mid-1990s. Neo-conservatism argued for a middle path between the traditional conservatism of the Old Left and the "radical reformers" who pushed for wholesale marketization. Neo-conservatism accepted market economics, but demanded a greater role for the state in its push for incremental reform, recentralization, and state-centered nationalism.[3] Neo-conservatism was rooted in the neo-authoritarianism of the mid-1980s to the early 1990s, which advocated a strong central government to push for marketization against local forces that supported decentralization but not marketization. The neo-authoritarians endorsed the 1989 Tiananmen Square crackdown on demonstrators and proclaimed the need for strict political control to ensure the success of the economic reforms against any protests at its injustices.

China's political and cultural landscape from the 1990s to the present has been defined to a large extent by the Tiananmen Square crackdown in 1989. Tiananmen marked a turning point, ending China's first reform decade, 1978 to 1988, and ushering in the second, from 1992 to 2002.[4] The interval between the crackdown and Deng Xiaoping's tour of Southern China in 1992 was a time when the Chinese intellectuals struggled to grasp the causes and ramifications of Tiananmen. Currently, all the most influential schools of thought are in rough alignment with the main lines of President Hu Jintao's "harmonious society" project, which will be discussed extensively in the second half of this chapter.

The intellectual discourse of the 1980s endorsed the state's economic reform efforts, which seemed to be turning the country around after the extended malfeasance and stagnation of the Cultural Revolution. The economy received an impressive kick-start, but the benefits of rapid economic development failed to reach large segments of Chinese society as corruption, income inequality among urban dwellers, and economic polarization between the coastal and inland provinces set in and worsened. All this discontent exploded in 1989 in the student-initiated mass demonstrations against corruption and privilege and for democracy. The demonstrators gradually stretched the Party's patience past its breaking point, provoking the infamous Tiananmen crackdown. This muted the intellectual ferment of the 1980s, forcing a period of silent introspection later termed the "interval period."

One school of thought that gained currency during the interval period saw the failure of 1989 as inevitable, the result of extreme radicalism dragged forward from the May Fourth movement into modern Chinese politics.[5] The 1989 movement was equated with other discredited mass movements as well, including the Cultural Revolution. This view echoed the "Neo-authoritarian" stance in vogue in the late 1980s that deemed the May Fourth intellectuals too radical and out of touch with China's long history. Neo-authoritarians value stability for economic growth over all else and advocate the use of state authority and elites to further the rapid expansion of the market. They regard Tiananmen-style social chaos or disorder as the greatest threat to economic prosperity and gradual political reform.

Neo-authoritarianism grew out of discussions in Shanghai in the late 1980s.[6] An important Neo-authoritarian figure, Wang Huning insisted that political reform is part of a complex process of change and that a given political structure must fit local historical, social, and cultural conditions. For China this means a strong central government managing gradual reform. Another leading Neo-authoritarian, Xiao Gongqin agreed that political reform in China must work toward a point somewhere between Western democratic development and Chinese cultural tradition.

Neo-authoritarianism became "Neo-conservatism" when, at a 1990 conference "China's Traditional Culture and Socialist Modernization," Xiao Gongqin added incremental political change to the Neo-authoritarian agenda, while still opposing the wholesale political reform pushed by liberal intellectuals sympathetic to the student movement.[7] A student of Ming and Qing history, Xiao argued that, beginning with the constitutional reform of 1898, leading reformists Kang Youwei and Liang Qichao had mistakenly chosen the radical path, while only the gradual reforms pursued by ranking local officials succeeded.[8] Rejecting direct democracy, Xiao supported building toward indirect (elite suffrage) democracy.

Neo-conservatism thus emerged as an intermediate ideology for intellectuals who no longer accept Marxism but who also reject the liberal call of the 1980s for a "New Enlightenment" inspired by Western liberal democratic theory. Both the Neo-authoritarian and Neo-conservative schools agree that for now China is best served by an authoritarian government. In the face of popular resistance and cultural inertia, they believe, only an authoritarian government can direct and enforce the broad economic reforms necessary.

The rejection of "New Enlightenment" thinking is shared by yet another school of thought that began to take shape in the mid-to-late 1990s, the "New Left." A precursor to the New Left was the inauguration in late 1991 of the independent journal *Dushu* (The Scholar), which attempted to retrieve the history of modern Chinese scholarship, a tradition some felt was in danger of being obscured by the explosion of interest in Western thought.[9] One of *Dushu*'s editors, Wang Hui, later became the leading figure of the New Left.[10] Wang Hui rejects the idea that the Western version of liberal democracy, linked to the free market, is the only viable course of societal progress. As Wang puts it, it is simply "utopian" to think that fairness, justice, and democracy can grow naturally out of an unchecked market.[11] Under his editorship *Dushu* proposed that China's future rests upon pioneering a "third way," rejecting both Marxism-Leninism and Western capitalism.

As Wang and others came into greater contact with Western academics and scholars, they were made increasingly aware of problems not just in European and American societies but also in post-Communist countries that try to bring their planned economies closer to Western liberal models.[12] Among other problems, they noted an unsavory alliance of elite political and commercial interests in China that mirrors similar alliances in the United States and many East Asian countries.

For the New Left, the intertwined nature of China's political and economic elites is the root cause of the social ills associated with corruption and uneven development in the 1990s, including nepotism, bribery and the embezzlement of public funds. The New Left urges political reform that serves the people instead of self-serving interest groups, including the intelligentsia. Wang advocates renewed attention to the underprivileged, asserting that their immediate needs are more urgent than the need for token democratic reforms. He also contends that the state will change only under pressure from a large social force, meaning China's workers and peasants. Democracy in China, he says, has to be based upon the active consent and mobilization of the majority of its population, and must be able to ensure social and economic justice for them.

Wang uses the term "Neo-liberal" (*xin ziyouzhuyi*) to describe opponents who insist on the primacy of market-driven growth over all other considerations. He also links Neo-liberals with Neo-conservatives who in the late 1990s called for strict governmental controls to ensure the success of economic reform against popular protests over its injustices. The New Left rejects this single-minded reform effort pursued at the expense of a social safety net and any prospect of building a civil society based on grassroots democracy.

The New Left and Neo-authoritarians share the same belief in a strong central government for a strong China. The difference between the two lies in the New Left's call for state intervention in order to make the market more socially responsible, as against the Neo-authoritarians' bet on putting the same strong central authority at the service of an unhampered, all-out market economy. Wang's "third way" demands social equality and justice across the board, and extends these to gender equality, the relations between humans and nature, and even to the conduct of international affairs.[13]

For the New Left, the immediate responsibility of the state is to bridge the gap between the haves and have-nots. Freedom of speech will come later. The key therefore is not to make radical political changes as strong leadership is still necessary to keep the economy on a path that is fairer, more democratic, and more humanitarian.[14]

By the mid-2000s the New Left's advocacy of a welfare state was gaining attention within a Communist leadership fearful of social instability and keen to consolidate its power and legitimacy. In March 2006, the National People's Congress convened in Beijing as legislators accused government officials of selling out to market forces. Such was the anti-market mood that a bill to defend private property and grant land titles to farmers was not even discussed.[15] Describing major new investments in rural areas, Chinese Premier Wen Jiabao emphasized that "building a socialist countryside" was a major historic task.[16] He also outlined steps to balance economic growth with environmental protection. After the meeting there was speculation about a possible re-centralization effort, changes that would return power to the central government and counter resistance from local governments still pushing for economic growth at all costs.

From Neo-authoritarianism to the New Left to Chinese President Hu Jintao's call for constructing a "harmonious society," regardless of their differences on the role of the market, the call for a strong central government at the expense (at least for now) of civil rights and freedom of speech has been consistent, in line with the Confucian ideal of cultivating disciplined individuals and responsible leaders who adhere to rules and rituals for the sake of the larger society. Though the New Leftists have never directed government policy, their concerns are increasingly echoed by Hu Jintao's new central leadership in its harmonious society rhetoric, and New Left intellectuals are unapologetic about converging, ideologically, with the authoritarian state.[17]

The New Left's current tenure in the limelight should not obscure the fact that the thinkers who are called "liberals" in China have persisted throughout the reform era. Recoiling from the excesses of Maoism and the failures of the old planned economy, most Chinese intellectuals, even those with no connection to the state, see the market economy as indispensable to China's modernization and revival. Zhu Xueqin, a history professor at Shanghai University who is one of China's best-known liberal intellectuals, wants more, not fewer, market reforms.[18] For him, China's present instability is caused not by economic forces but by a politically repressive regime that has prevented the emergence of representative democracy and a constitutional government.

As Joseph Fewsmith notes, contemporary Chinese liberals identify themselves with the May Fourth enlightenment tradition, which they understand not as a nationalistic project but as a modernization movement.[19] In the 1980s, they championed marketization and political liberalization. They opposed orthodox Marxism-Leninism, the bureaucracies that lay at the core of the "planned economy," and the ideologues who supported and took advantage of the old system. Tiananmen did not change their understanding of the forces that need to be opposed, but it did mute their voices and relegate them to a marginal place in China's contemporary discourse, where they remain today.

Throughout the debate among China's various ideological camps, history has been an important battleground and metaphor in a common search for a way out of the current chaotic transformation. In a wave of revisionist historiography, controversial figures and episodes of the past are now open for rehabilitation, while established heroes may be subjected to harsh scrutiny. Eulogizing the Great Qing came more and more into fashion in the late 1990s, corresponding with the rise of the "New Left," and sympathetic to its call for a stronger central government.

TV dramas have cashed in on this renewed interest in the history of Qing, as well as the short-lived Republican era. Revisionist Qing dramas have taken cues from various ideological strands, but all the while remaining close to popular views endorsed by the state. The Chinese entertainment industry's subordinate relationship to the state imposes a selective filter on what TV dramas can remember of the past. As the main intellectual camps and the state converge on support for a strong central government, almost every Manchu emperor who worked for a strong state has been made the hero of a serial drama. In the following section, we will take a look at the television makeover of the previously notorious Emperor, Yongzheng.

Yongzheng Dynasty and Totalitarian Nostalgia

In *YD* the emperor's new clothes are real, giving the historically notorious Yongzheng a radical makeover. A wave of revisionist historiography of the Qing dynasty began to emerge in the mid-1980s. Qing emperors subsequently became hot subjects of literature and art. *YD*'s take on Yongzheng was very much informed by the revisionist historiography advocated by the leading figures of the pro-centralization Neo-conservative camp.

China was at a crossroads in the late-1990s, with international and domestic problems mounting. NATO's accidental bombing of the Chinese embassy in Yugoslavia, ongoing deliberations over the WTO accession, growing unemployment and layoffs, rampant corruption, rising income gaps between rich and poor, and a worsening environmental situation had created a sense of crisis. Though disagreeing on the economic model for China's modernization, Neo-conservatives, the New Left and almost everyone else was suddenly agreeing on the need for a stronger central government that would protect China's interests globally and eradicate social and economic problems domestically. Corruption was seen not as an isolated problem but as the root of all other problems. The various organized calls for reining in corruption under stern central leadership gained widespread currency among the public. *YD* echoed the call, portraying Yongzheng as an exemplary ruler who cracked down on corruption and rebellious Confucian scholars, putting the well-being of the nation and his people ahead of personal political gain and his historical legacy.

YD can be divided into two parts, with the first half focusing on Yongzheng's rise to power and the second half on his achievement as a ruler. The early episodes introduce Yongzheng's father, the elderly Kangxi, as a wise ruler on the lookout for a viable heir to his throne. As the drama unfolds, the Kangxi dynasty is plagued by Yellow River flooding that destroys thousands of acres in Central and East China and leaves millions of people dead or homeless. Yongzheng is introduced as the only son among the elderly emperor's fourteen sons who shows genuine concern for the well-being of his father's dynasty and the flood victims. Yongzheng volunteers and is sent to the flood zone to head the relief effort, a task that requires local bureaucrats to donate money as the financially beleaguered central government lacks sufficient funds. Yongzheng's hot pursuit of "donations" alienates many local politicians and merchants. Yet his diligence and determination catch the attention of Kangxi.

The deficit in the national treasury is due to the rampant embezzling of public funds by various government officials — an embarrassment to Kangxi, who is determined to recover the money. Since the corruption involves almost all the key government officials, including the emperor's own sons and loyal followers, the rectification job is shunned by everyone except Yongzheng. Recovering the funds turns out to be impossible, as many culprits either refuse to return the money or have already squandered it. The biggest abuser turns out to be the crown prince. Yongzheng's tough stand lead to the temporary abdication of the crown prince and the suicide of one of Kangxi's trusted ministers. Yongzheng inevitably makes more political enemies, earning his reputation as "the cold-faced king."

The first five episodes of the serial firmly establish Yongzheng as an upright and outspoken character. With no tolerance for corruption, he is loyal to his father and devoted to the people. These episodes also introduce Yongzheng's political opponents, many of them his own siblings who have formed various political factions in hope of succeeding Kangxi. After establishing the power dynamics among Yongzheng, the crown prince, and the emperor's eighth son Yongji, the serial devotes a considerable proportion of its first half to power struggles and political intrigues within the palace. Yongzheng displays extraordinary endurance, and detailed depictions of his daily life reveal his frugality, which contrasts sharply with his siblings' decadence.

Aided by his political adviser, Yongzheng eventually gains the upper hand and is designated Kangxi's successor. Yongzheng's assumption of power upon Kangxi's sudden death provides a transition for the serial. As the director puts it, "the personality of the ruler determines the fate of the nation."[20] In the Confucian ideal, good governance and wise statecraft are secured by the moral commitment of political leaders, and this is also the only safeguard against abuses of power. It is therefore up to Yongzheng to single-handedly salvage the debt and corruption-ridden nation after the passing of Kangxi.

Yongzheng proves to be up to the task. After ascending the throne, he initiates a series of economic reform policies aimed at consolidating the central monetary reserve while distributing wealth and labor on a more egalitarian basis. The old system of taxation based on the number of individuals in a family is changed to taxation based on landownership. This reform meets resistance from local bureaucrats and merchants. Yongzheng then sets out to strip away many of the privileges traditionally enjoyed by Confucian scholars and bureaucrats, even ordering scholars to earn their living by raising their own crops like ordinary farmers. While harsh to the scholars and local bureaucrats, the Yongzheng depicted in *YD* is lenient to loyal followers who support his reform agenda. He dispatches loyal supporters to the provinces to carry out the reform policies.

However, the commissioners sent by Yongzheng grow imperious and despotic over time, causing grievances among the local people. Complaints are filed, demanding the removal of commissioners from their local posts. Yongzheng's chief political opponent, Yongji, seizes the opportunity to rally local bureaucrats and Confucian scholars to demand that Yongzheng withdraw his reform policy. To ensure the implementation of the new economic policy, which he sees as the only way to a stronger dynasty, Yongzheng suppresses the revolt with an iron fist. Blood is shed in the name of stability and security.

The symbolic link between Neo-authoritarianism's justification of the Tiananmen crackdown and the drama's ideological positioning is apparent. Indeed, the leading figure of the Neo-authoritarian movement, He Xin, is rumored to have had a close personal relationship with Hu Mei, the director of the show. The serial's positive spin on Yongzheng's crackdown on political riots echoes He's aversion to the abiding "movement mentality" of Chinese intellectuals — something he regards as a destructive element of Chinese culture.[21]

The image of Yongzheng in *YD* bears a remarkable resemblance to that of China's first emperor. The ends-justifies-the-means message articulated by Emperor Qin (Shihuangdi) is channeled in *YD* through an emperor historically linked to paranoia and brutality. This new, improved Yongzheng is thus transformed into an extraordinary ruler whose determination to build a stronger nation comes at the expense of his personal reputation.

Yongzheng's antagonism toward Confucian scholars and his distrust of the Confucian-influenced bureaucratic system are also reminiscent of the iconoclastic Mao, whose disdain for and suspicion of scholars and intellectuals alike — along with his absolute demand for loyalty — resulted in the catastrophic Cultural Revolution. Interestingly, Mao enjoyed a renewed popularity from the late 1980s to the early 1990s amidst a wave of totalitarian nostalgia in China. As part of the post-Tiananmen campaign to inculcate a sense of positive nostalgia among the shocked and fatigued public, the state re-released old revolutionary films and classic revolutionary songs, and produced contemporary historical films featuring the founding fathers of the People's Republic. The remythologization of Mao in the popular media fed the public's yearning for an era of simplicity and purity. A strong leader who — at least in the popular imagination — was above corruption, Mao was for many the symbol of an age of economic stability, egalitarianism, and national pride. The rehabilitation of Yongzheng provided by *YD* in the late 1990s works within a similar framework, with Yongzheng becoming the representative of an age of determination and confidence, of cultural and political unity, and above all of economic equality and incorruptibility.

Throughout the serial, Yongzheng is portrayed in private as worn out and lonely. Indeed, he is defined by the director as a "lonely reformer," a tragic figure whose noble ambition alienates him from his contemporaries and dooms his historical reputation. In contrast to his father's more confident and relaxed ruling style, Yongzheng's impatient and inflexible approach cut a coarser image. His eagerness to crack down on government corruption, to reform the tax system, and to recover public funds makes him intolerant of whoever gets in the way. Yongzheng is aware of the reputation he is earning, especially by prosecuting Confucian scholars. In one scene he cautions his chosen successor, fourth son Hongli (later the Qianlong emperor), not to offend the scholars as this will forever tarnish his reputation. He then rationalizes his suppression of the scholars' revolt by arguing that it is imperative to act now in order to prevent his son from facing the same problem. In short, he sacrifices his own reputation so his son might one day be remembered as a benevolent ruler. Clearly, there is a masochistic streak in Yongzheng's personality that contributes to his remarkable endurance, his nearly ascetic lifestyle, his sexual restraint, and his single-minded devotion to work. The serial ends with his sudden death at the age of fifty-five, as a result of exhaustion.

The image of Yongzheng as an upright reformer tough on corruption and passionate about the well-being of ordinary people is also reminiscent of former Premier Zhu Rongji. Zhu's efforts to curb government corruption earned him the reputation of a contemporary graft-buster.[22] Tang Guoqiang, the veteran actor who portrays Yongzheng, commented that: "The period of the Yongzheng dynasty resembles the current situation with anti-corruption as the goal of the current government. We're still trying to finish up what Yongzheng left unfinished. Anti-corruption and good economic policy is at the heart of the drama and is also the most touching topic among the public."[23]

Conclusion

China's new day in the economic sun is clouded by a spiralling crime rate, unemployment, corruption, and an increasing wealth gap. Rampant political corruption is a major contributor to China's widening income gap, and is also the root cause of social discontent and the prevailing political apathy. Debates have raged at both the intellectual and policy levels concerning potential solutions to these problems. Despite their differences on the role of the market, China's main political camps have rallied around a shared apprehension about mass movements and their shared faith in a strong and upright central government. Chinese television has not missed the point. The revisionist Qing drama has been at the forefront in articulating these ideas. In its effort to engage audiences fed up with corruption and the society's perceived loss of its moral grounding, dynasty drama presents exemplary emperors from bygone dynasties. These narrative reappraisals of history have proven popular and profitable for China's television industry. *YD* was the first to capitalize on the popular yearning for models of strong leadership. Other dynasty dramas such as *The Great Emperor Hanwu* (*Hanwu dadi*, 2006) followed with more exemplary rulers.

The rise of dynasty drama is further facilitated by the commercialization and globalization of the Chinese television industry. Dynasty drama has become the PRC's niche export genre for the Pan-Chinese market, and with China's vast historical wealth still largely untapped, Chinese TV practitioners will no doubt continue to exploit history and to tailor cultural legacy to the contemporary concerns.

2

Family Saga Serial Dramas and Reinterpretation of Cultural Traditions

Janice Hua Xu

Chinese television has recently witnessed the spectacular successes of serials embracing epic themes. Dramas about traditional large families enduring turbulent times, mostly during the first half of the twentieth century, notably the Republican era (1911–49), have captured the imagination of viewers. Among these, *Grand Mansion Gate* (*Da zhaimen*, 2001), *The Story of a Noble Family* (*Jinfen shijia*, 2003), and *Moment in Peking* (*Jinghua yanyun*, 2005) enjoyed high ratings nationally. These family sagas usually revolve around the rise and fall of family fortunes and the unity of the extended family in the face of threats, including plots by outsiders, problematic family members, and changes in political climate.

The genre of melodrama offers a way through which we can understand such dramatic events. A television melodrama is characterized by sentimental presentations of artificially plotted stories that appeal to the emotions of audiences and end in a morally reassuring note.[1] Serials about the fate and the fortunes of extended families over lengthy periods of time generate a wide variety of dramatic conflicts that draw audience emotions. In contrast to tragedy, melodrama is amenable to redemptive endings. In early television history in the West, producers of prime-time soap operas believed kinship and romantic liaisons in wealthy families were the basis for attracting female viewers, while business intrigues and power struggles would draw adult males.[2] One of the key features of television melodrama is the way it addresses the moral senses of the audience through "its hunger to engage or represent behavior and moral attitudes that belong to its particular day and time, especially behavior shocking or threatening to prevailing moral codes."[3] Characters are perceived both as individuals serving the development of the story and as bearers of social and moral values. For example, audiences can easily categorize a character as a "good son" or a "bad son," a "traditional woman" or a "new woman."

The multiplicity of plots and interpersonal relations of family sagas allow a variety of narrative possibilities and potential trajectories of identification for viewers. According to Newcomb, the narrative structure of family-theme television depends largely on the dissemination of knowledge about the complex kinship patterns in a story. Any event that causes an alteration in relational connections, such as an affair, divorce, or childbirth, "ripples through pairs and triads of human binding ties, shifting power relations, accumulated knowledge, and emotional response."[4]

This chapter examines the popularity of family saga dramas in China in recent years, analyzing their major themes and cultural significance in the context of the nation's modernization drive. These dramas highlight and contrast old and new ways of life, offering opportunities for expression of popular conceptions of Chinese cultural identity and contentious moral standards.

Melodrama and National Culture

Television is a focal point around which the anxieties over "national culture" in many developing countries are played out in the age of globalization. Many policymakers and intellectuals feel a need to take action to conserve and safeguard their national identity in the cultural front against the possibility of erosion. "While advancing the cause of 'development', television at the same time holds out the promise of defending national tradition, and serving as a line of defense against foreign culture, or against any other elements defined as negative; television culture becomes a key site for discerning symptoms of the national mood."[5]

In today's China where the idea of the "cultural industry" (*wenhua chanye*) has received a new wave of governmental support, there is a trend toward cultural revivalism stressing an essential national character, as well as the importance of traditional cultural values. "Traditional" folk genres have absorbed elements of mass culture and other invented traditions, offering an idealized display of "native culture" for mass consumption. The hybrid and reconstructed images of "traditional" Chinese customs are invoked to produce a national discourse about Chinese-style modernity.[6] To analyze the phenomenon of "native revival" in the emerging Chinese cultural industry, it is necessary to see it as a part of a reaction to the growing presence of Western media. It must not be assumed that the process of mass media penetration and the transnationalization of markets would necessarily mean the homogenization of cultures or identities. The appropriation of popular culture for political, ideological purposes — nationalistic, revolutionary, or communist — has been a distinct feature of modern Chinese political culture.[7] This process is demonstrated in the field of contemporary television industry, where market forces interplay with cultural policies and national sentiments.

The history of twentieth-century China, particularly the decades leading up to Liberation in 1949, contains rich material for televisual spectacles and ideological elaborations. Social transitions were disrupted by clashes of power and multiple contending interests. With the late Qing political and cultural order fractured by the turbulence of new ways, modern Western elements and traditional Chinese practices mingled and conflicted on diverse fronts. The emergence and coexistence of Nationalist, Communist, and many other introduced political ideologies also affected how people confronted change and selected their individual paths. In terms of story lines, character portrayal, and visual aspects like costumes and rituals, this period provides plenty of resources that can be packaged and marketed to contemporary television audiences. In current China, many people fear the disintegration of the social fabric in the modernization process. Furthermore, because of the impact of the global economy, the value system and symbolic meaning complex that used to tie individuals to society are losing their cohesive power. A retrospective look into China's past seems to bring possibilities for connecting past and present and for contemplating and responding to rapid transformations.

Grand Mansion Gate, a forty-episode television serial, was first broadcast on Chinese Central Television (hereafter "CCTV") during prime time in 2001. It enjoyed the highest ratings among television dramas in China that year. The drama centers on a prominent family in the Chinese medicine business, which had served in the imperial court and established the Tongrentang brand name, now three hundred years old. The narrative is based on real stories of the family, adapted from a novel written by Guo Baochang, a descendent of the Tongrentang medicine family. Guo also directed the show and claimed that it was a culmination of his forty years of effort.[8] The story begins in the late Qing dynasty, depicting the tribulations of the family over more than half a century. It has been rebroadcast by CCTV and other stations a number of times. This success led to the creation of an expensive sequel of thirty-two episodes, which was broadcast in 2003. A second sequel is under production, and this will bring the total number of episodes to one hundred.

Equally popular was *The Story of a Noble Family,* a serial about aristocratic life in Beijing during the 1920s and the romance between the premier's youngest son and a girl from an ordinary family. This family saga was based on a novel by Republican Era writer Zhang Henshui, who was a representative of the "Mandarin Ducks and Butterfly School" in Chinese literary history.[9] Well-known for portraying urban life and romance, his novels were popular and often serialized in newspapers in the 1920s. The extravagant show was produced by a private television production company in Guangdong Province, who later sold the copyright to CCTV due to budget difficulties. When CCTV screened the show in 2003, it held the highest ratings of drama for two years, and was subsequently rebroadcast by many provincial stations.

In 2005, CCTV scheduled *Moment in Peking,* a controversial adaptation of Lin Yutang's 1938 novel, which was originally written in English for a Western audience. Lin Yutang was nominated for the Nobel Prize for Literature for this work in 1975. He writes in the preface that it is "a story of how men and women in the contemporary era grow up and learn to live with one another, . . . how certain habits of living and ways of thinking are formed, and how, above all, they adjust themselves to the circumstances in this earthly life where men strive but the gods rule."[10] The forty-four-episode drama promotes traditional Chinese virtues such as tolerance and harmony through a panoramic view of Republican-era Chinese society, in particular the life of three couples and their extended families in the turbulent period leading to the beginning of the Sino-Japanese War (1937–45). The producers convinced China's foremost television drama actress Zhao Wei to accept the leading role. Though not as successful as *The Story of a Noble Family*, this high-budget drama generated interest from audiences in Chinese-speaking regions across the world.

Common to all of these dramatic works are the major lines of conflict — between individual desire and family interest, between modernity and tradition, and between family life and political turmoil of the nation. In addition to clear references to, or even direct participation of the characters in historical incidents, the dramas also make full use of glamorous settings, sophisticated character development, and star-filled casts. These works also embody regional specificity in that they resonate with local flavors of Beijing, including colloquialisms and popular pastimes such as Beijing opera.

In the following sections I discuss *Grand Mansion Gate* in detail in order to illustrate the textual components conducive to the popularity of such shows.

I also point out how these dramas provide a vehicle for nostalgia and reinterpretation of Chinese culture. For many people these elements are the key to balancing conflicting forces within society.

Individuals and Traditional Values

Family saga serials depicting individuals and groups in the middle of social changes can dramatize the interaction of individual fate and historical forces. This is particularly evident when depicting a time when the old system is falling apart and traditional values are in question. The dramas highlight the constant efforts by leading figures to maintain control and preserve family status and honor in the face of crises, conspiracies, and betrayals. Melodrama is "complicated and immensely enriched because its discourse is aesthetic and broadly popular: a forum or arena in which traditional ways of feeling and thinking are brought into continuous, strained relation with powerful intuitions of change and contingency."[11] The dramas often present individual choices — or lack of choices — at the intersections of personal fates and social events, carving out complex characterization through intense psychological activities and motivations.

Co-produced by CCTV and Wuxi Zhongshi Company, *Grand Mansion Gate* was advertised as a dense, well-crafted masterpiece — unlike many of the low-budget, roughly-made television dramas that currently circulate across television channels in China. The show failed to win the highest national award in television drama — the Golden Eagle Award — even though it achieved the year's highest ratings. This failure was no doubt due to controversies surrounding the "feudal garbage" (*fengjian zaopo*), key elements of the narrative such as family feuds, prostitution, and polygamy. The commercial success of *Grand Mansion Gate* did not translate into recognition among cultural elites.

This forty-episode drama begins with a series of incidents affecting a prestigious household in late Qing-dynasty Beijing. The head of the household, Grandfather Bai, is an herbal medicine doctor serving the royal court who lives with his three married sons under one roof. The family's medicine products are regarded as the highest quality in Beijing. After the birth of his grandson Bai Jingqi, a series of disasters occur and the family is caught up in deadly political struggles within the royal court. As a consequence of a feud with a powerful Mandarin family, the family business closes and one of Grandfather Bai's sons is sentenced to death. The old man falls ill in distress and the family faces the possibility of splitting up. Bai Jingqi's mother manages the family affairs throughout the crisis, eventually restoring the family status through her wisdom and perseverance. But nothing is as difficult as keeping the reckless Bai Jingqi out of trouble with the law. To uphold traditional rules and pacify family members who fear the consequences of his actions, she drives Bai Jingqi and his pregnant bride out of the family and orders them to start lives on their own. Later Bai Jingqi establishes his own medicine empire in a provincial capital before moving back to Beijing on the death of his father. However, his second marriage to a former prostitute and his business style continue to generate conflict within the large family. The episodes afterward focus mainly on Bai Jingqi's relationships with several women and his efforts in leading the extended household through the chaotic years prior to the Japanese occupation of Beijing (then known as Peking).

A character personifying the will of the individual confronting the values of the times, Bai Jingqi struggles between personal desires and obligations to family tradition. This is vividly demonstrated in the disputes around his marriages. He falls in love with three women at different stages of his life, and each of them seems an impossible choice in observing family honor and tradition. In spite of powerful objections by the whole household, he marries each of them. As I have mentioned above Bai Jingqi was driven out of the mansion by his mother after marrying his first love, the daughter of a rival family. Though she and her child were later accepted into the family after years of hardship and poverty, poor health results in her death on the day of her mother-in-law's funeral. When Bai Jingqi's takes up a concubine named Jiuhong, a famous prostitute in the city of Ji'nan, this sparks more disputes. Jiuhong has to live outside the big mansion after moving to Beijing, and her newborn daughter is even taken away from her at the instruction of the mother-in-law. The baby grew up in the big mansion, forbidden to have any ties with her low-status mother, an edict that breaks Jiuhong's heart.

While Bai Jingqi is portrayed as daring and rebellious during his early years, he eventually becomes a filial son and tries to fulfill the wishes of his mother in all kinds of ways. There is a key scene at his mother's large birthday party in which Bai Jingqi is sitting by her side watching her favorite Beijing opera performance. A servant enters to report that a humiliated Jiuhong is trying to hang herself. Bai Jingqi hesitates for a while, but after taking a look at his mother he continues watching the performance. Fortunately Jiuhong does not die. The ailing health of the mother-in-law brings a ray of hope for Jiuhong to have her status reversed, but the will left by the old lady dictates that Jiuhong cannot wear the funeral attire, which adorns everyone in the family during the extravagant funeral ceremony, even the pets. Years of miserable treatment twist Jiuhong's personality and she becomes addicted to opium. When she discovers Bai Jingqi's love for a servant named Xiangxiu, his mother's dog groomer, she vents her anger on Huaihua, another servant girl, who is appointed by his mother on her deathbed as concubine to Bai Jingqi. This rage eventually leads to Huaihua's suicide.

Chinese moral legacies are highlighted and examined through the yearnings, anguish, and pains of the individuals in the drama. However, it is noteworthy that Confucian traditions and the characters' motivations are not presented as simple right or wrong, good or evil. When Bai Jingqi was almost sixty years old, he announces his determination to break tradition and formally marry Xiangxiu, consequently raising her status above that of the estranged concubine Jiuhong. In an ironic moment, Jiuhong begins to miss the tough mother-in-law whose adherence to family rules had been the primary source of her miseries in the Bai household: "If she were alive she would not have allowed this to happen!" The moral ambivalence and contradictions in the actions of the characters provide a rich source of dramatic conflict, as well as points for audience engagement on ethical and emotional levels.

Hero Image: Reinterpretation of Cultural Identity

The television characters engage viewers and provide a focal point for identification, with their social and national status clearly marked through their speech, appearance, mannerisms, and the way they interact with other characters.[12] *Grand Mansion Gate* places Chinese entrepreneurs center stage as heroes. Traditionally, merchants had played important roles in social lives in China, but according to Confucian moral discourse they were usually considered as putting profit above righteousness. In other words, commerce was depicted in opposition to morality. Here their values and mannerisms are positively presented as emerging patterns in China, and they are accorded a prominent role.[13] Bai Jingqi, the leading character in the drama, personifies masculine qualities that have been rarely staged in national-level prime-time Chinese television. In the character we can see a combination of both traditional Chinese masculinity and modern ideals of enterprising individualism.[14]

According to Kam Louie, Chinese traditional conceptions of masculinity have been structured by two archetypes operating in a productive tension:

> One is *wen*, associated with the gentleman-scholar or *junzi* promoted by Confucius, who is the patron saint of *wen* masculinity. The emphasis here is on the maintenance of civil order and the promotion of vertical bonds

of hierarchy and filiality. The second archetype is *wu*, . . . *Wu* masculinity
is associated with the outlaw space of the *jianghu*, familiar to martial arts
movie fans, and it emphasizes the horizontal bonds of brotherhood . . .
an ideal balance of *wen* and *wu* emphasizes the skill and strategy that comes
with learning as a means of avoiding descending to the use of violence.[15]

While *wen* and *wu* shape the two sides of the ideal of traditional Chinese
masculinity, they are associated with the emphasis on moral character.
Therefore one needs the ability to make personal choices when the multiple
Confucian demands on somebody encounter a dilemma, for example, a
conflict between loyal obligations to the emperor and filial duties to one's
parents. One of the central values in Chinese folk culture for men in public
spaces is *yiqi*, which comes from a combination of the character *yi*, meaning
"righteousness," and the character *qi*, meaning "air." It refers to the moral-
intellectual quality of knowing right from wrong, together with the firmness
of character necessary to act consistently on the basis of such knowledge. [16]
It is also tied to the value of brotherhood, as symbolized in the story of
"meeting in the peach garden" of the three main characters in the ancient
novel *Romance of the Three Kingdoms* (*Sanguo yanyi*). Men with *yiqi* implicitly
reject the conservative social hierarchy dictated by the state authorities and
the elite by honoring fraternal fidelity. They are noble, generous, and
courageous. In traditional Chinese popular culture, the quality of *yiqi* can be
often found among heroic men who have little respect for the rule of law,
as in the story of *The Water Margin* (*Shui hu zhuan*) about 108 bandits who
take the vow of brotherhood. These men eat and drink together from big
bowls, fight fierce battles together, and care little about their own material
possessions.

In *Grand Mansion Gate,* Bai Jingqi risks his life to help friends get out of
danger, gives away all the money in his pocket to a suffering beggar, and
destroys low-quality medicines that harm the reputation of the family business.
Mischievous as a child, he is reckless and daring in pursuing his heart's desires,
even violent on some occasions. He is enterprising and extravagant; he is a
passionate lover and womanizer who breaks traditional restrictions on personal
freedom while maintaining filial obligations — eventually at the price of the
happiness of women around him. He also has little fear of spending time in
jail if he believes what he wants to do is right.

In an early episode, the Boxers are besieging foreign embassies. The Allied
Expeditionary Army[17] enters Beijing and one of the daughters of the Bai
family is raped by foreign soldiers. The streets are chaotic. Bai Jingqi kills a
German soldier who pursues his beloved private tutor — a close family friend

who had earlier saved his life. After the Japanese occupation of Manchuria, Bai Jingqi refuses attempts by a Japanese acquaintance to invest in the Bai family business, warning family members never to reveal their secret recipes. He declares that he would rather burn down the whole business rather than cooperate with the Japanese. Later when the Japanese army occupying Beijing asks Bai Jingqi to serve as the head of medical business association, he declines the request even though his shop is harassed every day and is forced to close. He and his sister also help hide a Beijing opera actor who refuses to perform for the Japanese. In the fortieth episode, Jingqi's brother agrees to serve as the head of the medicine association, but at the opening ceremony he commits suicide in public after denouncing the Japanese bombing that killed his son, thus bringing the whole family together to join in efforts to resist the Japanese.

It is evident in the drama that "gutsy" manhood and instinctive judgements are valued higher than "book knowledge" and formal education. Meanwhile, the traditional divisions between the elite class and the lower classes make little sense and receive no respect. When Bai Jingqi wants to expand his new business to take over more than two dozen small workshops, he had insufficient assets to secure a loan. He manages to borrow 2000 taels of silver from a bank by pawning a box containing his so-called "family treasure," using his grandfather's reputation as the royal court doctor. Years later when paying off the loan he confesses to the stunned bank owner that inside the box was his own excrement. In another scene he pays thousands of taels of silver to a brothel for its top prostitute (Jiuhong, who will become his concubine), but discovers that she was kept by a provincial government official. He kidnaps Jiuhong with a gun and wins her heart. Later he calmly goes to jail, eating and sleeping well until his well-connected cousin finds a way to get him out.

From the reception of *Grand Mansion Gate* it can be concluded that while orthodox moral standards are disintegrating, as multiple cultural elements contend in an evolving meaning system, "low-culture" values and the folk heroes representing these values are achieving status within the entertainment media. Together with the rising power of entrepreneurs, a new notion of masculinity is emerging, which seems to be associated with building a fortune from zero, winning the woman one desires from the hands of rivals, squandering money for one's close friends and aging mother, and disregarding or standing up to powerful authorities and enemies. To a certain extent, "bandit air" is gaining an upper hand over "official air." It is good entertainment.

Family Life and Social Turbulence

The Bai family fortune was closely connected to their service and association with the Qing royal court, and later to the political and social upheavals affecting China during the Republican era. When the protection of the dynastic empire disappeared, the family was subject to a combination of misfortunes including banditry, kidnapping, blackmailing, and the fallout of foreign invasions. The drama provides a showcase of the vulnerability of private life in chaotic times. Government authorities — both the imperial court and the Republican bureaucrats — are portrayed as corrupt and inept. Protection by powerful figures is the key to survival of family and business, and these figures are usually greedy and decadent. Law and order barely exists. Only bribery and personal networks are effective in getting family members out of trouble. Personal sacrifice and endurance of hardship are treasured moral virtues that hold the family together, while characters who can take advantage of fleeting opportunities in a chaotic world to bring fame to the family name are portrayed as heroes.

Throughout the family saga, traditional civilian values such as retribution, filial duty and personal loyalty are emphasized and dramatized. "Secret recipes from ancestors" and the "old brand name" become the keys to the livelihood of the family. They are to be protected at all cost. Individuals who put the interest of the whole clan above their own to help tide over crises are honored. Although nationalism is an element that heightens the conflict of the individuals in their social environment and brings a dramatic ending to the show, the characters are defined more by their handling of obligations, money, reputation, as well as clashes with family members, business partners, and rivals.

In the drama the characters engage in all kinds of secret scams for the sake of family fortune and status, such as bribing eunuchs to get access to the empress, replacing a family member on death row with a poor man's dead body, using government connections to throw business competitors into jail when they do not yield to monopoly. Any means benefiting the family status and security are justifiable, including sacrificing low-status family members. This indicates a departure from the Confucian-literati concerns expressed in many historical dramas in Chinese television, which tend to focus on the battles between virtuous and corrupt officials and which draw a clear line between the imperial power structure and average citizens at its mercy.

On the one hand, *Grand Mansion Gate* seems to involve obvious "main melody" themes such as patriotism, embodied by the *minzu qijie* (national integrity) of the leading characters who refuse to cooperate with the invading Japanese forces. On the other hand, the appeal of the drama to audiences might derive from aspects not promoted in official lines, for example, the scheming and business strategies used in dealing with officials and business competitors, as well as the characters' daring but convincing deeds in pursuing their personal desires. Throughout the drama, pragmatism and entrepreneurship characterize the actions of the characters more than pure Confucianism or even nationalism. It can be seen that the drama advocates cultural values that depart from Chinese official ideology, highlighting folk wisdom and individual existentialist philosophy. While some viewers have expressed negative opinions on the moral messages of the drama, the overwhelming popularity of *Grand Mansion Gate* indicates that these traits and values resonate with the preferences of contemporary Chinese serial drama audience.[18]

Romantic Love and Stability of the Family

The late Qing and Republican era of China witnessed tremendous upheavals in every aspect of social and cultural life, whereas the mixture of old and new ideologies and values dramatically impacted on the fate of the young generation. The circumstances under which they made choices and the interactions of class, gender and individual personalities provide rich resources for televisual depictions. While revisiting and reconstructing traditional ways of life, the family saga dramas bring into focus the desire, pleasure, and passion of personal growth, as well as the restrictions and sufferings people endured in the Confucian system.

Two other family sagas are worth mentioning in brief. In the CCTV version of *Moment in Peking* broadcast in 2005, the serial begins with the marriage entanglement between the prominent Zeng and Yao families. The two families had maintained close relationship, because years ago the Zengs had saved the eldest daughter of the Yao family, Mulan, from the hands of abductors during the chaos of the Boxer Uprising. Madam Zeng is fond of the graceful and talented Yao Mulan, but the three sons of the Zeng family were already engaged. When Pingya, the eldest son of the Zeng family, falls sick beyond the help of the best doctor in Peking, a fortune-teller advises that the only way to save his life is to have a wedding celebration and in this way fend off bad fortune. But Pingya's intended fiancée is unavailable on a journey at the time. An anxious Madame Zeng goes to the Yao house and begs for permission for the marriage of Pingya and Mulan. This poses a dilemma for the Yaos. Out of a desire to relieve the elders in both families, Mulan agrees to marry Pingya, even though she herself likes a young man named Kong Lifu from an ordinary family who shares her interest in ancient Chinese written characters. To add to the celebration, the Zengs arrange their second son to hold a wedding on the same day. When everyone in the three families is busy preparing for a huge ceremony proper for their social standings, Pingya's fiancée suddenly returns, declaring that she is willing to marry him in spite of his illness. At this change of event, instead of withdrawing wedding invitations (which indicate only the family names of the bride and groom), the Zengs decide to marry Mulan to their third son, the carefree Sunya and bring three brides into the family simultaneously.

Soon after the wedding, eighteen-year-old Mulan faced severe challenges from multiple fronts — Madam Zeng, grief-stricken by the death of Pingya, entrusts Mulan with the daily affairs of the large family; Mulan also finds herself the target of jealousy of her own sister and one sister-in-law; meanwhile her husband Sunya starts an affair with an art student named Cao Lihua. Although Mulan tries to resolve the matter by befriending Cao Lihua, the birth of a son to Sunya and Cao Lihua leads Mulan to contemplate the possibility of ending her marriage. However, despite encouragement from her friend Lifu for her divorce plan, Mulan gives up the idea upon the unexpected suicide of Cao Lihua, whose son was taken away by Madam Zeng. Mulan eventually reconciles with her husband and has a daughter with him, while raising the boy of Cao Lihua.

In this drama Mulan constantly places the family interest above that of her own, bearing personal sacrifices and the wrong accusations of family members. She plays a perfect role of good daughter and daughter-in-law, loyal to her husband even though he was passionate for another woman. On the other hand, she is not afraid of being the target of gossip. When Lifu was imprisoned for exposing corrupt officials, Mulan takes great risk to visit a warlord, and negotiates the release of Lifu. She also helps Lifu to marry her sister Mochou, although the marriage did not last due to the tragic death of Mochou in the chaos of the Sino-Japanese war.

The drama underscores the contrasts between traditional virtues and the modern values of individual freedom through the choices made by different characters in the story. Among the three brides of the Zeng family, one fulfilled the Confucian demand of chastity by staying as widow after her husband's death; one left her husband and later lived off a warlord; one endured all kinds of challenges and became the pillar holding the whole family together through wartime crises. Lin Yutang, author of the original novel *Moment in Peking*, indicated in its preface that "it is neither a glorification of the old way of life nor a defense of the new." While there are obvious differences between "good" and "bad" characters, each of the characters was struggling within specific social circumstances and deserved some degree of sympathy from the audience.

The elusiveness of romantic love is also a major theme of another CCTV serial, *The Story of a Noble Family,* adapted from Zhang Henshui's popular novel. In the drama, Jin Yanxi, the seventh child of the prime minister, rejects the affection of the willful daughter of his father's political ally to pursue Leng Qingqiu, a classic beauty from a common family. He manages to win her heart after lengthy efforts, including teaching literature in her high school, purchasing a courtyard house next to the Leng residence, forming a poetry society, and befriending her relatives. Later they gain approval from both families to marry and begin a new life in the huge mansion, but the independent-minded Leng Qingqiu finds it difficult to adjust to the family rules. As Yanxi's father loses grip of political power, Yanxi's career setbacks and financial troubles emerge, leading him to seek help from his former admirer. His marriage eventually collapses due to the couple's irreconcilable differences, and the prominent Jin family disintegrates after the sudden death of Yanxi's father. The children, concubines, and servants of the household move on with their lives in separate ways.

The success of these television serials is partly due to the reputation of the original novels, but they also brought in attacks from literary elites for not doing justice to the sophistication of the originals. Television's pursuit of ratings leads to producers searching for themes that echo popular concerns and satisfy audience desire for spectacle and fantasy. *The Story of a Noble Family* was criticized for focusing on creating "youth idols" for popular consumption instead of presenting a faithful picture of the complexities of social life in Beijing of that period.[19] Similarly, the CCTV version of *Moment in Peking* in 2005 received considerable negative response for the way in which the storyline and characters were erased or altered from Lin Yutang's novel covering four decades of historical events. Some critics even lament that the drama reduces a panoramic masterpiece to a story of love triangle.[20] Nonetheless, the television broadcasts of these family sagas achieved great commercial success, and more shows following this formula are expected to appear on screen.

Conclusion

In contemporary Chinese society, in which consumer culture has become predominant and state ideology is losing its power as the spiritual pillar of the public, it is timely that television serials highlighting the value of tradition receive so much acclaim. According to Michael Schudson, broadcast media can promote a more unified national culture by conferring status on nationally prominent people, places, rituals, and issues.[21] Melodramas open symbolic opportunities for expression of popular conceptions of gender ideals and national identity, reflecting public sentiments and contentious moral standards in contemporary society. In the process of reconstructing a Chinese cultural legacy in popular media such as television, folk tradition and "low culture" elements have emerged to find their share in mainstream entertainment forms to contend with intellectual elitism. Ideals of masculinity and femininity have become fluid and multiple, enabling the public to find inspirations from non-contemporary sources. For modern audiences seeking heroic images in the realm of imagination and fantasy, traditional materials can glitter with special appeals. Glazed with extravagant spectacles enhancing historical features, they generate elements of popularity for the entertainment industry.

The popularity of these shows can be seen as an illustration of the larger-scale tension and ambivalence about the consequence of modernity and "development." While societal changes bring uncertainty, feelings of yearning, reflection, and nostalgia are expressed through the reconstitution of the traditional family values. As Shuyu Kong demonstrates in Chapter 5, Chinese television drama of the last two decades has increasingly reflected a renewed popular fascination with domestic space and familial experience. This occurs when the image of a harmonious large family with its legacy honored from generation to generation becomes increasingly elusive in reality. In essence, the popularity of family saga dramas reflects the competing demands that contemporary individuals must face when attempting to keep pace with a "modern" world while preserving the importance of tradition. While these stories of characters in the early twentieth century have the direct appeal of universality in terms of dramatic qualities, in a more indirect way they address public sentiments in current China.

3

"Clean Officials," Emotional Moral Community, and Anti-corruption Television Dramas

Ruoyun Bai

Corruption is one of the most emotionally charged issues in China. In the shadow of two decades of double-digit GDP growth, corruption has reached endemic proportions, permeating the Chinese Communist Party and government agencies at all levels.[1] In the 1990s, millions of CCP members and cadres were punished by the Party's discipline inspection system. In the latter half of the decade, corruption was more and more likely to be found at high levels. The most infamous scandals brought death sentences or severe prison terms to a former party secretary of the Beijing Municipality (Chen Xitong), a vice provincial governor (Hu Changqing), a deputy secretary general of the National People's Congress (Cheng Kejie), a minister of Public Security (Li Jizhou), and many more. In 2006, corruption was thrust into the limelight again by a scandal that involved high-level Party leadership in Shanghai. On September 24, Chen Liangyu, the party secretary of the Shanghai Municipality, was removed from office for offenses ranging from misappropriating social security funds to seeking illicit gains from businesses

I would like to thank the anonymous reviewer for his/her suggestion about including some findings on audience responses. Obtaining such data presents a methodological difficulty as it would be difficult for the viewers to recall how they felt when watching *Pure as Snow* six years ago. A more realistic way to address the issue would be to interview viewers of recent anti-corruption dramas. While it is beyond the scope of this chapter, I hope to explore the issue in a future study.

for his family members.[2] In July 2007, Zheng Xiaoyu, Chief of State Food and Drug Administration, was executed amidst the wave of international controversies surrounding unsafe exports made in China.

Corruption has been featured in television dramas from the mid-1990s. These "anti-corruption dramas" typically revolve around one or more major corruption cases in a medium- to large-sized fictitious city, portraying Party and government officials engaging in embezzlement or misappropriation of public funds or assets, and taking bribes from favor-seekers. Corrupt officials include party secretaries, mayors, department chiefs, customs officials, police officers, and directors of state-owned enterprises. When bribery is involved, a private businessman or entrepreneur is often shown showering officials or their family members with gifts and cash in exchange for regulatory lenience, or scarce resources such as an exclusive right of land development in a highly valued urban area. The main perpetrator is often the most powerful or second most powerful leader of the city with strong backing in the provincial government. While anti-corruption dramas generally conform to the legal definition of corruption as abuse of public office for private gains — the typical forms of which are bribery, embezzlement and misappropriation of state assets — other types of official deviance are also featured, such as wining and dining on the public coffer, keeping mistresses, and falsifying statistics.

Given tight political control over prime-time television, all anti-corruption dramas subscribe to the same narrative framework, that is, no matter how powerful corrupt officials might appear, there will always be someone within the Party who remains incorruptible, fights resolutely to expose the corrupt schemes, and triumphs with the crucial aid from higher-up Party authorities, most likely the Central Discipline Inspection Commission ("CDIC," i.e. the Party's highest anti-corruption body). But this narrative structure collides with a civic culture that distrusts the ruling party. Producers of these drama serials inevitably face the question of how to handle the official discourse in a way that does not violate viewers' perceptions and opinions. A frequently employed narrative strategy is to cloak sensational stories about corrupt government officials in a layer that ostensibly adheres to the official discourse. Such a layer usually consists of one or two honest but bland government officials and the victory of the good ensured by the *deus ex machina* of officers from the CDIC. The real focus of interest, though, is on the bad guys.

Interestingly, however, this narrative strategy is absent from very popular anti-corruption dramas such as *Heaven Above* (*Cangtian zaishang*, 1995), *Pure as Snow* (*Daxue wuhen*, 2001), *The Procurator* (*Guojia gongsu*, 2003), and *The Year of the Dragon* (*Longnian dang'an*, 2003), among others. Instead of half-heartedly adhering to the Party line, these drama serials unequivocally put honest Party and government officials in a positive light and align themselves firmly with the official discourse. These characters resonate strongly with an age-old but still powerful, pervasive ideology, known as "clean official" (*qing guan yi shi*). According to this set of beliefs, society is bettered and justice restored by "clean officials," a minority of officials who are honest, fair, and who care for social underdogs. At the core of this ideology is a yearning for officials who pit themselves against powerful criminals to preserve the interests of ordinary people. Stories about clean officials in various art forms have enjoyed enduring popularity.

Many critics have attacked the so-called "clean official ideology," believing that it promotes an illusion among ordinary people that social injustices can be eliminated by individual government officials rather than by institutional safeguards, thereby undercutting people's desire for the rule of law. Such criticism, however, provides little insight into why narratives about clean Party officials in anti-corruption dramas are more appealing to viewers than notions of democracy and the rule of law. Resolving this puzzle may shed light on the nature of the Party's hegemony in contemporary China.[3] By hegemony, I refer to the process by which the Party seeks to create a consensus on the issue of corruption and to secure moral leadership by representing itself as standing on the side of "the people." To understand the appeal of these politically conservative anti-corruption dramas, it is imperative to examine the role of these clean officials in the narrative. I will argue that clean officials give rise to, and are central to, an anti-corruption moral community. By "moral community," I mean a group of men and women who fight corruption in a collective manner in the drama serials. In a broader sense, it includes each concerned citizen-character *across all* anti-corruption drama serials. At the most general level, it refers to the larger imagined anti-corruption community, to appropriate Benedict Anderson's formulation,[4] which includes viewers who make the moral decision to applaud the good characters and become part of the moral crusade against corruption. In this moral community, clean officials articulate the moral consensus with emotion that viewers experience as "real." Ideologically, as representatives of the Party-state, they help anchor the Party in the role of moral leadership and create a sense of moral unity between the Party and the people. Thus the reactivation of the cultural icon of "clean official" is central to the remolding of the Party's image in the mass media. Nevertheless, the appropriation of the clean official ideology incurs a price for the Party. It foregrounds ideological fissures and renders the official discourse vulnerable to deconstruction. As clean officials challenge authorities by definition, there is a strong tendency in anti-corruption drama serials to regulate the characters of the clean officials.

The Icon of "Clean Official"

To understand the appeal of clean officials, it is useful to explore briefly the prototypical clean official character in traditional popular literature: Bao Zheng, popularly known as Lord Bao (*Bao gong*). As an historical figure, Bao Zheng (AD 999–1062) was a high-ranking bureaucrat in the Northern Song dynasty serving Emperor Renzong as fiscal minister and governor of Kaifeng. During his years in the government, he combated crime, injustice, and corruption, and wrote numerous memoranda to the emperor impeaching wayward officials, including those with ties to the imperial family. While governor of Kaifeng (AD 1056–1058), he gained a reputation as "a strict and scrupulously fair administrator, so much so that eunuchs, powerful families, and courtroom clerks supposedly shrank back at the very sound of his name."[5] Morally, Bao was upright and severe. He was described by a contemporary chronicler as such:

> Stern and impatient by nature, he hated the high-handedness of clerks and strove toward sincerity and generosity. He loathed evil, yet he was ever ready to apply good faith and sympathy. He would not toady to the opinions of others, nor would he try to please them with false words and manners. Because he never responded to personal requests for favors, his friends and relatives all broke off relations with him. Even when he was in high position, his clothing, utensils, food, and drink were like those he had used as a commoner. He once said, 'Should any of my descendants be guilty of corruption in office, they may not return to their home, nor may they be buried in the family plot. Whosoever does not follow my ideals is no son or grandson of mine.'[6]

His devoted service to the government was recognized by the emperor, who, upon Bao's death, honored him with the posthumous title of "Filial and Reverent Duke" and suspended attending to royal court matters for one day as commemoration.[7] Bao's reputation as a stern, humorless judge who pitted himself against the corrupt and the powerful was to provide the basis for later Judge Bao stories in popular literature.

In popular literature, Bao Zheng's power and character assumed legendary proportions. Although official chroniclers recorded only three major court cases solved by Bao, the fictional Judge Bao resolved seventy-two mysteries.

It was reputed that he was able to do so because of his conscientiousness and clairvoyance; it was also said that he had the aid of magical objects such as a mirror to detect devils, a pillow to transport him to the Underworld, and another pillow to bring ghosts to life.[8] The elevation of Bao Zheng to the status of deity would not make much sense if not for his association with justice. In popular culture, Judge Bao always appears as the foe of injustice and corruption perpetrated by imperial families. Some of the most popular Judge Bao stories are about his relentless pursuit and punishment of powerful criminals related to the emperor by matrimonial ties. Judge Bao's hatred of the corrupt powerful is paralleled by his concern and commiseration for the downtrodden. To prevent corrupt courtroom clerks from making threats against people who might wish to present cases to him, he reformed the court decorum so that ordinary people could appeal to him directly by pounding the petition drum outside the courtroom. In response, people held him in high regard and always turned to him in times of need. A noted literary historian, Sun Kaidi, once observed, "In popular beliefs, Judge Bao commands respect in the same way that God of Martial Arts does. If one were to match a civil god to the martial god, Judge Bao would be the only choice, for ordinary people are far more familiar with him than with Confucius."[9]

Clean Officials and Anti-corruption Dramas

With few exceptions, the heroes of anti-corruption dramas can all be considered as clean officials. The hero is likely to be a Party leader or government leader in a sizable, fictitious city. In some cases, the hero is a Party's disciplinary official. Less frequently, he or she is a low-ranking Party or government official. No matter what position is occupied, however, the lead character is the single most important driving force in the resolution of corruption cases. Moral strength enables the hero to resist evil influences and fight corruption to the end. Evil influences include corrupt Party bosses, crooked cohorts, materialistic family members, and manipulative personal secretaries. These nefarious influences would sometimes exert their influence on the clean official, creating temporary confusion. But with his or her moral strength the hero of the story is able to regain perspicacity and control.

What seems intriguing is that Chinese viewers, including those I interviewed, believe that there are very few clean officials in reality. They consider Party cadres and government officials to be generally corrupt. So why do people still tune into anti-corruption dramas that exhort clean officials? What is so appealing about clean officials and their stories? In order to tackle this issue, in the following section, I provide an analysis of an anti-corruption drama serial, *Pure as Snow* (hereafter, *PAS*), broadcast by CCTV in 2001. It is a dual-plot twenty-episode drama serial. One story concerns a vice mayor who commits a murder at the beginning of the drama to cover up a corruption case in which he is implicated. The other narrative thread is about how a government official-turned-whistleblower doggedly pursues the general manager of a large state-owned enterprise who is guilty of stripping state assets. As an indicator of its official approval, *PAS* won Feitian, the highest government award for China's best television dramas of the year. Moreover, it was one of the most popular television shows in 2001. Audience surveys show that more than 120 million people watched the show.[10]

The following is a brief synopsis of the serial. An employee in the office of a municipal government is murdered. The employee is an insider in a major bribery case that implicates high-ranking officials in the city and the province. Fang Yulin, a detective at the city's police bureau, quickly targets Mayor Zhou as the primary suspect. Although Detective Fang and his colleagues successfully gather a great deal of incriminating evidence against Mayor Zhou, their detective work is in vain unless the highest authority in the province authorizes further investigation about Mayor Zhou. On a separate front, workers at a state-owned enterprise accuse their manager, Feng Xianglong, of embezzling factory assets. They know — albeit without substantive evidence — that Manager Feng sold off part of the state-owned enterprise's assets at one-tenth of their real value. But because of Manager Feng's relationship with key city government officials whom he heavily bribes, no serious investigation is conducted. Indignant, Ms. Liao Hongyu, a medium-ranking factory official, decides to investigate on her own by stealing the accounting book of the company. She finds solid evidence of Manager Feng's crime and mails it to the city's anti-corruption bureau. Unfortunately, the letter somehow falls into the hands of Manager Feng, who then hires some thugs to kill Ms. Liao. Having escaped death, Ms. Liao manages to bring her case to the personal attention of the head of the CDIC in Beijing, whose intervention leads to Manager Feng's defeat in the end.

In *PAS*, all the major crimes — embezzlement, bribery, and murder — take place by the end of the first episode of the show, and the identity of the major culprits soon becomes clear. Detective Fang, highly experienced and fully devoted to his duty, convinces the audience with his waterproof analysis of the evidence that Mayor Zhou is the murderer. Then in the third episode, factory workers charge that their Manager Feng conducted a murky deal through which he sold a large chunk of their factory assets to a private businessman at a ridiculously low price. This charge is confirmed by Manager

Feng himself when he explains to Mayor Zhou why this transaction occurred. Moreover, there are many suggestions that the highest authority in the province — a person named Gu — is also deeply implicated in both Zhou's and Feng's cases. So early in the show, the criminality of Mayor Zhou and Manager Feng is established, and that of Gu is strongly implied. In short, there is no "whodunit" suspense. Instead, the suspense is mostly about how such powerful villains will finally be punished. In other words, if viewers derive any pleasure from *PAS*, the source of pleasure seems to lie mainly in justice being done especially when powerful corrupt officials are involved.

In *PAS*, workers, laid-off workers, middle-class urban citizens, and government officials join together to fight the anti-corruption cause. At the center of this community is a group of clean officials, notably Detective Fang and Ms. Liao. Once an official at a state-owned enterprise, Ms. Liao loses her job because she reports the corruption in the management of the enterprise. But she lands a new job in Feng's company, where she can actively carry out investigations into a corruption case. Detective Fang receives various disciplinary sanctions and demotions because he often investigates local officials without authorization. Despite their relatively low status in the official hierarchy, they identify themselves as "officials" or *guan*, a category that sets them decidedly apart from "people" or *min*. Liao identifies her as a "government cadre" (*guojia ganbu*) with an administrative status of departmental chief, whereas Fang frequently reminds the audience that he is a "people's policeman" (*renmin jingcha*). Once, as Fang confronts his boss about the police bureaucracy, he says in exasperation, "I know it's time that I went home to sell yams." "Going home to sell yams" is an expression familiar to most Chinese people. The full expression of it is: "if you are an official and do not resolve people's grievances, then you'd be better off going home to sell yams." This ditty originated in a folklore story called "Seventh-Grade Sesame Official."[11] In this story, this county magistrate defends commoners' interest by challenging the overbearing gentry and powerful criminals. This expression is reserved only for officials in the Chinese context, and the fact that Fang employs such language indicates that he sees himself as an official.

Liao and Fang think and behave in a way expected of clean officials. They both demonstrate care and a strong sense of responsibility for the "people." Workers go to Ms. Liao with their grievances; she receives them into her house, listens to them, and, upset by the magnitude of corruption, makes up her mind to redress the gross injustices. Like Ms. Liao, Detective Fang harbors populist sentiments. Resentful of the fact that officials and their relatives are so privileged that the criminals among them are frequently condoned, he single-mindedly pursues powerful criminals such as Mayor Zhou. In short, these two protagonists represent a category of low-ranking clean officials who fight valiantly against corruption and injustice to protect social underdogs.

Fury and Anti-corruption Moral Community

A striking characteristic of these characters is their capacity to be emotionally aroused. This is illustrated clearly in the following segment in Episode 11. Ms. Liao is searching for concrete evidence of Manager Feng's illicit sale of factory assets. By coincidence, her former husband, Jiang Xingfeng, heads the officially assembled investigation group. But the investigation is just a puppet show directed by higher-up authorities who want to cover up the corrupt sale. Moreover, rumor circulates that the investigators take bribes from Manager Feng. Indignant, Ms. Liao confronts her former husband in his apartment, and a fierce argument ensues:

> *Ms. Liao:* So, you are here just to tell me that you, Jiang Xingfeng, are not at all responsible for the current situation [. . .]? As the team leader, all you can do is just to bottle up anything and everything when faced with all that is going on? [. . .]
> . . .
> *Jiang:* . . . You should have known how complicated this whole thing is, without me telling you so . . . I can only ensure that I, Jiang Xingfeng, enter and then leave this place with a clean record.
> *Ms. Liao:* As the leader of the investigation team, you don't do your best to investigate when there is such a mountain of problems? How can you say you are clean?
> *Jiang:* I want to investigate, but . . .
> *Ms. Liao:* But someone from above asked you not to investigate, so you stopped investigating, right?
> *Jiang:* I didn't say that someone asked me not to investigate.
> *Ms. Liao:* Jiang Xingfeng!!! Don't you play with such bureaucratic shibboleth!!! [. . .] [Music] If . . . if you can only promise to live a clean life of your own, then quit the position, go home and sell yams!!![12]

Particularly noteworthy in this emotionally charged scene is the manifestation of anger. Furious, Ms. Liao not only condemns corruption, but blames the government investigator for his cowardice. She challenges him as well as viewers to act bravely according to their conscience. She states plainly that a clean official does not just keep him/herself clean, but also stands up to corruption, and that otherwise he is little different from a corrupt official. Here, the meaning of corruption is shifted from the legal arena — where corruption is defined as abuse of public office to seek private gains — to the realm of conscience and morality, where failure to fight corruption is itself an instance of corruption.

In Episode 2, a similar encounter transpires between Detective Fang and his colleague named Guo Qiang. Upon preliminary investigation into the murder case, Detective Fang decides that Mayor Zhou was probably implicated, and he confides his findings to Guo. Terrified about the potential political repercussions of these findings, Guo dashes up to Detective Fang, seizes him by the collar, and yells, "You do want to invite trouble, don't you"? Upset about Guo's trepidation, Detective Fang yells back in fury, "Take a look at the uniform you wear, and think about the national emblem on your cap"! Guo responds cynically, "So you think just because I wear the police uniform, I can police everybody"? Detective Fang then presses Guo on this point, asking in an even angrier tone, "So who can you police and who can you not"?[13] Here, Detective Fang's sharp remarks resonate well with Ms. Liao's condemnation of her former husband. What they have in common is that they both take the populist stance and condemn cowardice in the face of justice crushed by willful power. On several other occasions, Fang expresses the same indignation toward powerful criminals and frustration about not being able to punish them. As a result of the heavy dose of moral indignation injected into the show, *PAS* enriches and expands the official discourse of corruption by bringing to life the affective dimension of the issue of official corruption.

As the clean officials in fury take up the anti-corruption cause, their courage spreads to the "people," i.e. non-officials. Doctor Su, who rescues Ms. Liao from Manager Feng's murder scheme, used to be — in his own words — "neither good nor bad." He suffers from fits of cowardice, but as he witnesses the bravery of Ms Liao, he turns into an anti-corruption hero. Not only does he successfully resist Manager Feng's demand that Ms. Liao be killed in her hospital bed, but he also personally escorts Ms. Liao to Beijing and helps her to find Dong Lin, the CDIC head, through personal connections. Another telling example concerns the family of Ms. Liao's accountant friend. After Ms. Liao secretly makes a copy of the accounting book of Manager Feng's company that is eventually to incriminate Manager Feng, she desperately needs to find some specialist who can read and interpret it. She finds her accountant friend, but the friend's wife is initially rather hostile to her. Yet, as soon as she learns the purpose of Ms. Liao's visit, her attitude undergoes a complete reversal. She sends her daughter to buy some evening snacks, and a new 40-watt bulb so that her husband and Ms. Liao can work overnight in well-lit conditions (apparently this is a poor, working-class family). Soon Ms. Liao is in tears, and so is the friend's wife, who emotionally exclaims: "In the future, whenever you need to check the accounts of these bastards and jackasses, you just come to us, OK? We'll provide room and good food for you no matter what!"[14] Upon this, Ms Liao breaks down. The tears shed together by these two women show solidarity between disparate social classes. Class differences are overridden by moral consensus.

The enactment and reenactment of the "clean official" myth in contemporary Chinese media can be seen as media rituals that confirm and consolidate moral values in the era of rampant corruption. According to Cottle, these rituals are "those exceptional and performative media phenomena that serve to sustain and/or mobilize collective sentiments and solidarities on the basis of symbolization and a subjunctive orientation to what should or ought to be."[15] Through these rituals, "collective solidarities are summoned and the media stage becomes populated by voices and views that reference an imagined moral community."[16]

What I want to further highlight about this moral community is its emotional dimension. In *PAS*, we see a moral community characterized by shared indignation based on moral consensus. This emotional moral community provides an important dimension to the popularity of *PAS* as well as other anti-corruption drama serials that exhort clean officials. In her study of the popularity of *Dallas* among Dutch viewers, Ien Ang argues that what is real for viewers of *Dallas* is not the literal content of the *Dallas* story, but "a subjective experience of the world: a 'structure of feeling'."[17] She defines such realism as "emotional realism." Similarly, even though Chinese viewers do not see these "clean official" stories as realistic, the anger expressed by clean officials is recognizable by viewers. Such emotion speaks to the angry or frustrated structure of feeling among many Chinese people who are not capable of taking actions to right the wrongs in real life. In this particular sense, clean officials are extremely realistic to viewers. Thus emotion is central to the anti-corruption moral community within the drama serial, but also central to the relationship between the drama serial and its viewers. It feeds into the larger anti-corruption imagination in the Chinese society.

What are the political implications of this imagined anti-corruption moral community? How is the Party situated in relation to it? Crucially, the Party leadership in *PAS* partakes of the collective solidarities. As the CDIC leader, Dong Lin represents the Party Center in its anti-corruption drive. When Ms. Liao eventually finds Ms. Dong, she is in hospital receiving medical treatment.

Despite her doctor's protestations, Ms. Dong receives Ms. Liao into her room. Attentively, she reads Ms. Liao's written report about Manager Feng's corruption and personal retaliation. Upset, Ms. Dong requests that Ms. Liao show her the wounds on her body. At the sight of the scars from the knife wounds, Ms. Dong is visibly troubled. After she sends Ms. Liao away, she makes a phone call to the highest disciplinary leader in Ms. Liao's province, and censures him for negligence of his duty. This phone call becomes the turning point in the narrative.

In *PAS* as well as other anti-corruption dramas, the heroes are always Party and government officials who are recognized as clean officials. It is through clean officials that the Party establishes its connection to the public. Clean officials are situated between the Party and the people, and by way of their proximity to both, they bridge the gap between leaders and the led. As representatives of the political order, clean officials convey the Party's anger about corruption; as advocates for public interest, clean officials express the indignation felt by a large segment of the Chinese population. So whenever anger wells up in clean officials, they are expressing the anger of the public and the anger of the Party simultaneously. By dramatizing anger, anti-corruption shows make it appear that the Party's interest is aligned with that of the general population, and thus provides the moral basis for the Party leadership of the community. In another sense, clean officials provide a locus and a definitive shape for the otherwise shapeless, fluid emotional display of anger. The anger now is directed toward the corrupt, and framing the central conflict as one between clean and corrupt officials clearly has benefits for the ruling party. Social conflicts and class stratification that are bound up with the issue of corruption are reduced into a morally unambiguous and politically innocuous form of melodrama. In doing so, anti-corruption drama serials reconstitute the Party's moral leadership or hegemony in the Gramscian sense. This is a specific instance of how "people's affect — their attention, volition, mood, passion — is organized, disciplined, mobilized and ultimately put into the service of specific political agendas."[18]

Thus, this imagined moral community is in the service of the Party's anti-corruption campaigns. Clean officials are the key to this community. Being popular heroes, they mediate and reduce the gap between the propaganda and the popular. They blend the Party's need for good publicity with a powerful popular belief in and desire for the redemptive power and heavenly justice embodied by clean officials. Because of the "clean officials," a dose of affective power is transfused into the Party heroes in the "clean official" image. It does not necessarily make the Party as an organizational entity lovable, but it does encourage attachment to these Party heroes. Such attachment is predicated not on realism in the sense of one-on-one correspondence to actual conditions, but on "emotional realism" enabled by the combination of public sentiments for justice and the charisma of "clean official" as embodiment of justice. This at least partially accounts for the fact that whereas the Party is out of favor with the public, many Chinese people accord deep respect for individual Party cadres. For example, the former Premier Zhu Rongji has been held in very high regard by the Chinese, despite the socially disastrous economic policies that he initiated, not least because of his "clean official" image — stern, fearless, iron-handed, clean and with a love of people, an image cultivated jointly by himself and by the media.

Containing Anger

Yet, by definition, "clean official" defies the powerful. In Hanan's words, Judge Bao is "the very model of a courageous official."[19] Although he or she does not question the dominant political and social order in its totality, the "clean official" occupies a moral universe that conditions him or her to question and defy authorities especially when the authorities are corrupt. When leading a moral community to confront corrupt political elites, they challenge, to appropriate Cottle's words, "the strategic power of institutions and vested interests, and even lend moral gravitas to the projects of challenger groups within society."[20] In this sense, the "clean official" myth can "open up productive spaces for social reflexivity and critique,"[21] and potentially disrupt the authoritarian political order. The characters of Detective Fang and Ms. Liao illustrate this point well. They are outspoken critics of corruption. Faced with outrageous forms of corruption, they make statements that are almost invariably embarrassing to the ruling elites. On more than one occasion Ms. Liao castigates corrupt managers in state-owned enterprises and expresses her contempt for those who tremble in front of authority. Likewise, Detective Fang frequently confronts his superiors about privileges enjoyed by powerful criminals and questions the qualifications of the Party leader at the police bureau.

To what extent can clean officials question higher-up authorities without calling into question the Party's authority? How furious can clean officials be without directing anger toward the political order itself? Ms. Liao is a brave fighter, but her temper and behavior often demonstrate a lack of maturity and rationality. Following the emotional confrontation with her former husband, she reflects to her daughter that he actually made a good point when he asked her for evidence to support her corruption charge. It is exactly through this climatic encounter that she is "enlightened" by Jiang that in order to successfully punish corrupt officials, one must not be carried away by anger or make charges without hard evidence. Thus reason triumphs over anger. After all, uncontrolled anger in a rebellious spirit is the last thing that the dominant elite want for Chinese television. So would be a Mao-style campaign nostalgia that rebels' anger may breed. Although Detective Fang is the best detective in the police bureau, he is often represented as naïve, immature, and prone to hasty judgement. In contrast, Detective Fang's boss, Chief Ma, is admired for his wisdom and sophistication. A cool-headed and self-controlled man in his forties, Chief Ma knows better than to openly confront his superiors, and he knows how to steer his way through the labyrinthine structures of the police bureaucracy to get things done. Because of his pragmatism, Chief Ma is able to protect Detective Fang and clear the way for the latter's investigation. Therefore he is portrayed as superior to Fang. In a word, at the textual level, emotion is subjected to rationality. Those who do not know how to control themselves emotionally are not so great after all. Though affect is a defining feature of the moral community, emotion is ultimately directed and contained.

Conclusion

In this chapter, I have demonstrated how tradition is reinvented and rearticulated to the affective plane so as to turn a source of political crisis into an opportunity of reconstructing the Chinese Communist Party's moral leadership. As the prototypical clean official in the Chinese folklore tradition, Judge Bao has contemporary parallels in anti-corruption dramas. Good Party cadres and government officials lead in battles against political corruption, in a similar way that Judge Bao punishes high-ranking officials and imperial family members in pre-modern Chinese literature. But the resemblance between Judge Bao stories and anti-corruption dramas must be understood at a level deeper than the plot and the narrative. In anti-corruption dramas, the promotion of good Party officials as moral paragons would fall flat without the presence of the emotion of anger and the anti-corruption moral community that such anger calls forth. With emphatic displays of anger toward social injustice and political corruption, these good characters enact and reenact moral dramas that differentiate the bad few from the good majority. Again and again, these moral dramas reinforce the hegemonic discursive framework of defining corruption. Whereas political corruption in contemporary China has largely resulted from the thoughtless marketization of a socialist economy coupled with the lack of political democratization, the moral dramas attempt to have us believe that corruption should be attributed to the moral failure of despicable public officials, and that the Party is determined to carry out a moral crusade against them in the people's interest.

4

Global Imaginary, Local Desire:
Chinese Transnational Serial Drama in the 1990s

Li Zeng

The twenty-one-episode Chinese television serial drama *Beijingers in New York* (*Beijing ren zai Niuyue*), was first broadcast on China Central Television (CCTV) in October 1993, quickly capturing the attention of much of the nation.[1] The first Mainland drama to be shot completely in a foreign country, the narrative revolved around the aspirations of a Chinese immigrant who struggles to be successful in business, and in doing so defeats his American rival. The serial contained images which would not have survived the censor's attention had it been located in Beijing.

Its popularity with Chinese audiences, and the somewhat unexpected high praise from the government, inspired a number of similar stories about cultural dislocation. This new subgenre of television serial featured Chinese abroad, as well as foreigners in China. Titles such as *Russian Girls in Harbin* (*Eluosi guniang zai Haerbin*, 1993), *Shanghainese in Tokyo* (*Shanghai ren zai Dongjing*, 1995), and *Foreign Babes in Beijing* (*Yangniu zai Beijing*, 1995) soon appeared.[2] I classify these serials as "transnational" more in terms of their imagery of cultural encounters than because of their production and distribution.

To understand *Beijingers in New York*'s representation of cultural encounters and foreign images, we must locate its emergence within a framework of globalization and transnational culture. There are essentially three contrasting approaches to framing global flows of capital within media and communication studies: culture, images, and ideology. The first unreservedly embraces global corporate ideology.[3] In this view, transnational corporations bring about development, progress, and modernization, while transnational media play a central role in promoting the virtue of global corporate ideology — commercialism and the market. This is certainly a problematic view. A second view is that globalization results in uneven power distribution and neocolonialism, and produces "cultural imperialism."[4] The view of globalization as hegemonic is problematic too. In many cases, the critical emphasis has been on a one-way flow from the advanced capitalist countries (particularly the United States) to the Third World. What has been ignored or undervalued is agency. This partial account of globalization is criticized in the third approach, which places the audience/consumer/user at the center. Ang's study, *Watching Dallas*, shows that the success of *Dallas* owes a good deal to the intrinsic pleasure derived from its melodramatic narrative structure, rather than its ideological message of consumer capitalism.[5] Homi Bhabha is one of many who have demonstrated how people of the Third World appropriate, reorganize, and transform the modern Western forms of technology and culture for their own uses.[6]

Based on these perspectives, this chapter shows how Chinese television meets the challenge from transnational competition and how Chinese people engage with changes brought by China's greater integration into the global economy. I analyze the Chinese "transnational" serial in relation to the state, the television industry, and the Chinese audience. I show how Chinese television appropriates, and in particular how domestic serials localize, international images and the foreign "other" to compete with international media. I show how the desire of local viewers for the unfamiliar and the exotic is expressed, how gender and sexuality are redefined, and how the state's shifting ideology and concerns are accommodated. Far from being simply Chinese nationalist propaganda promoted and enforced by the government, as scholars such as Geremie Barmé[7] have argued, the transnational serial dramas provide a culturally useful site of commonality where media institutions, audiences, and the state apparatus converge to negotiate for their individual interests. While participating in this fascinating and intriguing common experience each competing interest manages to achieve its own level of satisfaction.

Confronting the Challenge: Appropriations for the Native Pleasure

Before the advent of the "open door policy," Chinese people had little information about life in the West; the impressions they did receive were filtered through the state propaganda system. In the 1980s, television became the most important source of images of the world — Chinese viewers were able to compare their lives with the televised images of the citizens of foreign countries. Some writers have even suggested that, when watching international news, audiences paid far more attention to street scenes from foreign cities than to the political reporting that accompanied the pictures.[8]

The 1990s witnessed China's accelerated integration into the global capitalist system (eventually formalized by World Trade Organization accession in December 2001). Many Chinese, however, had already gone abroad by the mid-1980s, seeking education qualifications, new careers, "green cards," and a more exciting life than was possible at the time in China. This "craze for going abroad" (*chuguo re*) introduced a discourse of success and failure overseas. Some of the new "overseas" Chinese became models of success, their lives in foreign lands inspiring fanciful dreams for millions confined to the homeland. Book markets featured numerous literary and documentary accounts by and about Chinese overseas students. Television producers recognized the prevailing sentiment, and responded with the creation of a new television subgenre: the transnational serial.

Beijingers in New York was the first television serial to portray the experience of Chinese people in a foreign country. The story can be summarized as follows: Wang Qiming, a musician, and his doctor wife, Guo Yan, come to New York from Beijing to fulfill their American dream, to become successful and bring their daughter to a better life in America. Their expectations are immediately frustrated by the harsh reality of survival. Guo's Chinese relatives in New York offer little help as Wang looks for work. With no language and qualifications, Wang finds work as a waiter in a Chinese restaurant; meanwhile, his wife lands a job in an American garment factory run by David McCarthy. Life becomes more complex as Guo Yan is seduced by, and eventually marries, David. Humiliated, Wang Qiming plots revenge in the sphere of business. He finds emotional and financial support from A Chun, a resourceful emigrant from Taiwan who owns the restaurant in which Wang finds work. The serial culminates in Wang Qiming's success over David McCarthy, thanks to inside information from the estranged Guo Yan, who soon separates from David. In the final episodes we see the collapse of David McCarthy's business and the arrival of the couple's teenage daughter in New York. Following this, Wang Qiming becomes overconfident, gets caught in the stock market crash of the late 1980s, and turns to a last throw of the dice at the casino to pay his staff. He loses and eventually closes his business. The dream is ultimately a failure.

This television serial was constructed on the Chinese fantasy of capitalist metropolitan life. The representation is at times cinematic. In the opening credits, and throughout the twenty-one episodes, New York City is represented as a First World capitalist city. The juxtaposition of images of the Brooklyn Bridge, the Statue of Liberty, Times Square, and Fifth Avenue are repeated. The serial showcases American "lifestyles," grand high-rise buildings, spacious private homes, luxurious automobiles, and glamorous fashions. Low-angle shots and crane shots are frequently used to highlight the grandeur of office buildings. Tracking shots of New York streets create an illusion of direct contact between the viewers and what they see. The televisual images and objects of the "other" become fetishized commodities ready to be consumed by local viewers.

Lydia H. Liu claims that the secret of the serial's instant success lay in the producer and director's "intuitive grasp of television as a powerful media technology that can take the viewers almost anywhere in the world within the familiar surrounding of their homes."[9] The impact of this "transnational serial" was to break down the physical boundary of space constructed by the national serial. It created an illusion of being in two cultures at the same time. Many forms of media do this, now more than ever. In 1993, when this serial was broadcast, the internet was not available to Chinese people. For this reason, the gap in understanding was "filled in" by imagination. In his explanation of "mediascapes," Appadurai says: "The line between the reality and fictional landscapes they [the audience of the Third World] see are blurred, so that the farther away these audiences are from the direct experiences of metropolitan life, the more likely they are to construct imagined worlds that are chimerical, aesthetic, even fantastic objects, particularly if assessed by the criteria of some other perspective, some other imagined world."[10] The "local" viewer tends to glamorize, fantasize about, and idealize life outside his or her country. Appadurai's observation can be applied to *Beijingers in New York*, which perpetuated a glamorized and idealized image of the advanced "other." This serial reduced the distance created by the propaganda wars, but it displayed the foreign landscape through a Chinese viewpoint. Using well-known Chinese actors such as Jiang Wen, it provided the home audience with a virtual experience of an adventure in a foreign country.

Beijingers in New York also de-exoticized foreign images by encouraging viewer identification with the main character, Wang Qiming, whose views and experience of the foreign city are filtered through Chinese culture and ethics. His response to American people, his attitudes toward love and friendship, his life goal of working for the happiness of the next generation, and his response to humiliation are embedded in the conventions of Chinese culture and are shared by Chinese viewers. The representation of Western society is wrapped up in traditional Chinese morality. As Keane points out:

"Despite the depiction of the West as a dog-eat-dog society, many viewers registered an acute shock of recognition, the nation staring back at itself through a narrative which on the surface was an exercise in Occidentalism, but on a more concrete level, a reflection of the changing nature of social relations in China in the wake of economic reforms" (497).[11] Displaying New York through Wang's point of view and highlighting his success on the economic battlefield, this serial to some degree familiarizes and localizes the objectified foreign capitalist land.

Western Woman: Chinese Desire and Longing

While *Beijingers in New York* focused on a Chinese success story, serials about "foreigners" in China dramatize romance between Western women and Chinese men. The conspicuous presence of the Caucasian female is a significant selling point, symbolizing in different ways the desire and longing of Chinese men and women. In the 1990s, Chinese popular culture began to redefine gender roles. The reasons for this could be both the increasing influence of Western ideology and the gradual collapse of traditional values. Serials such as *Beijingers* and its imitators interrogate identity, gender, and sexuality. In most serials in this subgenre, the body of the Western or Caucasian female becomes the site where masculinity and femininity are reconceptualized, and where desire is released.

Foreign women are exoticized, eroticized, and objectified. In *Russian Girls in Harbin*, the Russian girls work as waitresses and entertainers for the pleasure of Chinese consumers. The main protagonist, Olia, is eroticized in numerous shots throughout the serial. Similarly, Jessie, a wealthy American exchange student in *Foreign Babes in Beijing*, is displayed as a sexualized object. In this twenty-episode television serial drama, Jessie — wild, sexy, and promiscuous — chases and seduces a married Chinese man, Tian Ming. In a culture and tradition that advocates restraint on explicit expression of sexuality, Jessie is portrayed as a temptress, the erotic "other." In an interview, Rachel DeWoskin, who played Jessie, said that she was often asked by Chinese journalists whether Jessie was a typical American girl.[12] The inquiry indicates that many Chinese fantasize American women as erotic and promiscuous and that their fantasies were confirmed by viewing this serial. Although *Beijingers in New York* does not feature a Caucasian female character, there is a scene where Wang Qiming goes to a motel with a prostitute. The close-up shots of her body and her sexual postures contrast with the traditional decorum of the Chinese female characters.

Chinese women characters are seldom portrayed in "sensuous" shots. They may be objectified, but they are not eroticized. For example, in *Beijingers in New York,* Guo Yan is always under the gaze of David McCarthy, but she is not portrayed in close-ups, nor does she appear in any scene as an erotic object. In *Foreign Babes in Beijing,* nearly all of Jessie's love scenes with Tian Ming are juxtaposed with scenes of his dutiful wife — in the factory, cooking for the family, and taking care of their child. Nevertheless, there are exceptions. A Chun, another main female character in *Beijingers in New York,* is portrayed as a sexually confident and liberated woman. She is different from traditional Chinese women who passively wait to be courted by men. More like Jessie in *Foreign Babes in Beijing,* and Olia in *Russian Girls in Harbin,* A Chun is straightforward about her love for Wang Qiming, pursues the man she loves, and eventually wins him over. The love scene on the sofa in episode eight is an explicit representation of her attitude toward love and desire. She invites Wang Qiming to her apartment and keeps him waiting in the living room while she takes a shower. Then she appears in her bathrobe and kisses him passionately. The scene clearly shows that A Chun makes the first move in their sexual relation: she flirts and seduces him.

Nevertheless, this serial drama makes it clear that her behavior is understandable because she has been in the United States for many years. The character of A Chun embodies Chinese people's imagination of a Westernized woman. More importantly, it emphasizes that she still adheres to Chinese tradition and ethics. One good example is that she insists in curing her son's illness with traditional Chinese medicine, even though her American ex-husband threatens to sue her. Thus the balance between her Westernized behavior and her Chinese identity is elaborately achieved. In other words, her body is Westernized but her soul is still Chinese.

Television was not the first medium to circulate images of Western females. In the early 1980s, pictures of international film stars appeared in magazines which were widely consumed. *Popular Cinema (Dazhong dianying),* the most highly circulated national film magazine, is an example. Following the state's call for opening to the world and speeding up modernization, *Popular Cinema* devoted considerable space to foreign stars and films. Sexuality was expressed through foreign images: Western women were often dressed erotically and framed in enticing postures, forming a sharp contrast with Chinese female stars, who were plainly dressed to look docile and demure. Sex was a sensitive issue, and sexual representations in cinema and television were subject to strict censorship; the Western female body became the site where Chinese men released their repressed sexual desire and reclaimed their lost masculinity through possession of the images.

In serials about foreigners in China, the Western women marry Chinese characters and are then domesticated. Although free-minded and actively seeking their dreams, they are conquered by their love for the Chinese men who defeat their Western rivals. For example, in *Foreign Babes in Beijing*, Louisa falls in love with Tianliang and rejects the courtship of her American classmate Robert; Jessie rebukes her bigoted, anti-Chinese father — another kind of rival — and marries Tian Ming. Film scholar Sheldon H. Lu suggests that this type of television serial caters to a large number of male viewers, and the victories that Chinese men score with foreign women are meant to represent a resurrection of Chinese masculinity.[13]

On the other hand, Chinese women who are seduced by foreign men are condemned and punished. In *Beijingers in New York*, Guo Yan is such a "fallen" woman and pays a high price for her submission. In episode eight, shots of Guo Yan and David McCarthy spending their honeymoon together are juxtaposed with images of the cuckolded Wang struggling for survival. It appears that these extravagances are intended to draw audience sympathy for Wang Qiming and condemnation for Yan for her betrayal — her contamination by the Western capitalist male. After much suffering, she is eventually forgiven, but only after she chooses to leave David and give up David's property. It is Wang Qiming's money that helps her to enter a graduate school, but she can never earn back his love. The disgrace of submitting to David McCarthy is an unbearable humiliation which finds a satisfactory resolution in the fallen Chinese woman's punishment.[14]

Chinese Women and the Gaze at the West

But how do Chinese women audiences view the representations of sexually liberated Western women? While directly associating such representations with Chinese (repressed) masculinity, critics of this type of serial have also neglected the female audience. I would argue that viewing the erotic "other" gives many Chinese female viewers pleasure by providing an expression of their own liberated sexual desire. Chinese women's pleasure in viewing eroticized Western women should be put in the context of the socialist discourse of gender. The Chinese Communist Party emphasized women's equal rights, and promoted slogans like "Whatever men can do, women can do." However, one consequence was that women were masculinized. During the 1960s and 1970s, women were dressed in shapeless, drab Mao-suits and dull uniforms, and wore no cosmetics. In other words, there was little concern for appearance, let alone fashion. Laura Mulvey's feminist criticism of

Hollywood cinema that women are represented as the object of male gaze
— "to-be-looked-at-ness" — is problematic when applied to Chinese socialist
cinema, which undermines the association between women and the sexual
body.[15]

In the 1980s, the widely circulated visual images of Western stars
contributed to Chinese women's reconstruction of their identity and viewing
expectations. There was a sudden rediscovery of the difference between the
female self/feminine and the male/masculine. The desired and different
qualities of the feminine were outwardly symbolized by choice of color, style,
and fashion. As Elisabeth Croll observed: "In addition to dressing fashionably,
there is a great interest in make-up, skin care, jewelry, cosmetics, and hair-
style, all accentuating the enhancement of physical appearance that is the new
attribute of women who '*know how to be women*'."[16] The great interest in
physical appearance formed a peculiar feminine-seeking phenomenon in
China in the 1980s. When Western feminists criticized objectification of
female bodies in advertisements and other popular discourses, a large number
of Chinese women — particularly young women — were embracing this
new culture, regardless of whether it was capitalist, and reconceptualizing
their bodies.[17] The pictures of Western female stars — in magazines, on
postcards, and in films — played an important role in catching up with fashion
trends and reconstructing sexuality. Distanced geographically from the erotic
"other," Chinese women were able to displace their desire for free sexual
expression on to the sexualized body of the Western woman.

Although making use of images of Western countries is a marketing
strategy to achieve the best audience ratings, these serials can be read as a
counter-discourse against the West's stereotypical representation of Chinese
men and women. In Western media and literature, Chinese men are usually
feminized (an early example is Cheng Huang in Griffith's film *Broken Blossom*),
and Chinese women are extremely eroticized (such as Anna May Wong in
Piccadilly and *Limehouse Blues*, and Joan Chen in *Tai-Pan*).[18] Interestingly, New
Chinese Cinema has employed the strategy of "self-exoticization," to use
Rey Chow's term, to break into the international market. Contrary to the
view that the fifth-generation directors' films such as *Red Sorghum* (dir. Zhang
Yimou), *Raise the Red Lantern* (dir. Zhang Yimou), and *Farewell to My
Concubine* (dir. Chen Kaige) promote the stereotype of China through
sumptuous displays of primitive landscapes and sexualized women, Rey Chow
argues that this new approach is a "tactic": "In its self-subalternizing, self-
exoticizing visual gestures, the oriental's orientalism is first and foremost a
demonstration — the display of a 'tactic'."[19] Similarly, Lu claims that Chinese
New Cinema produces alternative images and narratives for the Western

audience, deconstructs the monolithic, ethnocentric vision of history, and breaks "the closed circuit of First-world cinema in the political economy of global film culture."[20] The New Cinema uses this strategy of self-exhibition to gain access to the global market rather than submitting to the Western stereotype of China.

What differentiates the Chinese transnational television serial from the New Cinema is that the former objectifies and eroticizes the West for the pleasure of the native, while the latter exhibits and exoticizes the native for the gaze of the West. Produced for a domestic market instead of an international market, the Chinese serial caters to the Chinese audiences' desire and pleasure, and creates a cross-border space to consume the "other" from their perspectives and to take account of their everyday life within a globalizing context.

The State in Predicament: Globalization versus Nationalism

Although I emphasize the agency of Chinese television production and the Chinese viewer in the encounter with globalization, I do not exclude the role of the state since the Chinese government still has a strong level of control over the media. It has been argued that television is one of the state's means to promote nationalism to ensure its control over the people. As David Morley and Kevin Robins state: "In the post-war years, it was television that became the central mechanism for constructing their collective life and culture of the nation."[21] When globalization threatens the power of the state, nationalism becomes an effective weapon of resistance. Chinese television programs are also thought to represent the state ideology. For instance, aired two years after the Tiananmen Square demonstrations, *Yearning* was interpreted as a nationalist message to reconstruct "nation-ness" after the trauma.[22] *Beijingers in New York*, with the central plot of a Chinese immigrant defeating his American rival, seems to be quite naturally subject to the same critique. This critique seems to be further validated by the fact that its production gained support from the government. It is reported that the Central Committee of the Chinese Communist Party facilitated a loan of US$1.5 million dollars from the Bank of China to complete the shooting in New York.[23]

Barmé argues that this serial is clearly the government's promotion of patriotism and nationalism against American capitalism.[24] To some degree, he is right. This serial does present a relatively negative view of America, and the narrative is driven by the success of a Chinese man and his revenge against the American rival. American society is exhibited as morally corrupt. For example, David is portrayed as a self-centered man who manages his business ruthlessly, has little concern for his employees, and cares about nothing beyond making money.[25] In one scene, Guo Yan asks David what he loves more — money or her. He replies: "Money." Although Miss Bai tries to help him, she does not gain his trust. In one scene, when David finds that his inside business information has been disclosed to Wang Qiming, he accuses Miss Bai of it even though she has spent days trying to save him from bankruptcy. American businessmen and lawyers are depicted as sly and selfish people who disregard the well-being of their partners or clientele.

Nonetheless, positive attitudes toward American culture are also explicitly conveyed in *Beijingers in New York*. New York is presented as a place where everyone can succeed if only they work hard, and where one can enjoy the most fanciful and modern lifestyle. After Deng Xiaoping's 1992 "Southern Tour," and his speech affirming the socialist commodity economy, economic achievement became an indicator of success and social status. This serial, broadcast one year after Deng's Southern Tour, was a promotion of the trend of economic success. When Keane conducted a survey on audiences' responses in 1993, over half of his respondents said the significant message of this serial was that resourcefulness and independence led to success in a commodity economy.[26] Wang Qiming starts from nothing — he goes from a penniless waiter to successful businessman. This encapsulates the Chinese fantasy of the American dream. In the last seven or eight episodes, David is more positively portrayed than in the first half of the serial. He starts all over again and wins Wang Qiming's respect back in an honest way.

This television program is therefore not a completely negative portrayal of America. At the beginning of each episode, there is a replay of the theme verse read in English: "If you love him, bring him to New York, for it is heaven. If you hate him, bring him to New York, for it is hell." If this serial is an embodiment of the state's ideology, the ambivalent confrontation between the Chinese (Wang Qiming) and the American (David) can be read as the government's uncertainty about the accelerated reforms, rather than simply as propaganda of nationalism.

While embracing economic progress brought about by globalization, the state is attempting to maintain a balance between its control and the market: "a commodity economy with socialist characteristics" — the official term of China's new economic system — is itself an explicit articulation of the government's predicament. Never has the government been so perplexed by the changes. Lisa Rofel makes an important observation which helps to explain the presence of these contradictory representations in the mass media in the 1990s. She argues:

> The rejection of Maoist socialism and the introduction of a market economy have meant that in the current period of economic reform the state may be clear about speaking in the name of a social body, but it is much less sure about what it is speaking for. *The goals and desires of the state have never been more fraught with ambiguity and uncertainty.* At one moment, productivity and the pursuit of wealth are lauded by party bureaucrats; in the next moment, "socialist morality" is applauded as the antidote to undue worship of money.[27]

Beijingers in New York embodies these contradictory tendencies and presents a complicated cross-cultural encounter. It captures the state of China's predicament: embracing the global economy and fearing its hidden dangers.

While interpreting the program as an embodiment of the state's ambiguity toward globalization, I do not intend to argue against its nationalist message. However, I would question the predominant view of nationalism as a hegemonic discourse, an ideology imposed on the people at a time when the state's power is threatened. Benedict Anderson's concept of nation as "imagined communities" has frequently been used as the theoretical grounding for criticizing nationalism — the internal hegemony.[28] I agree that "nationalism" can be manipulated by the state to strengthen its power, and that the deconstruction of "national identity" creates much free space for individuals to construct their identity at a global level.[29] Nevertheless, I do not think there is a clear-cut line between the state's strategy of nationalism and the people's free engagement in constructing nationalism. As I mentioned above, the television viewers have their agency, and are not manipulated passively by the state's power.

Discussing the nationwide enthusiasm for the best-seller popular political book *China Can Say No* (1996), Dai Jinhua comments that "the pioneer of this so-called tide of nationalism, emotionally beckons to those of the same generation to trace how the American dream, even during the latter part of the Mao Zedong era, penetrated the Chinese imagination, only to become an even greater lie over time."[30] She suggests that, since America has been embedded in Chinese aspirations, its constant betrayal to China (referring to changeable Sino-American relations) frustrates the Chinese people: "We have time and time again been injured, continually encountering betrayal. Therefore, a choice is made, in a tone filled with injury, based on resentment to abandon the abandoner: China can say no."[31] Her explanation provides an insight into the relations between global television and the discourse of nationalism. Although nationalism can be an ideological tool manipulated by the state to reinforce its own hegemony, it can also be the articulation of the people who contemplate and engage with the encounter between their own cultural identity and the "other."

Conclusion

I have tried to emphasize that the Chinese transnational serial cannot simply be viewed from the perspective of the state's control over media and ideology. It is best understood as a cultural site where Chinese media, the state, and most importantly the Chinese audience engage with the social and cultural changes inevitably produced by the penetration of the global into the local, and project their disparate but interlocked desires through transnational bodies and images.

Serials such as *Beijingers in New York* and *Foreign Babes in Beijing* became popular at a particular historical moment: this was the early 1990s when China moved closer to integration into the global capital community. With increased exposure to foreign images, ideologies, and commodities, Chinese people were eager to know the outside world, and particularly the more advanced capitalist countries. This television subgenre continues to be popular. However, with the increasing global flow of capital, technology, images, and ideology, and greater possibilities for cross-border traveling, the distance has become more familiar and less exotic. The transnational serial, characterized by its ability to mobilize Chinese viewers into the global space, will presumably take another track to address Chinese people's desires and aspirations at a new stage of globalization.

II

Gender and Domestic Sphere

5

Family Matters:
Reconstructing the Family on the Chinese Television Screen

Shuyu Kong

Family is central to television soaps in the West. Not only does domestic space constitute the primary site for the majority of soap opera plots, but the melodramatic interwoven desires, troubles and joys of family life provide much of the content and rhythm of these TV dramas. This defining feature of Western soaps, however, does not necessarily apply to Chinese TV serial dramas, which originated from a very different narrative tradition and have developed a quite different social function from Western soaps within the sphere of contemporary life. Until the 1990s, narratives of social change and public events constituted the mainstream among Chinese television dramas dealing with contemporary life. Groundbreaking television dramas of the 1980s, such as *Eighteen Years in the Enemy Camp* (*Diying shi ba nian*, 1981), *New Star* (*Xinxing*, 1985), and *Plain-clothes Police* (*Bianyi jingcha*, 1987) all framed their stories within a much broader social space, be it revolutionary history, rural and urban social reforms, or law and social justice. Rarely did the more "secular" and private concerns of family life become their central subject matter.

The downplaying of family in Chinese TV drama during the 1980s was a residue of the socialist realism tradition — the direct result of a highly centralized and politicized national culture. From the late 1940s, the socialist state had sought to transform the national economy and culture, both through the reform of private property ownership and enterprise, and through appropriating and erasing private space from social imagination and artistic representation. With such a cultural legacy and narrative tradition of socialist realism, it is not surprising that the personal sphere and domestic space of the family did not immediately become the central focus of Chinese television serial drama.

Yearning (*Kewang*), produced by the Beijing Television Arts Center (hereafter, BTAC) in 1990, was influential in many ways in the development of Chinese TV drama. Utilizing the concept of "indoor drama" (*shinei ju*), the fifty-episode *Yearning* was produced with limited resources and budget, and developed a new mode of commercialized production of television drama. *Yearning* also caused a paradigmatic shift in the evolution of Chinese television narrative by zooming in on family life and domestic space. Centered around the "intertwined lives, loves and tragedies of two families" and the tension between a young woman's romantic relationship and her maternal love, the phenomenal popularity and success of *Yearning* lay in its effective borrowing of the format and conventions of family melodramas from other parts of the world,[1] including "coincidence of fate, hyperbolic figures, mysterious parentage, romance and tragedy, and the quintessential location in domestic space, as well as the symbolic construction of woman, the maternal and the feminine, through stories of desire, personal relations and daily family life."[2]

Throughout the 1990s and early 2000s, "family drama" steadily gained popularity. More and more TV dramas focused on family relationships and everyday experiences of individuals in contemporary urban family settings, resulting in a profusion of subgenres, among them "urban romances" (*dushi qinggan ju*), "family values dramas" (*jiating lunli ju*), and "dramas of urban ordinary folk" (*dushi pingmin ju*).[3] According to a recent industry survey, the *China TV Drama Market Report 2003–04* (*Zhongguo dianshiju shichang baogao 2003–04*), these subgenres rank very highly on the broadcast and reception ratings. For example, in 2002, what the report calls "urban life" (*dushi shenghuo*) dramas ranked second in broadcast ratings (16.5 percent) and third in reception (12.1 percent), coming just after crime dramas (20.7 percent and 19.4 percent respectively). And ordinary folk dramas ranked fifth, with broadcast and reception ratings of 8 percent and 8.2 percent respectively.[4] Unlike crime and costume dramas, both of which achieved sudden success mainly due to expensive marketing campaigns and the political controversy surrounding their subject matter, family dramas have been less dependent on such external factors. Hence, the consistent and growing popularity of these family subgenres clearly demonstrates the deep and broad appeal of family issues among Chinese audiences today. So much so that Yin Hong, a Chinese film and TV critic, in a recent study of the general characteristics of Chinese TV drama, claims that family stories dealing with mundane quotidian concerns have become the core subject matter (*hexin ticai*), and this thematic preference has directly affected the aesthetic experience of viewing Chinese TV dramas.[5]

So if family has become such an important trope in representing contemporary lives, what kinds of families are articulated in Chinese soap operas? How has family drama responded to the recent changes in Chinese society? How are different social agencies involved in constructing family in Chinese TV dramas? And what ideological and social functions does this construction of family serve? In the rest of this chapter, I will discuss the representation of contemporary urban families in recent Chinese TV drama and how this new discourse of domestic space is implicated with gender issues, class concerns, and state ideology. By examining the rise and acceptance of the "domestic space" in television culture and public discourse, I will argue that Chinese family drama has opened up a cultural forum for various social groups and ideological agents to make sense of dramatic social changes and to address the everyday emotional concerns of Chinese viewers.

Urban Romances and Women

Among television dramas that depict contemporary family life, a substantial number deal with love and marriage in the urban middle-class family. Some of these "urban romances" depict new forms of sexual relationships and family values evolving among young and fashionable urban Chinese. Well-received works include *Live Life to the Limit* (*Guoba yin*, 1993), *Sunrise in the East, Rain in the West* (*Dongbian richu xibian yu*, 1995), *Love Comes First* (*Rang ai zuo zhu*, 2001) and *Gallery of Passion and Love* (*Qing'ai hualang* 2004). Others explore the collapse of family relationships and moral dilemmas facing the middle-aged. In this category we find *Holding Hands* (*Qianshou*, 1999), *Coming and Going* (*Lailai wangwang*, 1999), *Ten Years of Married Life* (*Jiehun shi nian*, 2003), and *Chinese Style Divorce* (*Zhongguo shi lihun*, 2004). Still others focus particularly on women's self-identity and growth in the context of their romantic and family relationships, such as *Lipstick* (*Kouhong*, 2000), *Mirror* (*Kong jingzi*, 2002), *Empty House* (*Kong fangzi*, 2004), and *Romantic Affairs* (*Langman de shi*, 2004).

This overt preoccupation with romantic and family relationships in TV dramas clearly reflects peoples' concerns about the impact of urban social transformation on the personal and familial level. During the 1980s and 1990s, Chinese society experienced enormous changes caused by the economic reforms and the government's "open door" policy. One obvious effect of these changes on ordinary families has been the destabilization of the institution of marriage and the breakdown of family life in urban China. The deterioration of the traditional family structure, coupled with more social mobility and "contemporary" moral values which prize individualism and materialism, have placed great strains on ordinary Chinese families. The fragile foundations of the contemporary Chinese family based on revolutionary socialist ideas have made it even more vulnerable to the various temptations and challenges of an increasingly materialistic and individualistic society. As a result, many urban Chinese families have endured relationship crises in the last two decades. Rising divorce rates, an increase in extramarital affairs, and the revival of illegal sexual practices such as prostitution and concubinage are symptomatic of these crises.[6] They are a frequent topic of media commentary, and — not surprisingly — they provide the recurring plot motifs of television dramas too.

Another factor that has directly contributed to the emergence of the urban romance subgenre is the major impact of women writers.[7] Drawing on their personal experiences and sensitivity to women's issues and family relationships, many women writers, including Chi Li, Zhang Kangkang, Tie Ning, Pi Pi, Wang Hailing, and Wan Fang, have chosen to set the majority of their works against the backdrop of marriage and family crises in urban society. Their sensitive depiction of the emotional upheavals and struggles of ordinary Chinese women within a rapidly changing society have won a loyal following among urban readers. With the conscious promotion and cultivation of these women writers by commercial publishers — a typical example being the popular Cloth Tiger Series of Urban Romances by Chunfeng Publishing House[8] — these works have created a new subgenre of "middle brow" romantic fiction. The popularity of these women writers' fiction subsequently led to adaptations of their works into TV dramas, and in several cases, to new works written specially for television.[9]

The name "urban romance" may conjure up a slightly misleading impression however, as a substantial number of TV dramas dealing with love and marriage in urban middle-class families are not "romantic" in the traditional sense. Mirroring the reality of moral collapse and unstable human relationships in a rapidly changing and greatly confused society, the family lives and sexual relationships represented in these TV dramas are often full of turmoil and tension, mid-life crises, extramarital affairs and marriage breakups.

Holding Hands and *Chinese Style Divorce*, by the female screenwriter Wang Hailing, are typical of this subgenre. Compared by some commentators to a Chinese version of *Kramer v. Kramer*, these two serial dramas depict the bleak sexual relationships and breakdown of seemingly perfect middle-class professional families. Unlike the family tragedies caused by political persecution or social disasters in previous Chinese literature and cinema, the family crises in these TV dramas arise from stressful work situations, "trivial" everyday conflicts, and unfulfilled sexual and emotional desires.

The husbands in these two serials, one of whom is a computer engineer and the other a doctor, have to pursue more highly paid jobs in order to improve their living conditions and get ahead in a competitive environment. Though initially committed to their marriages, work pressures and other distractions soon cause them to lose interest in their families. At the same time, their wives are also torn between work and family. But after they choose to give up their own careers to support their husbands and children, they find that they have lost not only economic independence but also their self-identity and confidence, especially when their husbands find success in their careers and begin extramarital affairs with younger women who seem happy to admire their achievements. The estranged marriage relationships deteriorate into hostility and endless fighting, and eventually the men flee their families, leaving the wives with not only broken marriages but also broken selves.

There is a unique feminine perspective and sensibility in the articulation of sexual and family relationships in these TV dramas. While not lacking sympathy for the mid-life crises and high pressures that Chinese men face in an increasingly competitive society, these dramas pay much greater attention to the middle-aged female characters torn between their careers and families, and struggling to reconcile all the conflicting demands that family and society throw at them. As a result, they directly address many of the pressing issues and concerns specific to women in a transforming society. Both Xia Xiaoxue in *Holding Hands* and Lin Xiaofeng in *Chinese Style Divorce* represent the dilemma of intellectual and seemingly independent women who have grown up in "New China": the contradictory and double standards demanded of women in China's puritan socialist-turned-capitalist consumer society make them suddenly vulnerable and confused. Despite being highly educated and employable, deep-rooted social conventions and their own self-imposed conception of "woman's virtue and duties" cause them to sacrifice their own interests for the sake of their husbands and families. In addition, growing up in an "ungendered" revolutionary society has also left them insensitive to the emotional and sexual needs of their husbands, and ignorant of their own sexual natures, which often puts them at a disadvantage compared with younger women. Their sense of insecurity, especially their sexual inadequacy in a society where sex appeal has again become important, is most intensely demonstrated in their marital relationships, as they face hostility and betrayal from their own husbands.

These urban romances are particularly successful in capturing the inner emotional world of the female characters with great sympathy and sensitivity. The anger, confusion, frustration, jealousy and even hysteria of middle-aged women are convincingly built up, episode by episode, ultimately reaching crisis point. In some dramas, the crisis can become a catalyst for revelations about self-identity and the meaning of intimate relationships — and frequently an opportunity for inner growth, personal development and independence (both financial and spiritual) beyond the bonds of family. In *Lipstick* the main female character Jiang Xiaoge undergoes a transformation from a dependent, naïve and weak wife to a mature, strong-headed and successful female entrepreneur. In *Empty House*, two divorced women form a strong sisterhood to support and console each other through difficult times, and finally realize that happiness comes from being true to themselves rather than constantly trying to meet other people's expectations.

Thus, although Chinese TV drama, unlike Western soap opera, lacks a separate "women's tradition," the emerging subgenre of urban romances has opened up a gendered space to portray many of the problems and concerns facing women in Chinese society today. Despite their sometimes over-idealistic endings, these dramas provide consolation for viewers and a sense of social bonding with other women going through a similar difficult transition within capitalist-consumer society.

Family Values Drama and Drama of Ordinary Folk

Besides the crisis of urban middle-class families and the dilemmas of middle-aged career women, another substantial concern of TV drama in recent years has been the everyday family lives of common people, or "ordinary folk" (*putong baixing* or *pingmin*). In particular since the late 1990s, urban working classes, retirees, and the unemployed have displaced some of the glamorous images of upwardly mobile groups — the successful business managers and "public relations girls" that previously crowded the TV screen in the mid-1990s.[10] These dramas of ordinary folk, which overlap to a large extent with another subgenre called "family values dramas," are often centered on materially poor families in urban settings, and vividly portray their mundane and difficult daily lives. The style is distinctively naturalistic too: they are often shot against very plain, even ugly, scenic backdrops and interior sets, with minimal performing by the actors. Providing a drastic contrast with the dramatic and fast-paced police/crime stories and glossy cosmopolitan "white collar" urban dramas (see Chapter 7, for instance), this new subgenre has quietly and steadily won loyalty among ordinary Chinese viewers, who can closely relate to the characters and events portrayed.

Garrulous Zhang Damin's Happy Life (*Pinzui Zhang Damin de xingfu shenghuo*, 2000, hereafter, *Happy Life*) exemplifies the narrative style. Originally a popular novel by Beijing writer Liu Heng, *Happy Life* portrays a poor urban family of seven living in a single cramped room in a back-lane courtyard (*da za yuan*) in Beijing. The main character is Zhang Damin, the oldest brother in this extended family. With the burdens of looking after his family — an elderly mother who develops Alzheimer's, and four siblings who frequently demand material and financial support — coupled with his unsatisfactory job as a factory worker who later becomes unemployed when the state factory goes bankrupt and shuts down, Zhang Damin is not the most attractive candidate for a "happy life." The story revolves around Zhang's constant struggle to find space for all the family in their cramped home and somehow keep the household going. The everyday troubles of most ordinary urban Chinese left behind by the reforms are realistically depicted and the often black humorous survival strategies developed by Zhang Damin to deal with his extreme poverty produce a tragicomic effect. The enthusiastic response of the novel's readers led to it being adapted several times: into a film comedy, a stage play, a local opera (*pingju*), and the television series.

The TV series was particularly successful, not only winning official recognition (receiving the Golden Eagle Award for best TV program and the Propaganda Ministry's Five Ones Project Award) but also becoming one of the highest rated TV dramas of 2000, especially in Beijing and Northern China.

The TV series retains the basic storyline of the original work, and by taking advantage of the extended serial form, it is able to vividly capture the quotidian details of everyday Beijing life. The narrow back lanes of the Beijing courtyard ghetto, the cramped and shabby room of the family, and the dusty streets and cheap restaurants all create a realistic environment and atmosphere with which ordinary viewers can immediately identify. Each episode deals with yet another struggle for the family with their limited resources: how to share a bedroom between two couples at night; how to find more funds for a small start-up business; how to obtain money to feed a newborn baby and then locate a good daycare center so that the parents can go back to work; or how to share the duties of looking after fading elders. At the center of the entangled relationships between siblings and different generations, with their trivial arguments, little tricks and power struggles, stands the sad but also resilient figure of Zhang Damin. He is constantly challenged to find ingenious methods to make the family's scarce resources go further, but he manages somehow to retain his optimism and humor to deal with the bleak realities of poverty.

The success of Zhang's characterization and the serial as a whole largely stems from the vibrant and humorous dialogue inherited from the original novel. Full of local flavor, the dialogue complements the earthy street life scenes, and its down-to-earth wit and black humor shows the characters coming to terms with the difficulties and trivial dilemmas of their life situation. This quality is best captured by the performance in the title role of Liang Guanhua, a veteran stage actor from Beijing People's Arts Theater.

Following the success of *Happy Life*, critics were quick to label its approach the "common person style" (*pingmin fengge*) and a whole group of works in this vein followed, including hits such as *Eldest Brother* (*Dage*, 2002), *Mirror* and *Mother-in-Law* (*Popo*, 2004). These ordinary folk TV dramas altered the aesthetic style of Chinese serials, and have contributed greatly to the emergence of what has been termed a "common style" (*pingmin fengge*) or "documentary style" (*xieshi fengge*) in Chinese TV drama as a whole. These dramas present intimate narratives of human relationships in everyday surroundings, with plain and simple story lines and very few scenes of high suspense or melodrama. Their shooting and performances are also realistic, even naturalistic in style, almost like "fly on the wall" documentaries. This approach to production contrasts drastically with the big-budget spectaculars of recent Chinese cinema, which are obviously inspired by Hollywood blockbusters. The plain style simply reinforces the sense that TV drama has become primarily an entertainment and leisure activity of the common people.

The common folk subgenre conspicuously reflects a populism that has recently emerged in the popular culture industry, and reveals the effect of class stratification on cultural production and consumption due to China's market economic reforms. While the internet and cinema, with their higher entry costs, have become popular among the middle, upwardly mobile classes — the affluent "white collar" techies, intellectuals and college students — television drama, which up to the early 1990s had appealed to a range of different viewers,[11] has more recently become increasingly attuned to the true "mass audience." According to one survey in 2002, TV audiences now primarily comprise viewers of lower educational levels, females, the middle-aged and the elderly, and the economically less affluent.[12] Television in China is cheap and easily accessible (a monthly fee for satellite or cable TV costs only RMB 10 or so), and as a result, it has become the ideal leisure and entertainment activity for less privileged, less mobile audiences, such as retirees or the unemployed. Television production and investment companies have been quick to recognize this social change, and have responded with new series aimed specifically at this audience demographic.

Dramas about ordinary folk not only attract the loyalty of broad demographics, but they are also a very safe card to play politically. Clearly the writers and producers of these dramas have recognized the emotional anxieties faced by the less well-off in an increasingly aggressive and individualistic society where morals and family values, whether traditional or socialist, have collapsed. To assuage this anxiety, common folk dramas offer a conformist view of family and family relationships, and therefore satisfy the emotional needs of their mass audience for a warmer and more stable representation of human relationships than they experience in real life. Not surprisingly, many of these dramas are concerned with moral issues, as they directly address how family relationships and values are threatened by an increasingly individualistic and materialistic society. Filial duties, in-law relationships, parental responsibilities, and maintenance of family harmony in an extended family are constantly recurring themes. The many difficulties faced by the central families lead to frequent ethical dilemmas and moral conflicts. Yet more often than not, the resolution of these conflicts promotes a more traditional and conservative moral outlook in which harmony and stability prevail.

A noteworthy feature of many of these dramas is the idealized woman character, who embodies the virtues of kindness, hard work, tolerance and good sense, and who puts her own interests last in order to maintain the harmony of the family unit. She is a combination of the traditional Confucian ideal of the "virtuous wife and good mother" (*xianqi liangmu*) and the self-denying "socialist morality" of Lei Feng. The obvious precedent for this character type was Liu Huifang in *Yearning*, but similar kinds of female characters appear in several recent series such as *Mother-in-Law* and *Eldest Sister* (*Dajie*, 2004).

Whether intentionally or not, the relatively conservative aesthetics and moral values of ordinary folk dramas tie in with the mainstream state ideology of "social stability" and building a "harmonious society," and this might explain at least partially the official recognition and promotion of dramas like *Happy Life* and *Mother in Law*.[13] While many other TV drama genres, such as anti-corruption or crime dramas, re-made red classics, and even some costume dramas, have challenged the legitimacy of the communist government by touching on sensitive political issues, and therefore faced suppression and attacks in the official press,[14] ordinary folk dramas have easily received approval from the official censors, and have won frequent praise from critics. This subgenre has thus managed to satisfy both the emotional needs of the mass TV audience and the political demands of cultural officials, a necessary balancing act for all successful cultural products in contemporary China.

Nation and Family in Main Melody TV Drama: *Year after Year*

As family drama has steadily won over TV audiences and addressed their emotional needs, the state has also attempted to appropriate the discourse of family to present its own agenda.[15] More recently, as state legitimacy and its reform discourse have been challenged from all sides due to social problems and serious inequalities arising from the economic reforms, the government has actively sought to take advantage of the trend by producing its own "main melody family TV dramas" as mouthpieces to justify and make sense of the difficult social changes that are taking place.

One such example is the 21-episode TV drama *Year after Year* (*Yinian you yinian*, 1999), made specifically for the occasion of the 50th anniversary celebrations of the People's Republic in 1999. The producer BTAC drew on its top human resources and best crew and its production enjoyed a high priority and a generous budget. In early 1999, the serial was broadcast during prime time on Beijing Television's Channel 2 and was relayed by many other provincial and municipal stations. It was commended by the Propaganda Department as one of the ten best 50th anniversary celebration works and won many official awards, including the Five Ones Project Award.

On the surface, *Year after Year* follows the typical recent Chinese TV drama trend of focusing on the family and everyday life. The story portrays the personal lives and relationships of two extended and interrelated families in Beijing over the two decades from 1978: the Chens, who represent ordinary citizens living in a typical traditional courtyard (*siheyuan*) shared by many families, and the Lins, who represent the elite and educated class living in a gated villa. Although these two families are loosely connected by a long courtship and subsequent failed marriage between Chen Huan and Lin Pingping, their true function is as foils for the public events that occur "year after year," and it is the passing of time and historical events that are the real focus of the drama.

The narrative device that this drama exploits to insert the official reform discourse into the domestic story of the serial is the clever use of a chronicle structure. Claimed by the producers to be "a chronicle of ordinary people, and annals of local (Beijing) life" (*wei baixing li zhuan, wei difang xie zhi*),[16] the serial devotes one episode to each of the twenty-one years of reform history from 1978 to 1999. Each episode records the activities of the two families' members in the chosen year.

For viewers familiar with the history of the last two decades, these episodes conspicuously cover all the major social events and trends that emerged from the political and economic reforms by inscribing them into the everyday lives of the Chen and Lin families. These include: the revival of university entrance exams after the Cultural Revolution; the introduction of the responsibility system in the countryside; the rapid inflation and panic buying during the early 1980s; the strange and often corrupt phenomenon of government officials going into business; young people going abroad to seek their fortunes; the stock craze; foreign investment and real estate development; the unemployment of state factory workers and the rise of private entrepreneurship. In fact, while preparing the script, Li Xiaoming, the veteran screenwriter who penned *Yearning* ten years before, claims to have drawn inspiration and material from reading *Beijing Daily* — the mouthpiece of the Beijing government — page by page, and making several books of notes and clippings.[17]

Thus, in this epic serial, the "everyday lives" of ordinary people are not introduced to get viewers to focus on individuals; rather, the characters are created to embody the national history and associated public events that reflect the progress of economic and political reform led by the Communist Party. As a result, these everyday lives and experiences are heavily selective and edited based on the criterion of "national importance". And the individual families here merely serve as a microcosm of a nation on the move. This is a marked contrast with the more individualistic approach of the other family drama genres that we discussed above.

Because of this pre-designed theme and purpose, it is not surprising that the characters in *Year after Year* ostensibly represent the different groups or "types" that emerged from the social stratification and restructuring engendered by reforms. Their social relations, economic status, educational background, and their attitudes and opinions toward Deng Xiaoping's reforms merely confirm the social identities they have been given. We can find almost every type in these two families: the Chens' father works as a film projectionist in a local theater, a model worker of the older generation; the Chens' mother is a warm-hearted but sharp-tongued housewife; older daughter Chen Qing is a state factory worker who later, after being laid off, starts her own community service company; her husband Dahai is a private entrepreneur who sells all kinds of goods, from clothes to furniture; the son Chen Huan continues to teach in a university as an economics professor after graduating. In the Lin family, the father is a retired high official who strongly supports the reforms; the Lins' mother is a senior literary editor; the son Yida works as a junior government official and later becomes the business manager of a state-owned company, his wife Chaoying starts out as a cook from a provincial town who eventually finds success by running a restaurant business; and the Lins' daughter Pingping goes abroad to study, later returning as a representative of a foreign company.

Being typical representatives of the different social groups in Chinese society, the characters' comments, opinions and attitudes toward the government reform project are also designed to "represent" the views and different voices of their types. For example, in the episode 1983, the Chen family experiences the government's increases in the prices of essential goods and the subsequent panic buying throughout the country. We see a scene where the radio announces the government's open price policy, and the Chen family members, especially the housewife mother, react with confusion, distrust, and complaints, and they immediately rush out to stock up on supplies. But the son Chen Huan, who is conveniently cast as an economics professor, explains to them how the adjustment of prices is a way to stimulate the economy, and in the long run it will benefit ordinary people like themselves. And as the story proceeds, supply increases and the prices stabilize, and the once confused characters finally see the point of the reform. Of course, the differing voices have been moderated in such a manner that they never develop into an alternative or oppositional discourse, but rather complement and interpret the mainstream voice, often represented by the radio and TV news that are inserted skillfully into the everyday scenes, and legitimate the state ideology of reform. The constant refrain is that, despite many frustrations, difficulties and problems, the reform project has eventually brought China into a new and prosperous era, and things can only get better from now on.

The narrative and visual devices that are used to construct and support the chronicle format in *Year after Year* are abundant. Overall there is a realistic, documentary feel to the production, which is liberally sprinkled with archival footage and reports from various media of past years. The live recording and naturalistic performances also contribute to this sense of documentary. Carefully researched domestic arrangements, decorations and passing fashions, radio and television news broadcasts, film clips, and popular songs appear in each episode as appropriate to the year being described. These details not only give the audience an illusion of their shared history and effectively evoke emotional identification with the story; but also, just as important, they give opportunities to insert the official or mainstream ideology, embodied in the media and public events of the time. Also, unlike many TV dramas which tend to use medium-length and close-up shooting to focus on personal relationships, *Year after Year* unusually uses numerous long shots to establish the panoramic sense of history and national scale, even when the main part of the scene is in a domestic setting. The establishing shot for each episode best represents this panoramic perspective: It starts with a broad city view of Beijing as a growing and changing landscape, and gradually focuses on the smaller scale of neighborhoods, finally moving into the courtyard where the Chens live, as stereotypical microcosms of China's social reforms.

Conclusion

For centuries, the basic social and ethical unit of the family has been central to and constitutive of the nation and state in Chinese culture. From Confucian teachings to socialist propaganda, the interchangeable and interdependent relationship between *guo* and *jia* (the family/nation or family/state) has been repeatedly exploited by those in power. In the socialist discourse that prevailed during the Maoist period, the individual private family was totally subordinated and eventually erased by the demands of the collective nation/state, and this was clearly reflected in the suspicion directed toward private relationships in cultural products of that time.

The collapse of the socialist economic system and ideology and the emergence of an individualistic consumer society during the 1980s and 1990s led to a new perspective on family. As we have seen, TV drama of the last two decades has increasingly reflected this renewed popular fascination with domestic space and familial experience after a long period of neglect. The centrality of the family and family relationships in TV drama not only reacts against the previous socialist discourse but also reflects and responds to the deep impact of recent social changes on this most basic human relationship. As real-life families increasingly succumb to the pressures of contemporary life, breaking apart under the strains of unemployment, social mobility and materialism, imaginary television families become still more important by providing a sense of solidarity and emotional identification for ordinary viewers.

At the same time, TV family dramas have also diversified into a variety of subgenres that focus on distinct audiences and articulate the views of different social agents. While urban romances largely represent the female point of view, especially that of middle-aged married women, the renewed interest in mundane life seen in ordinary folk and family values dramas clearly resonates with the poor, the unemployed, the retired, and all those left behind by the economic reforms. Thus, we see the cultural imagination, and more practically, the newly-commercialized cultural industries, registering the effects of social stratification and growing inequalities in China's post-socialist society.

While the state's cultural bureaucracy has retreated well into the background in most of these new family subgenres, we still occasionally see its influence even at this most personal and private level. Official awards tend to go to those commercial TV dramas that promote conservative family values and thus accord with the government's vision of social stability within change. And alongside their commercial TV dramas, the state-controlled TV production centers must continue to produce main melody dramas that use screen families to subtly disseminate the official ideology of historical progress and continuing economic reform.

Television family drama thus involves diverse social agencies and agendas, and appeals to a range of different audiences. It creates a complex narrative that both reflects the wrenching social changes and class stratification occurring in China today and at the same time attempts to make sense of those changes, especially for those who feel they have been left behind.

6

Maids in the Televisual City:
Competing Tales of Post-Socialist Modernity

Wanning Sun

Chinese television dramas over the past few decades have seen the rise and decline of various narratives: stories of successful entrepreneurs, stories of Chinese going to live overseas, anti-corruption political drama, crime and police drama, not to mention epic historical dramas reinterpreting Chinese historical figures and events. None of these, however, quite captures the imagination of urban residents as vividly as narratives of ordinary people living mundane lives in their homes on an everyday basis. And no other narratives speak to the emerging urban middle-class's fear and anxiety about the urban "other" more palpably than the stories of the maid. For the first time since the founding of the PRC, the relaxing of the *hukou* system unleashed massive rural-to-urban migration, which has permanently and profoundly changed the streetscape of the Chinese city as well as the habitat of its residents.[1] The insertion of the liminal but ubiquitous figure of the "stranger" and "foreigner" into various intimate crevices and interstices of urban space brings both uncertainty and fear for both the local resident and the migrant, albeit for different reasons. In spite of her low socio-economic status, the figure of the maid has become perennial precisely because of the liminal nature of her existence. Confronted with mobility — both physical and social — questions of social identity naturally become inevitable: Who am I? What have I become? Where do I belong? And the anthropological impulse to gaze upon, to know, the "natives" among us, and to document "our" experience of dealing with "them," becomes all the more urgent.

In other words, the ongoing fascination with the maid in the popular consciousness is hardly surprising. After all, although it is difficult to estimate the exact number of rural migrants who work as domestic helpers, statistics do suggest that more and more urban families are employing domestic help and the number of vacancies urgently in need of filling is forever growing. Many young families need child-care for their young child; a growing number of Chinese families with old people need domestic help to care for the old. Currently China has 130 million people over the age of sixty, and this percentage is growing at the rate of three percent each year.[2] In Beijing, as many as 200,000 households are using domestic help, and within the next few years, about 230,000 families are expected to need full-time live-in maids, whereas another 220,000 families will need part-time and casual domestic help.[3] It is estimated that about 100,000 positions for domestic help are waiting to be filled in urban Beijing.[4] Statistically, this need translates into one in ten families in Beijing are needing or employing domestic help in some shape or form. Nation-wide, it is estimated as that as many as one in every five urban families are prospective and current employers,[5] with around 85 percent of these families in need of help either for childcare or care for the elderly.[6]

While each maid's story is different and unique, her experience is written into a number of perennial narrative frameworks, ranging from the "little maid making it big time" — the happy Cinderella end of the spectrum — to "the maid from hell" — the unhappy end of the spectrum. As consumers of the actual goods or the product (i.e. the material service and servitude provided by the maid), urban residents are also avid consumers of the symbolism used to "story" the maid. In fact, as this chapter shows, it is through a wide range of consumption activities — including the consumption of the labor of migrant workers at both material and symbolic levels — that an urban middle class has begun to emerge.

There are usually three ways in which the maid, who is marginal yet indispensable in the social life in urban China, figures in these dramas. She may be a character in the television dramas, recounting the experiences of rural migrants eking out a living in the city. Alternatively, the maid is a character in the drama of sociality and social change, for which the narrative presence varies from fleeting and insignificant to crucial and profound. Finally, the maid can feature in these dramas as the central figure, and the sociality which this structurally powerless figure engenders is the locomotive of the main narrative. The three tales of the maid which are analysed in this chapter, namely *Professor Tian and His Twenty-eight Maids* (*Tian jiaoshou jiade ershiba ge baomu*, 2001), *Chinese Maids in Foreign Families* (*Shewai baomu*, 2002), and *Ultimate Justice* (*Cangtian youyan*, 2004), all fall under this category. This chapter is a close reading of the three tales with some questions kept in mind. How is the figure of the maid — many of whom are marginal and peripheral to the city — constructed in these urban stories, and in what ways does the maid in each story embody the urban anxiety and ambivalence toward its social "other"? Furthermore, how does the figure of the maid help us to decode competing tales of post-socialist Chinese modernity?

Three Tales of the Maid: A "Story Board"

Professor Tian, an academic in the Institute of Drama and Theater, lives in a spacious apartment in a leafy suburb in Shanghai with his wife, a deputy director of a textile factory, and his son, a bright young man who works as a designer in an advertising company. His daughter is married and comes to visit over the weekend. The family is also blessed with the presence of Tian's mother, who lives with them, takes care of the housework, and makes everyday life at home cozy and peaceful — until one day she breaks her leg while doing her daily morning exercises dancing in the "seniors folk dance" group. It quickly becomes clear to everyone in the family that hiring a maid is the only solution to the household chaos.

Enter the first maid. Xiaofang is a diligent, polite young woman from Anhui, a province well known for its export of maids to Beijing, Shanghai, and other big cities. She is hired for 300 yuan[7] a month as a live-in maid. However, as she eats little and looks jaundiced, it suddenly occurs to the family that she may have hepatitis. The thought throws the whole family into a state of panic. As it turns out, however, Xiaofang is not ill; she is merely pregnant. She begs to stay, but the family thinks it would not be appropriate to house an illegitimate child. Then enters the second maid, then the third, and so on. By the last episode, we have seen twenty-eight maids entering and leaving Professor Tian's home and, because of them, no one in the family is ever the same again.

Audiences are treated to a round of maids, each with a different story to tell, but each of whom is invariably found wanting. However, Professor Tian's luck turns for the better when Huijuan, a local factory worker-turned-domestic servant, arrives. Huijuan has been a factory worker in a state enterprise, but, like so many other factory workers, has been laid off work since the nationwide restructuring of state enterprises. She signs up with the training center for domestic workers and becomes a certified domestic worker in Professor Tian's home, to the embarrassment of her husband — a writer — as well as her daughter and her daughter's friends. Huijuan uses her own example to prove to the world that a laid-off factory worker can regain dignity and achieve independence by becoming a domestic worker. She also convinces Tian's family that domestic work should be a recognized line of employment in modern times, commanding just as much respect as other professions. For instance, her arrival changes the life of Yiwen, Professor Tian's daughter. Yiwen, a factory worker herself, has the habit of throwing her weight around with the maid, believing that maids are to be disciplined and treated with distrust. However, when faced with the imminent prospect of losing her job through the nationwide restructuring of state enterprises, Yiwen becomes increasingly insecure, putting a strain on her relationship with both her husband and her family. Huijuan then takes on the role of her de facto marriage counselor and life coach, helping her to regain her sense of self-worth in spite of imminent unemployment. Toward the end of the show, Huijuan has to give up her job at Professor Tian's house because she is now too busy training other would-be domestic workers, and Professor Tian's family is ready to meet the twenty-eighth maid. When the doorbell rings and Yiwen, Professor Tian's unemployed daughter, enters, everyone is stunned: she is the twenty-eighth maid.

Such is the story of *Professor Tian and His Twenty-eight Maids*, a twenty-two-episode television drama screened nationally on Chinese television at the beginning of 2001. The show was a runaway success — making Professor Tian a household name among Chinese viewers and a figure inviting instant recognition and identification among urban residents — and many provincial television stations repeated the screening within a very short space of time. Within months of its production, the video tapes of these episodes also found their way into the Chinese-language video shops in diasporic Chinese communities.

A couple of years after Professor Tian became a household name, another story of the maid hit the Chinese television, this time putting Chinese domestic workers in China's transnational spaces — that is, the households of foreigners and expatriates living in China. *Chinese Maids in Foreign Families*, a twenty-two-episode television drama also set in Shanghai and screened on Chinese television in 2002. The series features the frustrations and triumphs of three domestic workers: a rural migrant, Xiangcao, and two former state enterprise workers, Qiaoyun and Gengxiong, who have been laid off from their factories. The serial has a "happy" ending. Each of the three characters is transformed by their experience of working for foreign families, and by the end of the story they have all become more "modern," proud of their work, and ready to take on bigger and more exciting challenges in life. The serial ends with Qiaoyun and her American employers boarding a United States-bound plane.

Not all tales of the maid have a happy ending. *Ultimate Justice*, another twenty-episode television drama centering around a maid, evolves around the conflict between the humble maid Wang Yan and the powerful Wu Lei, a CEO of an IT company. The story starts with a gratuitous death in the courtyard of the Wu family. The killer is Mr Wu, and it so happens that Wang Yan has the incriminating evidence. From deceit and betrayal to blackmail and attempted murders, the battle between David and Goliath is fought between the powerful CEO and the maid; tactics and strategies are deployed, according to the logic of dignity and respect on the part of the maid, and that of money and power on the part of her opponent. While detectives and policemen are busy trying to identify the killer, Wang Yan the maid has the answer all along. However, she is neither on the side of the killer nor that of the law, since — as she intuits soon enough — neither is willing to deliver — or indeed capable of delivering — the justice and fairness she wants. She takes bribes when it suits her, and yet provides no moral or practical alibi for anybody. Similarly, rather than relying on the state and its authorities to confer dignity and respect on her, as is the case with Huijuan in Professor Tian's home and Gengxiong in *Chinese Maids in Foreign Homes*, both of whom become state-selected "model domestic workers," Wang Yan chooses her own way of living a dignified life as a maid. The story has a tragic ending, however, with Wang Yan going insane, and her opponent, unable to cover his crime, killing himself. Produced by Beijing Broadcasting, Film and Television Pty Ltd, and screened on many television stations throughout China toward the end of 2004, *Ultimate Justice* gained its popularity partly due to the fame of a number of celebrities starring in the show. That aside, it is also an undeniably gripping tale of the modern city, mixing intrigue, crime, romance, and scandal, and propelled by the pivotal role assumed by the humble maid.

Intimate Strangers and the Controlling Gaze

Professor Tian and His Twenty-eight Maids is marketed as a "comedy" (*xi ju*). To have as many as twenty-eight maids within the short period of a few weeks may well have been a narrative ploy of *Professor Tian and His Twenty-eight Maids*, as their coming and going facilitates the episodic story-telling and at the same time keeps the story fresh and interesting. However, a high turnover of maids is in fact typical of many employers' experiences with domestic workers in urban China. It is quite common, for instance, for a maid to last no more than a few months, only to be replaced by someone else equally fleetingly. Such a high turnover is also symptomatic of a social problem confronting the emerging middle class in Chinese cities. Television dramas such as this therefore serve a number of purposes, one of which is the documentation of the "uncivilized," "primitive," "not so modern," and in short, "different" thoughts and behaviors of the "other." They can also be read as the "first close encounter" type of documentaries, whereby the modern ethnographer turns the gaze of the camera on to the "tribal people." In this sense, the production of Professor Tian's story can be read as a significant text that captures the initial and growing sense of unease.

Professor Tian's story, a media product born out of the logic of the market economy, is instantly popular precisely because it caters to such growing collective need. In my multiple-year research project on domestic workers in China, involving extensive interviews and conversations with urban and middle-class residents who employ maids, I have again and again come across references to the well-known yet imaginary "Professor Tian" — a character whose predicaments and dilemmas engender widespread recognition and resonance among urban residents in China. Some comment that, although they are not professors and have not hired as many maids as he has, Professor Tian's issues, problems, and difficulties of living with and managing a maid are all too common and familiar.

If the maid is indispensable, a "good" maid is nonetheless impossible to find. The high turnover of maids in Professor Tian's home is indeed emblematic of an urban complex marked with dependence on one hand, and fear and anxiety on the other. The difficulty, if not the impossibility, of finding a "good" maid, the risk involved in using a *baomu*, as well as the trouble one has to go through to train a maid have become perennial topics in the urban media. Like the girls who turn up on Professor Tian's doorstep, each maid's arrival brings renewed hope to the employers only to end in frustration. She is either too clumsy — one of Professor Tian's maids cannot help dropping plates in the kitchen — or not competent enough, or not trustworthy, or simply not good-looking enough. Overall, in the imagination of many urban employers, a *baomu* needs to be sanitized — *baomu* now needs medical clearance for all contagious diseases before starting work — scrutinized — there have been a number of calls to record each *baomu*'s employment history and particulars on a centralized databank so as to "put employers at ease" — and disciplined.

Both the "indispensable maid" and the "impossible maid" tropes point to a profound ambivalence marking the urban middle class's collective psyche. This "foreigner" in the intimate domestic space of home calls into question the previously unchallenged divide between the self and other, inside/outside, private/public. An often-quoted explanation used to account for this disjuncture is the issue of the "low quality" (*suzhi di*) of the majority of maids. Professor Tian's wife more than once laments the "low quality" of her maids by comparing them to her staff — that is, workers in the state-run enterprises. Further, the urban media regularly relay urban families' laments about the low quality of maids, and these voices of discontent are acutely felt by domestic service agencies, whose attempts to recruit qualified domestic workers have become equally newsworthy when not successful. The effort to improve the quality of domestic workers has become not only a market initiative but, more importantly, an important state project. The notion of "quality" alongside concerted efforts to define and produce it points to a little-acknowledged complicity between the state, the *baomu* industry, academics, and urban middle-class consumers. Although it results in a concerted effort to educate and elevate the standard of work of domestic workers, such complicity seldom gives agency to the domestic servants themselves. Very often, the maid is little more than an object to be modernized and civilized.

"Useful" Citizens for the Modern State

Domestic workers are subject not only to the disciplinary regime of the market and workplace — that is, urban residents and their home — their objectification is also crucial to the building of citizenship for the modern state. Certain stories about maids in Professor Tian's home are narratives of journeys, growth, and the triumphs of the individual endeavor but, more importantly, they are also about the formation of a new personhood, about an individual improving her "personal quality," her literacy, job skills, and work attitudes so as to fit in better with the social life of modernity. For instance, Xiaoling, a young woman from the country, is studying hard while working as Professor Tian's maid so that one day she can go to university, an aspiration to gain better *suzhi* that is rewarded with the love of Professor Tian's son. In another instance, Huijuan — like so many other middle-aged workers in the Chinese cities — is laid off from her factory. However, unlike many laid-off female workers who lose their sense of self-worth and confidence in life, and who are unwilling to "lose face" by becoming a domestic worker, Huijuan has a realistic and positive attitude. She enrolls in the domestic service training course, becomes a qualified worker in Professor Tian's home, and gives moral support to Professor's Tian's daughter who, with much encouragement and support, becomes the twenty-eighth maid in the house. Huijuan then goes to "bigger and better" things by becoming a trainer in the domestic service training center. She uses her own example to show trainees — and other unemployed factory workers — that women should not lose confidence in life, and that they can regain strength (*ziqiang*), independence (*zili*), and dignity (*sizun*) through re-employment. These, of course, are all essential ingredients of good "personal quality," according to the state.

Huijuan, as well as her counterparts in *Chinese Maids in Foreign Families*, is thereby a "positive" role model from the point of the view of the party and the state. A "good" woman, in the mind of the state, is one who is happy to be "demobilized" from state-organized production work, just as she was happy to be "mobilized" into the labor force for the sake of socialist construction. Also, while not contending with fellow national subjects over access to economic and political resources, she should nevertheless still be doing her bit for her country and state. Gengxiong, who helps the government and the police to uncover the transnational drug ring in Shanghai while working for a Hong Kong family, is but one good example. Furthermore, once demobilized, a good national female subject does not complain. She is resilient and strong, finds alternative ways of generating income without waiting for a handout from the state, and in so doing supplies a much-needed service to the job market. Furthermore, a "good" woman is capable of not only making the necessary adjustment in her actions but, more importantly, engineering a paradigm shift in the way she thinks about her personhood. Huijuan has this to say to her class when she starts her training course as a domestic worker:

> When I first lost my job in the factory, I lost my psychological equilibrium (*xinli bu pingheng*). I couldn't sleep well at night. I lost that feeling of being the master of my own destiny which I had when I worked on the workshop floor in the factory. When I decided to become a domestic worker, there was a lot of resistance around me. My husband is old-fashioned and does not want me to become a domestic worker. My daughter's friends also give her a hard time. But I believe that it is up to yourself to realize your worth as a dignified human being. To spell the word "human being" (*ren*), you need to start putting one stroke after another (*yi bi yi ba xie ge ren*).

Clearly, the figure of the re-employed factory worker in domestic service is politically useful. As I have demonstrated elsewhere, economic difficulties facing women are constructed in the state discourses as individual rather than social problems.[8] Further, too much emphasis on women's equality and access to employment in times of economic reforms and enterprise restructuring would reveal the inherent inequity in the state reform agenda. For this reason, the figure of a laid-off worker who is prepared to accept losing jobs as natural and inevitable, to accept downward social mobility and seek alternative ways of making a living without much subsidizing from the state, is both desirable to the state and useful to the market. Qiaoyun, a Chinese maid working for an American family, has not only turned her misfortune of being laid off into a positive experience, she has also started to do her part — by initiating an export business selling *qipao* — to assist China to become part of the global economy. It is according to this political logic that laid-off female workers are often turned into "desirable entrepreneurs" in both state and popular media narratives. While these narratives praise these women for regaining financial independence or for their success in business ventures, they seldom acknowledge the women's psychological struggle to overcome their internalized feelings of the shame and stigma associated with domestic servitude. Nor do they acknowledge the financial sacrifices these female factory workers have had to make. As casualties of the state restructuring, these women may have dedicated the prime years of their working lives to a state enterprise, only to have their relationship to the factory severed for the meager amount of a "redundancy package."

Popular television dramas like *Professor Tian and His Twenty-eight Maids* not only articulate an adjusted subject position of the "national women," they also present a powerful discursive space in which to educate national subjects and turn them into "useful" citizens. In addition, as Lee Haiyan observes in her study of *Chinese Maids in Foreign Families*, the serial figures the Chinese nannies as apprentices in a modern, cosmopolitan subjectivity, and similarly figures the foreigners' homes as a training ground for that subjectivity.[9] These dramas are *powerful* both because they are stories of individual women coping with difficulties in their lives and because they are told in the melodramatic fashion well known to the genre of socialist realism, a mixing of entertainment with indoctrination. In other words, the change and transformation we have seen in the subject positions of these women is constructed to be not only desirable, but also natural and inevitable. Second, these stories articulate, on behalf of both the state and the market, what a "useful" citizen should be like. In the beginning, Yiwen, Professor Tian's married daughter, embodies counter-productivity or even waste to both the state and the market. She is a factory worker waiting to be laid off, has few re-employable skills and, to make matters worse, has an "attitude problem." She believes that maids are of an inferior class, and treats them accordingly. Although only coming to visit her parents over the weekend, she has the strongest opinions about how to treat a maid. She spies on a maid buying food in the store to make sure that she does not exaggerate the price of vegetables, warns her brother "not to go out with a maid, particularly maids from the provinces," and believes that maids are "servants" and that "if you treat them kindly, they will take advantage of your kindness." When the maid gives her son a birthday present, she declines it, her reason being that "it doesn't matter how much money she has, she is still a servant." At the same time, with the prospect of losing her own job more and more imminent, she has become increasingly neurotic and insecure as an individual. A predictable trigger point in the maid–family conflict, Yiwen also starts to inflict strain both on her marriage and on domestic harmony in Professor Tian's home. She starts to pick fights with her husband, and seeks refuge in her parents' home, whilst at the same time acting like a wounded child as she feels that the whole world — including the maids — is starting to look down upon her.

Like those maids from the provinces who are found wanting by their employers because of their incompetence, uncleanness, or untrustworthiness — thus becoming objects to be modernized, civilized and educated — Yiwen also has a serious problem with "personal quality" (*suzhi*). She is in need of an overhaul of her personhood in order to make herself acceptable within the parameters of the state discourse. Like the maids she despises, Yiwen embodies a similar challenge to those charged with the responsibility of "thought work" (*sixiang gongzuo*). Not surprisingly here, as is often the case in socially realistic melodrama, it is a role model — with her patient guidance and encouragement — that is entrusted with such an honorable task. Coming to work in Professor Tian's home upon losing her job, it is Huijuan who wins Yiwen's confidence and trust, gives counsel for her marriage problems, and helps her regain her confidence. More importantly, she demonstrates — using herself as an example — that being a domestic worker is not degrading but a way of becoming independent again. Thanks to Huijuan's influence, Yiwen has changed. As mentioned earlier, the last episode ends with her walking into her father's home as the twenty-eighth maid, a narrative and ideological closure that is at once surprising and predictable.

The Maid Who Returns the Gaze

The city where Professor Tian lives and where *Chinese Maids in Foreign Homes* work is undoubtedly an entrepreneurial city, inscribed with masculine power of both global capital and the post-socialist state. As such, the city is represented and visualized as a space which exists to make sense for and from a male and authoritative point of view. However, in *Ultimate Justice*, certain ways of looking are clearly reversed. There are a number of ways in which the text can be read as subversive.

First, unlike other dramas involving the maid, this is a story which simultaneously foregrounds and erases the "otherness" of the rural migrant. For both the self — the urban middle class — and the other — the rural migrant — the self–other boundary is drawn and redrawn. Wang Yan, like many other rural migrants, hopes to shed her country outlook and live like a city person. Her ambiguous status as both the maid of the Wu family and a de facto family member also seems to suggest that her aspirations may be achievable. Before the death which shakes the family, she is assured by various members, via both deeds and words, that she is "family," without whom the family is incomplete. The incident of a gratuitous death in the house, however, explodes this delusion, and the urban residents suddenly realize that this "stranger" has made inroads into every crevice of their private and domestic lives and, because of their presence, life will never be the same again.

Secondly, contrary to previous representation of the maid, whereby she is constructed as being subject to management, control, and "civilization" of the urban residents, Wang Yan turns this subject/object ratio on its head and turns the anthropological gaze on to the urban residents, powerful people, and urban life in general. In James Donald's work on the cinema and the city, he points to the notable cinematic tradition of using the character of a detective or an anthropologist as a way of understanding the city.[10] The detective or the anthropologist is necessary to the narrative of the city because, he argues, unlike "us," who are too much a part of the urban landscape, the detective and the anthropologist are able to maintain both a distance and an intimate knowledge of the city. Wang Yan shows us that, although peripheral in most narratives of urban life, the figure of the maid offers important clues to unraveling the dark side of the modern city — and, indeed, the dark side of certain people who assume power within it. An outsider embedded in the texture of the urban life, she is in the best position to assume the role of the detective and the anthropologist. Usually viewed from the perspectives of male, authoritative, and public figures such as academics, social and economic elites (such as Professor Wu and his business entrepreneur son) and the police (like Wu Lei, the CEO's brother), urban life may appear to be different. Wang Yan's ethnographic observations of city folks are sundry, many, and — unsurprisingly — not too flattering. For instance, it seems to her that urban elites are unable to treat outsiders with dignity and respect. As her arch-enemy is at pains to remind her: "I can give you anything you want, except for respect. You are a maid, remember?" She is equally bemused by their obsession with, and faith in, money. Wu Lei blindly assumes that his offer of large amount of money will buy Wang Yan's silence.

Third, the "humble maid" not only provides an alternative ways of visualizing, imagining, and commenting on the city, she also possesses the anthropologists' and scientists' skills in obtaining and archiving empirical data. As an eyewitness to the urban life and the crimes that are committed in it, Wang Yan's handling of evidence is both sophisticated and technology-savvy. Wang Yan's secret weapon is her possession of a computer disk, which contains criminalizing images of her opponent. Throughout the serial, however, Wang Yan uses her possession of the disk as a secret and silent weapon, and as an antidote to her arch-enemy. In doing so, she is seen to cleverly appropriate the technology of "looking" and return the gaze.

Clearly, the state discourse of the "useful citizen" is not able to hail her into place, nor does she want to turn herself into a productive worker in the marketplace. However, indifferent as she is to the seduction of a total ideological "makeover," Wang is nevertheless unable to resist the alluring prospective of becoming "modern." She leaves her village home, comes to the city, and deludes herself into believing that her rural-to-urban transformation is achievable, and that, protected by the city's anonymity, her past — humble as well as troubled — will not catch up with her.

The war between Wu Lei and Wang Yan can be read in terms of class, gender, and the rural–urban divide, and it is worth considering how such conflict is resolved in the story. Wu Lei, having realized that he has lost all there is in life — career, power, fortune, his family — and that he has to face the law, decides to end his life by jumping from his window of his opulent office in a high-rise building. Wang Yan, on the other hand, having lost her loved one — the youngest son in Wu's family — as well as her dreams for her future in the city, and her faith in justice and modern way of life, ends up going insane. Here, I suggest, lie clues as how to read modernity as a fairy tale. While Wang Yan is seen to beat the city people at their own games, she is ultimately punished for her intransigence and unruliness. In spite of her insanity, Professor Wu keeps her in his house and continues to treat her as "family." However, because of her insanity, the detached witness, detective, and ethnographic observer of the city and the modern life is no more. Unlike the previous television dramas, whereby the ideological closure is achieved through an ultimate reconciliation between the urban or middle-class people and their maids, *Ultimate Justice* offers no way out for either the corrupted power elites in the city, or the subaltern who dares to cross boundaries and threaten to speak out. This is the opposite of the grand finale of the modernist fantasia. Modernity, as we see here, is bound for a tragic ending, perhaps best read as a cautionary tale to the losers on both sides.

Conclusion

The maid is a powerful figure in television's narrative of social change in urban China precisely because of the socially powerless position in which she finds herself. Given that, at the turn of the new millennium, China has entered the "era of the maid" (*baomu shidai*), it is understandable that the wide-ranging, diverse, and complex experience of negotiating the intricate, sometimes difficult, and almost always ambivalent relationship between urban residents and their *baomu* has provided constant narrative fodder for popular cultural representations. The ubiquitous presence of the maid in urban China is a constant, and often uncomfortable, reminder of the unequal power relations marking gender, class, and rural/urban duality.

Juxtaposing these televisual narratives enables us to see that television dramas not only offer more than one way of telling a story about modernity, they also suggest that there is more than one story to tell. Television dramas, the most popular and accessible form of story-telling in contemporary China, have a dual responsibility to deliver both product advertisements to consumers and political messages to national subjects. TV drama is also a genre that has come to be associated with the everyday life of the suburban home.[11] This imperative of operating according to the logic of both the market and state ideology requires cultural productions to have "indoctri-tainment" value.[12] That is, it needs to be both entertaining and ideologically relevant.[13] Having emerged as a highly popular cultural artifact during the 1980s, the current phase of television drama in China is thus emblematic of the general paradox confronting the Chinese media as a whole. Equally emblematic is the important role assumed in these productions by intellectuals and "cultural workers" — members of an emerging urban middle class like Professor Tian, the main character in the drama serial. As one Chinese media academic and practitioner puts it: "Chinese television drama expressed power relations and conflicts within these cultural formations. While emerging market forces and the state were the two primary elements that governed television drama, intellectuals involved in production acted as representatives of political power and the market."[14]

It is important to remember that the marginalized social groups featured in these dramas usually have little control over major cultural production, including representations which feature their lives. In most cases, their only access to these cultural productions is as a media consumer — migrant workers, including domestic workers, are also avid viewers of television dramas — and as an object of representation. How to construct sociality and social conflict in television dramas — or what Yin calls "power relations" in television dramas — is both the privilege and responsibility of intellectuals, who are "involved in production" of these social texts, and act as "representatives of political power and the market."[15]

Indeed, as my reading of these stories suggests, all three drama serials want to persuade viewers to accept the unquestionable inevitability of global capitalism and market economy. They also seem to point to the state as the logical mastermind of the nationwide drive for modernization and urbanization. However, packaged as entertainment, these television dramas are at once cultural texts and commodities. As such, they naturally strive to, on one hand, achieve the widest possible resonance among national viewers and, on the other, resort to the marketing strategy of "product differentiation" by speaking to various segments of the audience. This is done by making available to viewers a range of reading/viewing positions, along the lines of gender, socio-economic status, and place (urban or rural), as well as a spectrum of subjects which the viewing positions produce. Whether viewers wish to identify with or distance themselves from a particular subject position, and whether they derive pleasure from resisting being hailed into place, they are assured that there is "something for everyone."

7

Pink Dramas:
Reconciling Consumer Modernity and Confucian Womanhood

Ya-chien Huang

There is a scene in the Chinese television drama *Falling in Love* (*Haoxiang haoxiang tan lianai*) in which two females in skintight gym suits are working out on the treadmills while exchanging their opinions on the modern femme fatale. One of them announces,

> This is the era of post-modernism and post-feminism. You, wake up! A new era will not stifle the start of new relationships. We should fully explore the diversity and possibility of love. It does not matter whether you love an old man or a young dude; you just have to love someone anyhow.[1]

These are the words of Mao Na, a well-known character in this popular Chinese "pink drama" (*fenhong dianshiju*). The pink drama is a subgenre of popular television serial drama which has shifted the emphasis on depictions of "virtuous wives and good mothers" (*xianqi liangmu*) — epitomized by the self-sacrificing character of Liu Huifang in the famous television soap opera *Yearning* (*Kewang,* 1990) — toward single, childless urban women who are successful in careers but nevertheless confused in personal relationships. Women in pink dramas have provided a vivid testimonial to China's growing consumerism and commercialized culture. Educated, independent, and enjoying Westernized lifestyles in cosmopolitan cities, they symbolize a generation growing up since the late 1980s.

Other important elements impacting on the production of pink dramas are the regulatory policies of the State Administration of Radio, Film and

Television (SARFT) and a sense of ambivalence toward Western-style consumerism and individual-centered modernity, which is most evident in China's bustling urban centers. Tension between modernization and tradition has been a reoccurring theme in Chinese history since the late nineteenth century. The sense of ambivalence is expressed in pink dramas in debates among female characters, often centering on personal relationships. In this sense, pink dramas do not only reflect the changing lifestyles of urban Chinese women, but also reveal negotiations between global influence and local meanings. Similar themes on negotiating an "acceptable" femininity, modernity, and national identity in recent globalization have been discussed in other Asian cultural contexts,[2] where images of modern women have been upheld as a sign of socio-economic progression while they have simultaneously been reconfigured to support a distinctive national identity through an "invented tradition".[3]

As China opens to the outside world, the power of the state to control people's thoughts is waning. This diminution of cultural authority has opened up discussions of the "Trojan horse effect", in which the influence of global media on individual development increases as representations are encoded in seemingly harmless new forms. Following examination of two pink dramas, *Pink Ladies* (*Fenhong nülang*) and *Falling in Love* (*Haoxiang haoxiang tan lianai*), I will sketch out the political, cultural and economic undercurrents beneath the production and reception of this genre. In the final section of this chapter, I will investigate how foreign programming offers a fertile arena to test gender identities and provides symbolic resources to (some) Chinese women as they grapple with real-life dilemmas.

Gender Identity in Transition: Consumerism versus Nationalism

While shifting gender identity provides the context for pink dramas, the narrative focus is undoubtedly women's empowerment. Socio-economic transformations, particularly the growth of a consumer society, have offered more opportunities to women, and have helped to redefine gender distinction. While Western visitors to China before the 1970s expressed surprise at the masculine clothes, hairstyles and body language of women and the relative lack of gender distinction under deliberate "state gender erasure,"[4] the post-Mao era (after 1976) has witnessed a decline in state influence over personal style. Market-driven representations of femininity soon began to appear after the "open door policy" of 1978. Women have since been empowered by consumerism and become targets of advertising. Following *ELLE,* the first

Western women's fashion magazine published in China in 1988, leading international magazines with glossy images of young models wearing the latest fashion and make-up have been available to Chinese women.[5] In 1995, China started its own fashion magazine industry by launching *Ruei Li Clothing and Beauty (Rueili fushi meirueng)* under a joint venture with a Japanese company. Up until 2006, the number of fashion magazines has expanded and there are numerous titles touching on different aspects of women's lives. The younger generations, especially those born after the late 1970s, have grown up with easy access to these magazines which promote personal styles and consumer goods, and which feature articles that open up new territories for women at work and in relationships.

When *Vogue,* internationally linked to an affluent niche readership, launched its first Mainland China issue in September 2005, it was a confirmation of China's progression toward a society in which people consume to establish their social status and self-image.[6] In the process of "consumer revolution," terms such as "pink-collar" *(fenling)*, "pink-collared pretty women" *(fenling liren)*, or "pink-collared new aristocracy" *(fenling xingui)* are used increasingly to address a new generation of women. While the term "pink collar" is often associated with women of lower education with secondary and less well-paid jobs in the Western context,[7] "pink culture" entails positive connotations. It refers to women who have benefited from better education and employment opportunities, and are consequently able to enter into fashionable professions. Capitalizing on this new niche, representations of pink culture have been used in advertisements to entice women to spend their salaries on commodities that symbolize elegance, individuality, independence and personal freedom. Images of "pink ladies," represented by successful female politicians, entrepreneurs, employers in Western-style business, models, and fashion designers, have outnumbered the "middle-class housewives" and "flower vases" to be new role models.

The Shifting Media Environment

The media environment in China since the 1990s, like many other cultural sectors, has seen growing interactions between market freedom and the regulating force of state censorship. The era of television drama production after 1987 has been dubbed as "the commercial period" to emphasize how advertising and sponsorship from business enterprises have replaced state funding as the main source of income and revenue.[8] Product placement, or "soft advertising" *(ruan guanggao)*, has increased in the past decade. However, despite the fact that production has become more market-oriented, the Chinese government still maintains a high degree of control over the ideological content of television dramas. In most cases, producers impose self-censorship to make money and avoid trouble.[9]

Ideological constraints on fictional forms and expression coupled with changing demands from a domestic market being transformed by commercialization have prompted Chinese producers to look elsewhere for materials. Cultural proximity — shared East Asian values — has enabled popular culture from Hong Kong and Taiwan to claim substantial loyalty from Mainland China consumers. Based on interviews with Chinese youngsters, Gold has argued that Hong Kong and Taiwan's popular cultural products succeed in China because of their intensively personal focus.[10] Playing on everyday incidents and feelings that people can relate to easily (*shenghuoxing*), they have reached out through a language of individual emotion and personal expression and have in turn persuaded Mainland productions into giving more attention to the private sphere. Appropriating other foreign formats has offered a convenient solution for Chinese producers, as format adaptations can often capitalize on program ideas with proven popular appeal; all that needs to be done is to tailor them for domestic consumption with successful local elements.[11] Studies have repeatedly found that audiences prefer domestic and regional content over foreign programming.[12] Being "culturally specific but nationally neutral"[13] formats assist in the recycling of program content across different television systems in the world.[14] However, in the case of China, producers often blatantly copy, or in their words, "borrow" or "make reference to" the original programming to varying degrees without paying fees to the creators. Chinese producers have rationalized this practice of copying, by presenting it in a positive light, as a kind of "cultural technology" which emphasizes the benefits of introducing new forms of expression and their added values to the recipient television systems.[15] With changes on the domestic terrain and inspirations from abroad, China's television drama landscape has illustrated an "interpersonal model of production" by the end of the 1990s, which incorporates and translates diversified materials into a greater awareness of personal experience and differentiated market segments.[16] The arrival of pink dramas is one example. Borrowing heavily from the post-feminist sensibility of high-achieving women in search of satisfying relationships as represented in successful Western media products, most notably *Ally McBeal, Bridget Jones' Diary,* and *Sex and the City,* this genre deals with women's issues and social mobility on the one hand, while on the other, signifies the niche production strategies adopted by television stations in targeting young privileged women as consumers.[17]

Chinese Modernity and Confucianized Women in Pink Dramas

Screened in May 2003 and featuring four young single women in Shanghai, *Pink Ladies* (*Fenhong nülang*) is a typical example of the pink drama genre. *Pink Ladies* was adapted from *Hot Ladies* (*Se nülang*), a comic book by the Taiwanese artist Zhu Deyong. Zhu, who made his name in Taiwan in the 1990s, is famous for turning real-life heterosexual relationships into bitterly witty caricatures. His works had sold millions of copies in China before *Hot Ladies* made it to the small screen. Another of his works, *Shuang xiang pao*, featuring irony in marriage and men's relationships with their mothers-in-law, was also adapted for television in 2004. The popularity of *Shuang xiang pao* won Wu Zuengde, the Taiwanese director of *Pink Ladies* and *Shuang xiang pao*, a place in the "double-ten award" (Shuangshi jiang), an award that is based on popular votes and is one of the three most prestigious television awards in China. Both dramas were produced under the supervision of the China International Television Corporation, but involved creative talent and investment from China, Taiwan, Japan and Singapore. Flows of finance, shooting locations and personnel across national boundaries reveal the ambition of China's television industry to engage with the dynamics of East Asia popular culture.[18]

The central character in *Pink Ladies* is Xiaoping, a twenty-seven-year-old nursery teacher who is obsessed by the idea of marriage. She fantasizes her dates as candidates, and is therefore nicknamed "marriage crazy" by her friends. The serial starts when Xiaoping's groom fails to turn up at their wedding and her journey to find Mr. Right begins. She meets three other single women and they move in together in a newly-built apartment. Runan represents a stereotypical "strong woman" (*nü qiangren*) or career women in Chinese society — capable but personally unfulfilled. She is ambitious at work and leaves no time to take care of her boyfriend, who consequently marries her sister instead. From this point onward, she disdained relationships and was known as a "manly woman" (*nanrenpo*). Wanling, an attractive cosmetic saleslady in a department store, enjoys being crowned as *wanrenmi*, literally a "fan of ten thousand people." She is confident and not afraid of manipulating men with her charm. She expresses sarcastic views on relationships and often speaks against traditional women's decorum and sexual taboos. Hamei is a twenty-year-old disc jockey who is rebellious, full of energy and enjoys foreign popular culture. Although she does not have any serious boyfriends, she has many friends. She expresses a certain naivety and curiosity about relationships. At one level, the story of these four women resonates with Western post-feminist productions. It is grounded in the pink culture movement in which (some) women are accorded freedom to determine their life choices while cushioned by the safety net of friendship. It is notrworthy that the series takes place in Shanghai — once referred to as the Paris of the East — where trendy restaurants, bars, discos, shopping malls, internet cafés, and skyscrapers in the newly-developed Pudong district are blended into a narrative that showcases change and rampant economic growth in China.

At another level, *Pink Ladies* reworks Western post-feminism by investing it with distinctively local meanings. Xiaoping's determination to get married is inextricably tied up with the responsibility to her family rather than the individual "choice politics." Her eager search for love is to fulfill a promise made to her mother that she would get married within three months. Unlike the story in the comic book where the four leads share more or less the same weight, the television serial focuses more on Xiaoping. Xiaoping, the ordinary-looking woman, is portrayed as having immense kindness and sincerity and is always sacrificing, both emotionally and financially, to bail others out. This attribute reflects "the virtuous wife and good mother" in a family setting and the narrative rewards her for this moral grounding on various occasions. Not only does she get a priceless gold fishing hook from the millionaire, Mr. Shi, to exchange for any wishes she wants, she also wins the heart of Wanghao, the handsome and rich entrepreneur admired by other women.

Another major strand within pink dramas is represented by a serial based directly on the format of the hugely successful Home Box Office (HBO) series, *Sex and the City* (hereafter, *SATC*), which revolves around the friendships and love lives of four single white female professionals in New York: Carrie Bradshaw (journalist/writer); Samantha Jones (PR executive and sexual libertine); Miranda Hobbs (corporate lawyer and relationship cynic); and Charlotte York (art gallery manager and romantic optimist). These four women are all their in mid-thirties, earn considerable salaries and socialize in fashionable bars and restaurants. Whenever they meet, they recount their romantic encounters and debate on a wide range of personal topics from marriage, pregnancy, compatibility, and commitment to their partner's preferences and performances in bed.[19] The recipe of the series can be described as an anthropological quest to discover the deeper meaning of human relationships and sexuality, spiced up with unabashed fashion consumption and novel representations of contemporary female sexuality, female friendship and female independence. Soon after the series was aired in Asia in 1999, its format was copied by television producers in China, Taiwan, and Hong Kong.[20]

At first glance, the popularity of the *SATC* format in Greater China is a puzzle, since one of its main textual elements, the intermittent casual sexual relationships, is hardly the ideal kind of programming desired by the public and regulators in a Confucian context. However, the process of adaptation has taken on board local moral and social realities. This element has been subdued, making the local version a prototypical instance of cultural "hybrid" in the recent exploitation of foreign formats. This customization — redesigning *SATC* to fit snugly with the officially approved conceptions of Chinese modernity and the new Confucianized woman — becomes more apparent when we look more closely at the Beijing version, *Falling in Love*. First aired on several major television stations in China in October 2004, *Falling in Love* is a forty-episode series focusing on the life of four urban women: Tan Ailing, Li Minglang, Mao Na and Tao Chun. As in *SATC*, the four heroines are in their early thirties and earn high salaries. Like Carrie Bradshaw, Tan Ailing is a writer on female topics. She is linked to her "Mr. Big", Wu Yuefeng, who does not want to commit to marriage. Their extended relationship forms the narrative core of the series while the other three women repeatedly try out different partners. Li Minglang is a highly-regarded television producer. Tough and aggressive, she is an oriental translation of Miranda Hobbs. She presents herself as a strong feminist and does not believe in marriage. Mao Na, a successful stylist, is ostensibly drawn from the Samantha Jones mould. During the day she displays fine style in her fashionable profession; while at night, she is conspicuous in social activities. She is not interested in long-term relationships but enjoys male company. Tao Chun is a computer software designer. She represents traditional Chinese womanhood and harbors hopes of marrying a gentleman and producing a family. In the early episodes, she articulates traditional values and aspirations for a better future. In the end she falls in love and gets married, only to find that marriage is not as straightforward as she has imagined.

Interestingly, the personal dilemmas of these four female leads are not presented simplistically as individual judgment or a lack of judgment. Rather, they cater for a media culture that has developed a keen interest in matters of everyday life as well as questions of intimacy. Their stories serve as an ideology of selective cultural revivalism which seeks to retain a balance between demonizing Western morality and encouraging Western practices that promote economic development. To start with, their fashionable careers and glamorous lifestyles are the results of expanding consumerism and in this respect illustrate how women have been offered new opportunities in the market economy. Their modern apartments are decorated in ways which exude individuality as well as a desire to imitate a Westernized living environment. Their frequent gatherings do not feature Chinese tea drinking, but are staged in bars accompanied by a culture of wine and cocktail sipping. Even in domestic settings, the backdrop to their conversations is afternoon tea English style, or cakes and coffee freshly brewed from Italian cappuccino machines. This image of sophisticated cosmopolitan citizens is constructed repeatedly in relation to universally recognizable logos, such as TGI Friday's, Gucci, Prada, MaxMara, and Mercedes Benz. The insertion of these commercial symbols is not solely due to cultural empowerment but also to commercial forces such as product placement deals and the exploitation of the pink-collared mentality. The latter in particular valorizes individualism and hedonism reflected in conspicuous consumption. In contrast to the traditionally-extolled virtue of devoting oneself to the communal good, the pink-collared woman pursues contemporary bourgeois lifestyles that provide personal realization and happiness. This is illustrated in a scene where Tao Chun's spending habits offend her boyfriend. When she buys yet another skirt for her already crowded wardrobe, he reproaches her for not being able to see frugality as a virtue and iterates his unwillingness to live with a woman lacking such quality. His anger, however, fails to bring a compromise; Tao Chun stands tenaciously behind her action and argues that she has the right to decide how to spend her salary. Her boyfriend finally caves in and somewhat bizarrely transforms into a person obsessed with lifestyle commodities such as perfume and exotic cuisine. Although ironically scripted on occasions, the condemnation and sarcastic comments made toward the moral shortcomings of China's fast-growing consumerism are reconciled by the narrative of women's social empowerment as a facet of China's modernization.

This does not mean that themes of material consumption are simply passed on without some refraction. Rather, they often become sites for further reproduction of local identities and meanings. Echoing widespread ambivalence toward the inflow of Western culture since the late 1980s, the representation of the commercialized femininity in the series has shown the propensity of moving from a wholesale acceptance of anything foreign to "repatriation and domestication of difference."[21] Like *SATC*, the made-up female bodies in *Falling in Love* are dressed by renowned stylists in a variety of costumes provided by commercial sponsors, but unlike *SATC* where the four women are dressed to emphasize their individual "sexy zones," the women in *Falling in Love* are purposely dressed in a less decorative style without excessive display of flesh. Mini-skirts, plunging necklines, ruffle laces and sequins, and contrasting color combinations are minimized. Consequently, whereas the fashion choices in *SATC* are described as the embodiment of the free-spirited "bohemian bourgeoisie,"[22] the style displayed in *Falling in Love* is relatively contained to match the traditionally desirable qualities of Eastern femininity — gentle, soft, and one that does not "flaunt her qualities." Perhaps the two major sponsors, MaxMara and Mushi, are chosen for a reason, as the former is internationally famous for designing classic-style clothing, while the latter is owned by a French designer who has long resided in Beijing and incorporated both Chinese and French cultural inspirations into her design. The fashion narrative not only duplicates the linkage between television drama and commercial product placement deals in images of modern women, but more importantly points to a negotiated taste and femininity that are suitable for modern Chinese women.

It is, however, the issue of "sex and sexuality" that remains an area where the translation between the two serials is interrupted. Despite the fact that the consumer culture of Chinese cities has encouraged a more liberated libido with direct manifestations of sexuality, such as make-up, clothing, and fashion, representing issues of sex and sexuality in China remains problematic and highly contested. Wei Hui's popular paperback, *Shanghai Baby*, is a vivid example. Born in Shanghai in the late 1970s, Hui produced a semi-autobiographical account of the spiritual and sexual awakening of a young woman named Coco, whose sensual relationships with two men involve conflicting feelings of love and betrayal. As Hui comments on the book's cover, "I was looking for a voice of my generation. The gap that divides those of us born in the 1970s and the older generation has never been so wide."[23] This voice was eventually dubbed as decadent, debauched and a slave of foreign culture by older commentators. In April 2000, Chinese cultural authorities banned the book and publicly burned 40,000 copies. It can be argued that government censorship, which aims to screen out unhealthy influences, remains grounded in Confucian ethics and judges sexual discourse and personal behavior within strict demarcations between public and private spheres. As a result, sexual expression in the public space cannot be tolerated, although sex in the private sphere is encouraged.[24] Content that is deemed to disrupt the maintenance of this separation is banned. To comply with this structure, the focus of representations of sex/sexuality in *Falling in Love* eschews depictions of or discussion about physical acts, and emphasizes spiritual (*qing*) elements and compassion. For instance, in a parallel episode to *SATC* about how to handle sexual favor in relationships, the contentious point has been toned down from a "blow job" that Charlotte refuses to perform, to a "lacy nighty" which Tao Chun refuses to wear. On another occasion, in a social outing to the restaurant, SATC's Mr. Big tips a skimpy-dressed belly dancer moving around him while the Chinese character Wu

Yuefeng tips a static-posed female guitar player from a distance. In contrast with the overtly sexualized adventures portrayed in *SATC*, sexuality is not used to engage audiences. Rather, the serial's appeal is built around the changing lifestyles of women coming to terms with careers and love in the modern city. Interestingly, a Hong Kong version of SATC, *Women on the Run* (2005), also contains no overt depictions or reminders of sexual activities within the screenplay. These local versions are in effect a dilution of the confrontational and "liberated" liaison narrative, and are written within the social and political constraints of the Chinese society.

The construction of a remodeled Confucianized womanhood is also evident in the representation of single women. While eschewing the stereotypical roles of housewife and good mother, the narrative of *Falling in Love* does not escape completely from the Confucian male-female gender roles and the strong traditional emphasis on family values. This becomes especially evident in the character Mao Na. At the beginning of the series, she is a rebel against conventional social values. A fashion stylist, she indulges in a luxurious (and apparently) promiscuous social life. Her motto is "only relationships (*lianai*), no love (*aiqing*)." In one early episode, she is watching *SATC* in the living room at her cousin's house. Her cousin, a married woman from the older generation, complains that she should be serious about her life and stop drifting from one man to the other. The older woman insists that no matter how society changes, a woman in numerous relationships will never gain social approval. Mao Na is indignant, defending her right to be single and independent. She argues that getting married is no longer obligatory for women, and accuses her cousin of being retrograde and jealous of her freedom. This scene not only depicts a fight between single women and married women, but also a struggle over approved gender roles between different generations. Ironically, toward the end of the serial, Mao Na falls ill. Bedridden, she calls all the men who have ever expressed love for her, but nobody shows up. Soon after recovering from illness, she marries a restaurant owner and moves to the southwest of China. She replaces her fashionable clothes with hiking gear and is last seen climbing mountains and visiting temples with her husband. She then writes to her friend, detailing how wrong she thinks she was before, and praising the warmth and calmness her marriage has given her.

Contested Gender Identities: The Foreign versus the Local

Falling in Love sets out a contestation between personal emancipation and

Confucian values within the context of a more broadly-based revival of popular culture. However, together with the introduction of new images of women, the media have also staged public debates and criticism. Some members of the *Falling in Love* audience have pointed out that the serial failed to address the dilemmas that Chinese women face. In one review widely circulated on the Internet, the author expresses strong disappointment with the narrative of *Falling in Love* for its implicit message that women need to get married. In her opinion, *SATC* portrays four independent women looking for love, but the Chinese version portrays four marriage-seeking women pretending to be independent. This interpretation becomes increasingly pertinent as the narrative develops, and the four women grow increasingly anxious about their single status.[25] Another review on the Internet questions the novelty of gender representations in *Falling in Love,* and regards them as capitalizing on the issues of "sex" and "flower vase women" while providing no profound thinking on women's sexual liberation.[26]

Comments like these are supported by research on women in Asian societies, especially young middle-class women. The contestation of gender identity is a complicated process of (re)inventing and adapting one's images and sense of self. This takes place within a social and psychological space in which familial responsibility, feminism, and state policies overlap and jostle for attention and supremacy.[27] Beneath this apparent conflict, however, lies the continuing resilience of the core separation of the public sphere from the personal sphere. While women are encouraged to achieve the same goals as men in education and at work, the mainstream culture discourages fundamental changes to either gender roles or dominant conceptions of femininity, especially when it comes to marriage and sexuality. For some women, the rigidity of this separation creates difficulties in anchoring their gender identity, which in turn makes Western conceptions of emancipation, personal freedom and individual choice attractive. To them, it is precisely those elements — freedom as single women, gender power reversal, and sexual liberation — which have *not* been transposed into *Falling in Love* that constitute a matrix of pleasure. The rebellion against conventions, as played out in *SATC*, has filled a space that is lacking in local culture. SATC has offered women symbolic resources to negotiate real-life tensions created by the separation of spheres. However, this pleasure with *SATC* is also ambivalent and fantasy-based. To the women viewers, watching a half-hour episode on their living-room sofa is like taking an imagined journey with the characters into what is deemed "inappropriate or immoral" in the Chinese context. Engaging with the tensions between local/foreign and reality/fantasy enables them to place the boundary under control. Their vicarious participation in the *SATC* lifestyle is both joyful and safe, but is again only cherished in the personal sphere.

Conclusion

The combination of political and socio-economic forces described above has played an important part in the development of pink dramas. While Western scholars have highlighted the role that post-feminist media products have played in transitional feminist politics,[28] I have argued that pink dramas are not only significant in exploring how media texts and media consumption construct gender identities, but are also important in examining shifts in gender representation as part of a broader debate on globalized cultural identities. In other words, one should not overlook the ways in which conceptions of modern Chinese womanhood are contested, and how Chinese cultural identity is interrogated and boundaries are redrawn in the recent growth of pink dramas and literature associated with women's culture, psychology and sexuality.

The emergence of pink dramas addresses the social empowerment and changing lifestyles of single urban women. However, representations of women's aspirations and dilemmas in this genre are not altogether innocent. They are strongly structured by the Western-influenced commercialization of gender and the television industry's role in this process. These serials are also informed by a form of cultural revivalism, in which modernity and Westernization are not so easily reconciled. Instead a new amalgam of modernity and tradition emerges. This inherent contradiction resonates strongly with the experiences of young women who are trying to figure out what it means to be modern and Chinese. Pink dramas address this tension by offering representations of "preferred" femininity. Yet, this settlement is constantly challenged by the way these dramas are appropriated by their audience. By offering a glimpse into the significant role that this genre plays in negotiating the social and emotional contradictions of transition in contemporary China, this chapter has hopefully pointed out a number of issues and connections that merit further reflection and research.

III

Production, Reception, and Distribution

8

A Brief History of Chinese Situation Comedies

Di Miao

The television situation comedy, or sitcom, was "invented" in the United States. Derived from the episodic radio format preceding broadcast television, the TV sitcom soon extended comedy genres. Hartley argues that there are two broad categories of sitcom: workplace comedies (often dealing with characters, relationships, and sexual exploration issues, at least in Western media) and family (or domestic) comedies (focusing on identity and individual roles within the family).[1]

This chapter will first explore how situation comedies have taken root in China, beginning with perhaps the best known workplace comedy of the early 1990s, *Stories from an Editorial Office* (*Bianjibu de gushi*). I will then discuss how the US sitcom format was utilized and modified in the mid-1990s in shows produced and directed by Ying Da. Ying was an influential figure in the development of the sitcom genre in China. The sitcoms which I will discuss are the successful *I Love My Family* (*Wo ai wo jia*) and the innovative but less successful *Chinese Restaurant* (*Zhongguo canguan*). Finally, I will examine an example of the more indigenous Chinese sitcom genre, *Tales of Jianghu* (*Wulin waizhuan*).

Stories from an Editorial Office

The commercialization of Chinese television began in the 1980s and accelerated in the early 1990s, resulting in changes in the way television drama was financed and produced. Prior to the 1980s, issues of cost and profit were marginal to production considerations. Television dramas were produced in-house by the state-owned television stations. From the late 1980s, state-owned enterprises outside the media sector, and even some private firms, were allowed to make television dramas in partnership with officially authorized production entities. Against this backdrop of entrepreneurial activity in media production, *Stories from an Editorial Office,* China's first influential television comedy, debuted during the Spring Festival of 1992.

Produced by the Beijing Television Arts Center, *Stories from an Editorial Office* was described as an "indoor drama serial" (*shinei dianshiju*) by the Beijing Television Arts Centre (BTAC). This twenty-four-episode comedy show was shot mostly in studios with multiple cameras and simultaneous recording — techniques that were then quite new to drama producers in China. Production costs were reduced because of these innovative techniques. Set in an editor's office of a magazine called *Guide for Living* (*Renjian zhinan*), the show follows the workplace sitcom model, that is, it touches on characters, relationships, social phenomena, and manners. A complete story is told in one or two episodes; each event in the editorial office revolves around editors with distinct personalities.

Similar to the well-known BBC sitcom of the 1980s, *Drop the Dead Donkey,* the cast is a mix of young and old, the entrepreneurial and conservative. While critics were divided on the show's value, audiences responded well to the creative use of Beijing street slang, fast-paced dialogues and witty parodies of Maoist values.[2] Of course, the satires were uncontroversial, shying away from overtly political content. In the lyrics of the theme song, it was said that the ultimate goal was just to arouse "a good laugh." Soon after the program aired, the main characters Li Dongbao (played by Ge You), Ge Ling (Lü Liping) and Yu Deli (Hou Yaohua) became household names. Yu Deli's classic line "Money is not everything, but without money you can do nothing" (*qian bushi wanneng de, dan meiyou qian shi wanwan buneng de*) became part of the lingua franca at the time. The success of the show proved that situation comedy had market potential in China. *Stories from an Editorial Office* contained all the basic elements of a typical situation comedy: serial narrative structure, indoor setting, contrasting characters, and good punch lines. However, *Stories from an Editorial Office* was shot in a studio without an audience.

At the time *Stories from an Editorial Office* appeared, the word "situation comedy" had not been translated into Chinese. In 1982, a US sci-fi sitcom *My Favorite Martian* aired on a number of local television stations. But it was only after ten years, when the US show *Growing Pains* was broadcast, that this type of "television drama serial" drew serious attention from the Chinese television industry. *Growing Pains* was the first American show to make a mark in China. The happy life enjoyed by the Seavers and the "democratic" domestic relationships provided a contrasting model for Chinese viewers, embodying fresh ideas about family relationships and upbringing. Most importantly, *Growing Pains* familiarized Chinese viewers with situation comedy. At the very least, it also accustomed Chinese viewers to the use of canned laughter.

I Love My Family, Ying Da, and the Localization of the US Sitcom Format

From 1985 to 1987, Ying Da studied theatre at the Eugene O'Neill Theater Center in New London, Connecticut. When interned in New York, he was once working close to a studio in which *The Cosby Show* was being recorded. Ying became so enamored with the content, format, and shooting techniques of US situation comedies that he decided to import this genre into China.[3] In 1992, when *Growing Pains* was at the peak of its popularity, Ying Da met with Wang Shuo, the well-known writer, and Liang Zuo, Ying Da's fellow Peking University alumnus who was famous for writing comedy cross-talks (*xiangsheng*) such as *Narrow Escape* (*Hukou xiaxian*) and *Thief's Company* (*Xiaotou gongsi*). The trio decided to create a situation comedy about an ordinary Chinese family. The following year, Hengda Real Estate, a company from northeastern China, was persuaded by Ying Da to sponsor the production. This was a risky venture. In the end, the show recouped ten times the amount of the original investment.[4]

When *I Love My Family* first aired, it met with lukewarm audience response in some cities. In 1994, it was voted one of the worst television dramas by viewers polled by *Chengdu Evening News*, although it did surprisingly well in terms of audience ratings. But in the subsequent years it developed a loyal following, and is now widely held to be a classical Chinese situation comedy. It has had frequent rerun.

The "ordinary family" presented in *I Love My Family* is far from common. Old Fu, the household head, is a revolutionary veteran with bureau-level administrative ranking (that is, he is a senior party cadre or *gaogan*). In the first episode, he is notified of his retirement, which means that he has to step down and start a life as an ordinary person. The older son, Zhiguo, works at a government agency. He is honest but a little too fond of money and power. Zhiguo's wife, Heping, is a low-brow drum-song performer, but nevertheless a good mother and wife. The younger son, Zhixin, is unemployed. He has little to do except loitering around, although he is extremely concerned about "losing face." There are also a granddaughter named Yuanyuan, an eighth-grader; a young maid temporarily staying in Beijing; and a daughter named Xiaofan, who visits the Fu's house occasionally. This is a "typical" Chinese family — three generations under one roof.

Following John Hartley's description of the family sitcom, each family member has an independent identity. The dialogues are witty and challenge the traditional familial order, which is associated with rigidity and generational hierarchy. According to one writer, this family is "an ideal family in which freedom, liveliness, humor, and joy abound."[5] As in *Stories from an Editorial Office*, the comedy of *I Love My Family* is achieved as words and phrases are dislodged from their conventional contexts. Also, like *Stories from an Editorial Office*, the show subverts the orthodox discourse of authority and hierarchy. However, *I Love My Family* sticks closer to the sitcom genre in that it has a studio audience and laugh tracks. Ying Da has said that if he had been involved in *Stories from an Editorial Office*, he would have produced it differently.

Like *Stories from an Editorial Office*, *I Love My Family* addresses contemporary social issues. It plays on people's confusions, hopes, disillusions, worries, and disorientations in an age of profound transformation. We see a false *qigong* (a type of traditional breathing exercise) master, a fraudulent scientist, a dubious broker, and a burglar, among others. The writers also play on the craze of *xiahai* (literally "going into the sea," that is, leaving the security of the public sector to become an entrepreneur). There are episodes about moonlighting, studying abroad, peasant migration to the cities, private tutoring, street peddling, and singing competitions. As in US sitcoms, the equilibrium in the family is disturbed in each episode, followed by a flurry of efforts to make sense of the situation and eventually a return to the initial equilibrium.

In 1995, Ying Da established the Ying Film and Television Arts Co. (*Ying shi yingshi yishu gongsi*). The new company launched a series of sitcoms, including *The Waiting Room* (*Houche dating,* 1998, 20 episodes), *The New 72 Tenants* (*Xin 72jia fangke,* 1997, 40 episodes), *Psychiatric Clinic* (*Xinli zhensuo,* 1998, 20 episodes), and *The Chinese Restaurant* (*Zhongguo canguan,* 1999, 80 episodes). Ying Da's productions have all been influenced by US situation comedies. According to a news report: "Ying Da acknowledged that each of his situation comedies was modeled on an American show . . . But he is proud of his ability of localizing and nationalizing those shows so successfully that the audience no longer sees any trace of their foreign origins."[6]

Nevertheless, *I Love My Family* is also strongly influenced by local factors.

For example, a unique linguistic feature is its appropriation of the traditional humor of comedic cross-talk. Liang Zuo, the first professional sitcom writer in China, used to be a cross-talk writer. When he turned to sitcoms, he was able to seamlessly incorporate many techniques linked to this traditional art form. In fact, it is imperative for sitcom writers to study cross-talk and to master its innovative language deployment.

Further Experimentation and Financial Constraints

Early Chinese comedies tended to feature family life in northern China. This gave rise to a problem: slang and dialects particular to the north made it difficult for viewers in the south to comprehend and appreciate the humor. At the time, it was said that sitcoms were unlikely to cross the Yangzi River to the south. Departing from this trend, *The New 72 Tenants* is set in a traditional Shanghai-style living compound housing four families — the Wang, the Zhang, the Qian, and the Su families. The cast consists almost entirely of native Shanghai actors and actresses, who reflect typical Shanghainese characteristics in their dialogues and their ways of thinking. In addition, *The New 72 Tenants* incorporated many elements from local comedies. This sitcom has been popular with both northern and southern viewers. It can be argued that *The New 72 Tenants* was the forerunner to southern sitcoms such as *The Old Uncle* (*Lao niangjiu*), produced in Shanghai, and *Daughters-in-law from Outside the Province* (*Waidi xifu bendi lang*), produced in Guangdong.

In the late 1990s, sitcoms represented a cheap kind of program costing no more than RMB 50,000 per episode. The shortage in funds for investment in sitcoms has led to many problems. The first is the uncertain quality of production personnel. The low salaries on offer are not attractive to most talented writers, directors and technical staff. The general manager of The Ying Co., Wang Xiaojing, said that "it costs RMB 10,000 on average to hire one director to direct one episode. If we want to hire a reputed director, the costs would double. We can only afford at most one such expensive director for a show."[7]

A situation comedy producer is inclined to be more generous when it comes to hiring actors and actresses. A good lead actor or actress has an immediate impact on the show's marketability. In a climate of restricted costs, perpetuated by a lack of distribution and syndication rights (see Chapters 10 and 15) it is imperative that salary costs are reduced as much as possible. This is usually achieved by minimizing the working hours of stars. Sitcom producers are guided by the belief that the faster the production, the better. When Ying Da was shooting *I Love My Family*, he divided the day into three units — morning, afternoon, and evening. Every episode was to be completed in five units, which meant that three episodes were made in five working days. But today the practice is to finish one and a half episodes within a single day; some shows (such as *Happy Family*) are produced at a rate of two episodes a day.

Under such circumstances, shows are made in haste. To accommodate the requirement of finishing three episodes in two days, scriptwriters have little time to polish the lines; actors have little time for preparation; technical crew members — though accustomed to the pace — make mistakes which generally remain uncorrected. Despite frequent complaints from viewers, the quality is unlikely to improve as long as poor production conditions prevail.[8]

Another effect of financial deprivation is the replacement of studio audience with canned laughter. According to Ying Da, a genuine sitcom is taped in front of a live audience. When shooting *I Love My Family*, Ying went to great lengths to gather studio audience, even performing stand-up comedy by himself during scene shifts to enliven the atmosphere.[9] But, after the experiment with *I Love My Family*, Ying — as well as other producers — dispensed with the studio audience. But the issue of cost persists even with canned laughter. Ying Da's company, which places more emphasis on quality, has laugh tracks that sound varied and authentic. Other production companies make do with perfunctorily recorded false laughter, which sounds flat and flaccid. An extreme example is *Happy Family* (CCTV-2), for which there are only three kinds of laugh tracks — explosive, medium-strength, and mild. These laughs are directly written into the script as a means of speeding up post-production.

Chinese Restaurant and the Problem of Censorship

It was only in 1999 that the second situation comedy was made in front of a live audience. *The Chinese Restaurant* was directed by Ying Da and modeled on the popular 1980s US situation comedy *Cheers*. Set in a Chinese restaurant in Los Angeles, it recounts the lives of a group of overseas Chinese. In the opening episode, titled "Assuming Office," a Chinese restaurant — appropriately named "Sichuan Garden" — is on the verge of bankruptcy due to mismanagement. To reverse the situation, the board of directors decides to replace the manager.

Unlike other television dramas about Chinese overseas students (see Chapter 4), this show provides an open window on the lives of expatriates.

People from all walks of life meet in the restaurant: people from Beijing, Shanghai, Taiwan, Hong Kong, American-born Chinese, and Americans who like Chinese cuisine. Stories revolve around the change of the restaurant's management, a false alarm concerning AIDS, the absurd manners of the rich, embarrassing moments associated with an old man and his young wife, and the grueling work in the restaurant.

Written by Liang Zuo and Liang Huan, this show gathered together a strong crew; it was Ying Da's most favored and carefully handled project following *I Love My Family*. It was shot in front of a studio audience.[10] Television viewers, the media, and Ying Da himself had high expectations. However, the show failed to generate an audience of sufficient numbers. One of the reasons for its failure, according to Ying, was that it was too distant from ordinary people's life (the story was based in Los Angeles). Ying also mentioned in private that the censors had hacked off many good scenes, which destroyed consistency and coherency in certain episodes.

This is a serious issue facing the industry, and not only in sitcoms. China's censorship policy differentiates "television program" from "television drama." "Television programs" refer to recurring programs — usually non-dramatic — produced or commissioned by television stations, and reviewed by television stations prior to broadcasting. The SARFT ("State Administration of Radio, Film, and TV") monitors programs during broadcasting and seeks out audience opinions. When "problematic" content is found, however it is defined, the SARFT issues criticisms or warnings. It sometimes even suspends a show. For television dramas, however, censorship takes place prior to broadcasting. The regulator examines television dramas, and in most cases requests cuts and revisions, or under some circumstances kills off a show entirely. Censorship is stringent and producers are frequently required to make unexpected changes.

The Chinese Restaurant is a case in point. When the show was initially reviewed, the Beijing Bureau of SARFT delivered a fairly positive appraisal of the show. But on the eve of its initial broadcast, the Chinese Embassy in Yugoslavia was bombed by the United States (May 8, 1999). In this sudden heightening of diplomatic tension, the large doses of positive content about American society, such as civility and prosperity, suddenly became problematic and sensitive, and in the eyes of the regulator, might trigger hostile reactions from the audience. As such, the distributor Yahuan had to undertake major revisions prior to broadcasting. Nearly every episode was reduced by about five minutes in length, and screening was delayed until June 30. The version of *The Chinese Restaurant* that was finally broadcast looked very different from the original.[11]

The fate of *The Chinese Restaurant* was arguably due to bad luck more than bad management. It highlights the sensitivities confronting Chinese sitcoms. There are many taboos that stand in the way of success. Whereas conflicts of values, status, and lifestyles are the ingredients of sitcoms in most countries, Chinese officials often take a dim view. Social conflict is not a topic that can be discussed casually in the mass media. It has been rumored that soon after *I Love My Family* was broadcast, some old party cadres complained that the characterization of Old Fu in the show damaged the image of revolutionary cadres. Old Fu is portrayed as somewhat misplaced, the subject of ridicule for his adherence to an outdated value system. In fact, the same strategy of satirizing the past was used, albeit using a different background, in *Stories from an Editorial Office*.

The Chinese sense of humor is quite complex. When watching a television drama, a Chinese viewer will tend to seek out representations of the social group to which he or she belongs and then feel obligated to defend the honor of the group. This may be a religious, ethnic, cultural, geographical, class, occupational, organizational, age, or gender-based group. While people are ready to ridicule others' values, identities and lifestyles, once they are the target, they can become very upset. For the government, this embedded sensitivity presents a dilemma; for writers, it is a hurdle. So long as there is someone — or some group — feeling unhappy or offended, social stability can be threatened. For this reason, the regulating agency takes great pains to restrict the limits of what is allowed. Over the past few years, this conservative cultural environment has led to the decline of cross-talk and comedic skits. Situation comedy based on satire also faces an uncertain future. Since *I Love My Family*, Chinese situation comedies have regressed in terms of the depth of social life explored and the strength of social critique.

Nevertheless, experiments with situation comedy have continued. Although none has outdone *I Love My Family* in popularity, the sitcom genre has been accepted by the market and the audience. A national program specifically devoted to sitcoms was instituted on October 30, 1999. The "630 Theater" was launched jointly by almost a hundred cable television stations on their flagship channels in the timeslot between 6.30 and 7 p.m. It was operated by the Yahuan Company and the National Association of Cable Television. The first show featured in the "630 Theater" was *The Chinese Restaurant*, followed by a series of popular shows such as *The Unemployed Sister Ma* (*Xianren Ma dajie*), *Old Wei's Plan X* (*Lao Wei de X jihua*), and *Diary of the Net Bug* (*Wangchong riji*).

Tales of Jianghu (*Wulin wanzhuan*) and the Future of Chinese Situation Comedies

Situation comedies make people laugh, and in doing so they lessen the pressures of modern life. In this way they meet certain needs of the audience. But currently, the quality leaves much to be desired. As mentioned earlier, among the many factors that affect this genre, the low level of investment is critical. On its better days, an episode can recoup less than RMB 150,000, and most of the time it does even worse. The primary reason for low price is that sitcoms are rarely scheduled in prime time. Until quite recently, very few sitcoms were screened between 7 and 10 p.m. Some are scheduled in the time slot prior to 7 p.m. or at noon, and the majority appears in marginal timeslots such as at midnight or in the early morning hours. Lack of access to prime time has become the major obstacle for Chinese situation comedies. Compared with US sitcoms, almost all of which are shown on the major networks at prime time in their initial broadcast, Chinese sitcoms are severely disadvantaged.

Sitcoms are kept off prime-time television in China because they attract fewer audiences than serial drama. The bottom line is advertising revenue for television stations. Despite the fact that a few shows occasionally deliver a large audience, television stations are not ready to take the risk. The inability of sitcoms to draw audience has to do with the viewing habits of Chinese, as well as low production values. Chinese television viewers prefer serials to series. As far as low production values are concerned, a vicious circle has set in. Low quality leads to unattractive screening time and low prices, which dampens investments to an even lower level and eventually results in even lower-quality shows.

A new development came about in late 2005 and early 2006. A show with characters clad in pre-modern costumes called *Tales of Jianghu*[12] was shown in prime time on CCTV-8 with little fanfare. This show had been accorded limited attention and had low expectations when it started. Even without much promotion, *Tales of Jianghu* garnered rapidly increasing audience share, and the average weekly audience ratings nationwide reached 1.72 percent, which was quite an accomplishment in the highly competitive Chinese television industry.[13] It also attracted a great deal of attention on the Internet. Leading characters such as Tong Xiangyu, Bai Zhantang, and Guo Furong have all established solid fan bases; the thousands of messages posted on several major websites are strong evidence of the appearance of the "culture of *Jianghu*." Originally produced for a niche audience, the show eventually gained popular acceptance and became one of the cultural highlights of 2005.

According to Ning Caishen, the scriptwriter, the eighty-episode *Tales of Jianghu* is narrated from the perspective of the teenage girl, Guo Furong, who is a new arrival in *Jianghu*. Contrary to her noble origins, Guo Furong desires to become part of *Jianghu* as a swordswoman. At one time, she tries to be helpful, but gets into trouble and ends up in a hostel, injured. The hostel is named Tongfu. From that time she stays in the hostel as a maid. The hostel's owner, named Tong Xiangyu, is a kind, good-looking, but very stingy woman. Her husband died shortly after her wedding, and she has taken it upon herself to raise her younger sister-in-law, Mo Xiaobei. She is more like a mother than a sister to Xiaobei. The waiter named Bai Zhantang is in an ambivalent relationship with Tong Xiangyu. The rest of the characters include a knowledgeable, bookish accountant, Sir Lu, a chef known as Jiang the Big Mouth, and a parade of the guests who come and go.

In terms of form and content, *Tales of Jianghu* has a strong Chinese flavor. Seeking a breakthrough style, *Tales of Jianghu* is distinct from classical Western sitcoms and from Chinese ones of the early period. Instead, borrowing from the chapter-based Chinese traditional fiction, it tells two related stories in each episode of over 40 minutes; each episode has a title that resembles chapter titles in a traditional novel — such as "Old Xing loses his administrative job by joining in a gang of beggars; little Liu imitates the official tone and gets promoted to police officer." While the typical sitcom uses canned laughter, *Jianghu* replaces laughter with Chinese traditional music. Shang Jing, the director, offers an explanation, saying that although the laughter in US sitcoms sounds spontaneous and appropriate, in Chinese shows is phony: "We did not use laugh tracks. When it gets funny, you will laugh any way, and need not be cued by canned laughs. There's no need to tickle the audience."[14]

Jianghu employs a unique cultural element — martial arts; this is unprecedented in the history of Chinese sitcoms. Yet, while one finds martial arts masters in this show, such as the Master of Theft, the Head of Heng Mountain School, and the Master in Guanzhong, these characters are portrayed as ordinary human beings. In fact, Tongfu Hotel resembles a microcosm of Chinese society, dealing with issues ranging from the education of minors, school pressures, and domestic violence to ruthless business competition.

The show is also characterized by a measure of post-modern absurdity. It blends the newest developments in Chinese popular culture, including Internet language, popular songs, commercials, entertainment shows, style and information programs, slang and dialects, and popular sayings. The show therefore has strong appeal to young viewers. In addition, its strong sense of pastiche is a crucial element, contributing to a distinctive sense of postmodernity. Tradition and modernity, East and West, humor and kindliness, indoctrination and post-modern deconstruction, satire of swordsmanship, and advocacy of the martial spirit are all smartly blended into a montage that is this Chinese-style farce.

Reportedly, it was this highly individualized style that impressed the person in charge of CCTV-8, who then made the decision to purchase the initial broadcast rights of *Tales of Jianghu* for prime-time screening. History proves his decision to have been correct. The show earned CCTV-8 more than RMB 100 million of advertising revenue. (Some analysts have observed that, because this show is watched mostly by urban youth, the advertising value is even greater.)[15]

Conclusion: The Road Ahead

It has been more than a decade since the first Chinese sitcom made an appearance. However, despite its rapid development, the Chinese sitcom remains a marginalized genre. According to an estimate by ACNeilson in 2002, of all the episodes of television dramas made in China, sitcoms accounted for just 5 percent.[16] The situation has not changed much since then. Except for a small number of first-rate shows, the majority of sitcoms do not make it to prime-time slots on major television channels. Most of the time, they are screened at marginal times.

Tales of Jianghu has ushered in a new way of thinking among producers in China and has pointed to a way out of the dilemmas of low-cost production for Chinese sitcoms. First, the fact that an incredibly farcical show like *Jianghu* has become a ratings bonanza demonstrates that innovation is the key to lifting Chinese comedies out of the current situation of stagnation. Sitcoms set in domestic and family settings — the quotidian urban setting model — can no longer attract large audiences. Second, situation comedies need to be retargeted to accommodate shifts in audience demographics. Based on this author's observation, the most popular US situation comedies such as *Friends* and *Seinfeld* have a huge following among college students and white-collar youths in China. These people normally do not watch any Chinese situation comedies, but they love *Jianghu*. The producers of *Jianghu* made it explicit that this show was not written for those born before 1970. Obviously, for a sitcom to secure a better timeslot and become a more marketable commodity, it is crucial for producers to target urban youth as the primary audience.

The success of *Jianghu* has brought a large number of contracts for scriptwriter Ning Caishen (who used to be a fairly well-known Internet writer) and director Shang Jing. It is likely that the dominance of the Ying brothers in these genres will come to an end and that the industrial structure will be changed. But can one show, such as *Jianghu,* lead to a real breakthrough in the development of Chinese situation comedy and bring the genre to new heights? That remains to be seen.

9

Carnivalesque Pleasure:
The Audio-visual Market and the
Consumption of Television Drama

Rong Cai

On a late Saturday afternoon, Miss Wu — a busy young lawyer in the capital city in her late twenties — goes shopping around the corner of her apartment complex in a residential area five minutes away from Beijing Normal University. She chooses to visit the supermarket and a nearby grocery store at dusk not to avoid the crowd but to find Mr. Zhang, the owner of a makeshift video stall. Zhang runs his business guerrilla style. He does not conduct business in the early afternoon when anti-piracy inspectors are likely to be around; he does not have a fixed spot among the stands along the street in front of the grocery store, yet he is never far away from the entrance; he does not hawk his wares — his customers come to him. Zhang stands quietly behind his display on a small folding table: music CDs, games software, and video disks, and many more bundled with rubber bands in a duffle bag by his feet. Miss Wu strolls over and they greet each other with a knowing nod. On this afternoon, Miss Wu spends RMB 32 and buys *The Jewel in the Palace* (*Da changjin*), an HDVD compilation of a fifty-four-episode South Korean TV drama currently running on Hunan Television.

What is described here is by no means an isolated case. Similar scenes take place daily in towns and cities across China. Obviously, television is not the only channel through which TV drama reaches Chinese viewers. What roles, then, does the video market — legal or illegal — play in the consumption of TV drama? And in what ways does this mode of consumption contribute to the flow and interrogation of meaning within the field of contemporary mass culture?

This chapter examines China's home video market for TV drama — a powerful alternative to the more formal broadcast model of consumption described elsewhere in this book.[1] I begin with an examination of a number of issues in the development of China's audio-visual market since the 1980s, and provide statistics to support the claim that there is a marked polarization in audio-visual publications. Consumption of traditional media such as audio cassettes and video tapes has rapidly declined while that of new digital media such as VCD and DVD has increased sharply. I look at the size and extent of the video market. Following this, I discuss recent trends in illegal recording, and examine anti-piracy offensives by the state and the video industry. The chapter concludes with a close look at consumers of TV drama on video and the socio-ideological implications of using video as an alternative medium to broadcast television. In looking beyond statistics and commercial arguments, I want to show how video viewing introduces unpredictability into viewer consumption, generating a dynamic relation between viewers and administered public television. This turns video viewing into an unofficial site of meaning production whereby consumers design their own modes of consumption to create individual definitions and hierarchies of knowledge.

China's Audio-visual Market

Under the World Trade Organization (WTO)'s Services Classification List, the audio-visual sector includes film, radio, television, and sound recording industries.[2] "Audio-visual industry" (*Yinxiang ye*) in Chinese practice excludes film production, distribution, and exhibition, as well as radio and television transmission services. As defined in Chinese law, audio-visual products comprise a wide array of materials such as audio tapes, video tapes, gramophone records, laser audio compact disks, and laser video compact disks with recorded content (which includes CDs and DVDs).[3] China practices a license system for publication, production, import, wholesale, retail, and rental of audio-visual products. The Ministry of Culture and cultural administration departments of local governments are in charge of the wholesale, retail, renting, public projection, and import of audio-visual products, while oversight of publication, production, and reproduction of audio-visual products falls under the jurisdiction of the General Administration of Press and Publications (GAPP) and the press and publication administration departments of local governments. Actual content of audio-visual products is vetted by a joint committee of the State Administration of Radio, Film, and Television (SARFT) and the Ministry of Culture. Broadcast television programming — programming delivered free to air to households — is monitored by SARFT and the Propaganda Department, and is the principal subject of television ratings companies such as CVSC-SOFRES Media (CSM), a joint venture founded in 1997 between CTR Market Research Ltd and Taylor Nielson Sofres. Missing from the statistics issued on behalf of ratings monitors, however, are broader audio-visual product consumption practices and the black market distribution of content.

China's audio-visual market only began to develop in the 1980s when the nation opened up to the outside world following the Cultural Revolution (1966–76). During the 1980s, audio-visual product consisted mostly of audio and video cassettes.[4] By the 1990s, China's audio-visual industry had entered a new phase, as China became a global base for the reproduction of CDs and DVDs. What is recorded in statistics is just the tip of a large and fragmented unofficial audio-visual industry that has been facilitated by the development of digital reproduction technologies. According to official statistics, there were over 320 audio-visual publishing companies in China by 2003, an increase of 28 over the previous year.[5] There were about 300 listed reproduction companies, 1,800 wholesale distributors, and approximately 140,000 retail entities.[6] Total sales of audio-visual products (including music CDs) reached RMB 2755 million in 2003, a growth that was more than threefold compared with the RMB 738 million in 1994. The number of titles increased from 9,298 in 1994 to 28,224 in 2003, while the total volume of items moved up from 79.8 million to 456 million in the same period.[7]

A close look at the breakdown reveals some notable trends in the publication of video products. The most significant development has been a decline in video tape sales and a sharp increase in VCDs and, more recently, DVDs. The developments reflect global trends. After the first home video device, the Sony one-hour Betamax, was introduced into the consumer electronics market in 1975, video cassette recorders (VCR) utilizing the VHS format quickly spread around the world. By 1989, VCR household penetration in the United States was estimated at around 70 percent.[8] China, however, was on a different trajectory. Even though VCR became available in the 1980s and video tapes began to be produced during the same period, home video was not popular. The VCR and video tapes were too expensive for the ordinary consumer. In addition, there was no efficient and extensive video tape rental system to help promote the medium.[9] When the much cheaper video compact disc (VCD) and VCD players entered China in the mid-1990s, production of video tapes dropped from about 3.8 million cassettes in 1997 to a mere 163,500 in 2003 — a plunge of 95.7 percent over six years. The number of titles published likewise fell from 513,700 to 29,600 during this period. Indeed, video tapes comprised a negligible 0.0035 percent of the annual publication of audio-visual products in 2003.[10]

The drastic decline in video cassette production was due to the steady rise of VCDs and DVDs in the market. The VCD format was first introduced by Sony and Philips in 1993. Aware of the emerging high-compression DVD technology, manufacturers decided not to pursue this option in many developed international media markets, but instead exported the technology to less developed countries, such as China and its Asian neighbors.[11] Since appearing in China in 1993, VCD proliferated at a speed faster than any new technology in the country's history. Sixteen percent of urban households had VCD players in 1998; two years later, ownership had grown to 36.4 percent. Production of VCD players peaked in 1998 when 18.5 million units were manufactured.[12] By 2003, the number of VCD players in China stood at more than 30 million.[13] The spread of VCD players in turn spurred a demand for VCD content, as demonstrated by the following statistics. Over 53 million VCDs and 6,281 titles were published in 1997, accounting for 26 percent of the year's audio and video products. Six year later, in 2003, over 300 million VCDs were sold — an impressive increase of 52.48 percent over the previous year.[14] The popularization of VCD shows that, from the mid-1990s, people became less dependent on regular television broadcasts for their leisure entertainment. The evolution of new digital technologies eventually signaled that the heyday of the VCD was coming to an end. By the time DVD was available in China in 2000, a new cycle of electronic entertainment consumption was in the offing. Although DVD still lagged behind VCD in terms of actual sales volume in 2003, its growth rate in the audio-visual market outpaced all other recording devices. While DVDs only made up 1 percent of national audio-visual production in 2001, output had quadrupled to 4 percent in 2002, and doubled to 8 percent by 2003. The year 2002 saw an increase of 249 percent in titles and 614 percent in quantity compared with 2001. The growth continued in 2003, with the total number of items published exceeding 485 million. Although VCD still occupied the largest share in audio and video production in 2003, analysts predicted that DVD would soon replace VCD and video tape to become the predominant recording device, and that video tape would eventually disappear altogether.[15] The prediction was well-founded. Sales of DVD players were catching up quickly; 18.74 million units were sold in 2005.[16]

The statistics on TV drama are difficult to extract from the data attributed to audio-visual output, as no precise percentages of TV drama in national audio and video production are available. Official statisticians lump TV drama and films together under the category of "feature stories" in audio-visual production. As reported, by 2003 video tape was no longer the dominant medium for TV drama or film; VCDs and DVDs were the major carriers.[17] In terms of quantity, 35.81 percent of DVDs and 34.3 percent of VCDs were devoted to "feature stories" in 2003. Foreign imported titles represent a considerable portion: 51.54 percent in titles and 47.62 percent in quantity in DVD production, and 16 percent in titles and 32.28 percent in quantity in VCD production.[18] Although the statistics did not specify the origin of the imported video products, we can make an intelligent guess based on information on foreign television programming. According to the *China TV Drama Report (2003–2004)*, published by CMS, Hong Kong, Korea, and Taiwan were the top three suppliers of imported TV drama broadcasted by major channels in 2002. Among the 327 titles aired, 40.7 percent were from Hong Kong, 20.5 percent from Korea, and 12.9 percent from Taiwan. Despite having enjoyed enormous popularity in the 1980s, Japanese TV serials had begun to lose their appeal for the Chinese audience by 1990, accounting for only 7 percent of the broadcast volume of foreign TV drama that year. Those from the West, United States, and Europe combined made up 15 percent of the imports, far behind Hong Kong.[19] It seems that linguistic and cultural affinity contributed to the strong draw of Asian TV dramas for Chinese viewers over their Western counterparts.[20]

Piracy on the DVD Market: The HDVD Effect

The most significant supply source for TV drama consumers, however, remains pirated VCDs and DVDs. According to one high-level source, while annual sales of TV drama on the audio-visual market in recent years topped RMB 2,700 million, sales from pirate copies are estimated at ten times the value of legal transactions.[21] As has often been pointed out, technological developments are inextricably linked to globalization — the flow of culture, knowledge, technology, and goods across cultural, ideological, and geographic borders. Unfortunately, piracy also benefits from technological breakthroughs and regional and international competition and cooperation. Audio-visual piracy has presented an ongoing problem ever since China allowed import of Western movies after the Cultural Revolution.[22] Contact with the outside world and the adoption of new technologies stimulated the growth of a market-oriented economy, but they also created conditions for piracy, turning China into the "piracy capital of the world" in the eyes of the international community.[23] Realizing that it must comply with international standards in order to be part of the global economy, China founded the National Anti-

Pornography Working Committee in 1989 to combat copyright violations, and later changed its name to "The National Anti-Piracy and Pornography Working Committee" (NAPWC) in February 2000.

Under pressure from the United States and the Western community, China enacted a Copyright Law in 1990 to protect intellectual property rights. Two years later, in 1992, new regulations compatible with the Berne Convention for Protection of Literary and Artistic Works went into effect. The establishment of legal and institutional mechanisms, however, does not guarantee success in the fight against piracy. Criminal enforcement remains a problem. Piracy in all copyright sectors (motion pictures, sound recordings, business software, entertainment software, and books) continues to be rampant, and has become even more fluid and efficient in recent years with the diffusion of new digital and Internet technologies. In the 2005 Special 301 Report on the People's Republic of China, the International Intellectual Property Alliance (IIPA) notes that, although anti-piracy activities have increased in most sectors, "piracy levels have not been 'significantly reduced' — they still are around 90 percent in all sectors."[24] The Office of United States Trade Representatives (USTR) kept China on the Priority Watch List in 2006.[25]

My focus here is on the newest anti-piracy front: the battle against the so-called HDVD (super DVD — or compressed DVD, as they are alternately named). If the Hollywood majors suffered most from the widespread piracy of the 1980s and 1990s, the arrival of HDVD (DVD *yasuodie*) in late 2004 has devastated China's domestic audio-visual industry, and the TV drama industry in particular. HDVD has become the preferred technology for drama piracy. Within just a few months after its appearance, illegal HDVD had left carnage, crippling giant video publishers and vendors and bankrupting smaller businesses. Using an MPEG-2 format, a compressed video disc can now store a huge amount of data — about six to seven hours' worth of film or TV drama. A forty-episode TV drama can be contained in four HDVDs — instead of forty VCDs. HDVDs can run on DVD players and computers — and while the viewing quality is no better than VCD, the compressed discs require little storage space and are easily portable.

Video producers, publishers, and retailers were quick to describe piracy on HDVD as a "SARS [bird flu epidemic]" for China's audio-visual market. Since becoming available in October 2004, HDVD has inflicted tremendous damage on the audio-visual industry. Chen Bin, CEO of Weijia Audio-visual Corporation, a Guangdong-based business which had established a reputation by winning the video publishing rights to the blockbuster film *Hero* in a fierce bidding war, disclosed that a month after illegal HDVDs hit the market, sales in the Beijing area were down 80 percent.[26] Weijia had plenty of company in its misfortune. Another leading audio-visual publisher from Guangdong, Qiaojiaren Culture Transmission Ltd, informed reporters that it only sold 20,000 copies of the drama, *A Century of Changes (Canghai bainian)* — 80,000 short of what had been expected — representing a loss of RMB 3 million for the company.[27] The experiences of Weijia and Qiaojiaren represented a nationwide trend. As a result of rampant circulation of pirated HDVDs, the Beijing Audio-visual Building, China's largest retail market for audio-visual products, had more returns than orders at the end of 2004.[28] In only a few months, legal sales of video products across the nation declined by 70–80 percent, an estimated loss of about RMB 100 million for China's video manufacturers.[29]

Piracy on HDVDs produced ripple effects. Video rights fees used to provide about 30 percent of a TV drama's production costs. Before the appearance of HDVDs, producers of popular TV dramas could create handsome revenues from video release. *The Kangxi Empire (Kangxi diguo)* sold for RMB 40,000 an episode, and *The Great Emperor Wu of Han (Han Wu dadi)* brought in RMB 10,000 an episode. The record, however, was achieved by *The Silver Valley (Baiyin gu)*, a story of feud between two Shanxi banking families set in pre-modern China: it reaped RMB 5.4 million for the producers. Industry insiders predicted that spectacular deals like this would never happen again. Wild circulation of illegal HDVDs forced TV drama producers to dramatically lower their copyright fees. But when only about 10 percent of video sales were legitimate, even 50-percent discounts on rights failed to persuade disheartened video publishers.[30]

The victims of TV drama piracy were not just drama and video producers. Individual consumers only accounted for between 20 and 30 percent of sales; the majority of buyers of legal video products were video rental agencies.[31] HDVD piracy led to significant revenue losses for the 140,000 or so retail rental outlets. Rental stores usually lease out TV dramas by the piece, the daily fee ranging from fifty cents to RMB 3 per disc. For an average-length drama (twenty episodes), a store could make a profit of between RMB 40 and RMB 60.[32] When a pirated copy of the same drama cost only about RMB10 or less, who would bother to rent?

In face of a grave threat to China's entire audio-visual industry, the official response was swift. On November 10, 2004, the National Anti-Piracy and Pornography Working Committee under the General Administration of Press and Publication issued a call to crack down on illegal HDVD production and sales to government offices at all levels. Four days later, it was followed by another notice from the Ministry of Culture entitled "Urgent Notice on

Clamping Down on Pirated Compressed DVDs." It was reported that the Minister of Culture facilitated the notice from draft to authorization within twenty-four hours. In December 2004, the state spearheaded a three-month nationwide sting operation in an attempt to stamp out HDVD piracy. The NAPWC instituted a reward of RMB 300,000 to informants who were instrumental in closing down seized illegal replication lines. Private audio-visual producers also contributed to the anti-piracy campaigns. In a coordinated offensive against piracy in late 2004, eleven large audio-visual companies in Guangdong amassed RMB 5 million — as well as an inspection team of 300 — to launch an all-out war against illegal video reproduction. Guangdong Zhongkai Culture Development Ltd, which paid RMB 5 million for the video rights to the film *No Thieves in the World (Tianxia wu zei)*, offered a reward of RMB 300,000 of its own to any individual whose information could lead to the arrest of people responsible for producing pirated copies of the movie.[33] The statistics from anti-piracy seizures were indeed staggering. Nationwide, 154 million pirated discs were confiscated in 2004.[34] *Nanfang ribao* reported that a raid on a village depot in Foshan, Guangdong uncovered 4.12 tons of pirated audio-visual products.[35]

To cope with unchecked piracy, audio-visual companies also came up with individual strategies. The producer of the TV drama, *Female Talent and Male Beauty (Nü cai nan mao)* decided not to release it on DVD to foil piracy.[36] Some companies chose to dramatically lower the prices of their VCDs and DVDs to reduce inventory; some attempted to buy out illegal copies, replacing two pirated discs with one legitimate VCD for their customers.[37] And some even tried to enlist help from their illegal opponents. An unconfirmed anecdote had it that, after purchasing the video rights to a new movie, the owners of an unnamed video company would first wine and dine the heads of piracy operations to secure their commitment that they would delay the release of pirated copies by a few days to give legitimate VCDs and DVDs a head start on the market.[38] In fact, some audio-visual plants were forced to use surplus capacity to produce both legitimate and pirate copies to stay in business.[39] Part of the failure to stop piracy was caused by the fact that demand outstripped legal supplies, and that profit margins from illegal sales were large enough to offset fears for punishment.[40] Eventually, after much debate and agonizing within the industry, legitimate HDVDs began to be produced in March 2005 to compete with pirated copies.

Consuming TV Drama on Video

Who consumes TV drama on VCDs and DVDs? How does this audience differ from that of regular broadcast television? To answer these questions, let us first look at the profile of the broadcast TV audience in China. A 2004 CSM report on China's TV drama market reveals that TV drama tends to attract female audience and people with lower level of education. Women spent eight minutes per day more than men on TV drama, and those with junior high school education watched sixteen minutes more than viewers with a college degree (fifty-seven versus forty-one minutes). Age and income levels were also factors. The age group of sixty-five and older watched more than other groups; and those with a monthly income of RMB 900 and less watched fifty-nine minutes as opposed to the forty-one minutes spent by people earning more than RMB 2000 a month.[41] Apparently, TV drama appealed more to viewers in the lower strata of society. Understandably, in the stratified and commercialized society of today, women, the elderly, and the less educated had more leisure time for television and less disposable income for other forms of entertainment.

Consumers of TV drama on video, on the other hand, belonged to a different socio-economic group. According to one investigation, the majority of buyers of pirated discs were white-collar workers with good education and high incomes. In fact, the higher the education level, the more likely a person was to consume piracy. Among those with a Master's degree, 78.6 percent admitted to having bought pirated videos in various formats. The next highest percentage, 65.8 percent, belonged to college graduates. The rest of the statistics are as follows: 52.5 percent among associate degree holders and 50 percent among high school graduates. Not surprisingly, the income level of consumers of piracy exhibited a similar pattern. The higher the income, the more one consumed pirated video products. Among those earning more than RMB 4,000 a month, 75 percent had bought pirated discs. The second place, 67.4 percent, went to people with a monthly income of RMB 2000–2999. Those between these two groups — that is, people earning between RMB 3000 and RMB 3999 a month — fell slightly behind the second group. Of this group, 66.7 percent had consumed pirated products. One superficial explanation for this consumption pattern is that the more educated people are, the higher is their demand for cultural products.[42] Another explanation is that the more educated have better jobs and the financial means to pay for cultural products, even if they are illegal goods. In addition, these people may consciously display ownership of DVDs as a status symbol.

Specific examples will help us to understand some of the cultural factors beyond the mere statistics. A certain Miss Sun spent RMB 30 on a pirated copy of the TV drama *Falling in Love (Haoxiang haoxiang tanlianai)*, a Chinese version of the HBO series *Sex and the City* (see Chapter 7). The reason for her purchase was to own a copy. Miss Sun did not have the patience to follow the broadcast schedule. A reporter by profession, she had a busy social life and high demands on her leisure time, just like the four female characters in the Chinese drama. Miss Sun wanted to watch the drama according to her own schedule. With a personal copy: "I can watch it whenever I want and however much I want. Besides, the video doesn't have those annoying commercials."[43] When asked why she purchased pirated HDVDs (as opposed to legitimate VCDs), a Ms. Xie informed a reporter that she preferred the compressed discs because they were convenient and portable. It was easy to carry them around, and she could be spared the trouble of having to frequently switch discs.[44] To many consumers looking for entertainment, the price difference between legitimate discs and pirated HDVDs was the major reason they favored illegal copies. The picture quality of compressed DVDs was good enough for ordinary viewers who were not connoisseurs and had no interest in collecting high-quality DVDs.[45]

As I have said, piracy inflicts extensive damages on all parties — a heavy loss in tax revenues to the government and deep erosions of the profits of TV drama producers, copyright-holders, video manufacturers, distributors, and leasing agencies. Aside from the economic impacts, what are the social and ideological ramifications of consuming TV drama on video? Although the video tape failed to spread in China the way it did in the rest of the world, research on the use of home video can help shed some light on our discussion at hand. One could argue that, while new domestic digital technologies improved the quality of data recording, enhancing the pleasure of home viewing, the basic function of the new technologies in the domestic space may not have changed dramatically. Hailed as a revolution, the introduction of VCR in the mid-1970s initially caused consternation in the media industry. However, it was soon embraced by both industry and consumers, and popularized all over the world. In a report to UNESCO on the use of VCR worldwide, Manuel Alvarado has identified three major uses (in descending order of importance): "a) Time-shifting (recording transmitted TV programs for later reviewing); b) viewing non-broadcast professional material (primarily, but not solely, movies); c) viewing non-broadcast non-professional material, i.e. 'home movies'."[46] The third use — viewing privately made materials — was negligible in China, as camcorders were luxuries beyond the reach of most people. The two examples of pirated HDVD purchases I have cited above indicate that Chinese consumers use the VCD and DVD primarily for time-shifting (though the viewers did not actually record the content) and, to a lesser degree, for viewing non-broadcast professional material.

No doubt convenience is foremost in the uses identified among Chinese consumers. But uses extend beyond providing cheap entertainment and innocent pleasures. Video technologies can be subversive devices – they can lead to social relaxations and even ideological challenges to the status quo. Video viewing, often of pirated copies, unsettles the relation between the viewer and broadcast television, giving the former greater freedom in content control. New home video technologies enable viewers to negotiate and anchor meanings at sites not necessarily approved by the state. In her study of copyright, piracy and Asian cinema, Laikwan Pang argues that copyright enforcement and infringement should not be addressed only within the boundaries of the international legal regime instituted to protect intellectual property and related commercial values within a global capitalist order. Pang points to an irony in the piracy of movies: Hollywood, aided by its dominance over technology, has fuelled the desire for Western cultural products in the developing countries. However, while hi-tech visual and audio effects have helped Hollywood maintain its supreme position in world cinema, degraded reproduction of these effects on pirated discs in Asia is "undercutting Hollywood producers' attempts to use high technology to control and manipulate the desires of global audiences."[47]

More relevant to my discussion of TV drama consumption on video is the impact of national politics on movie piracy in China. Government policy restricting expression has encouraged rampant movie piracy in China, and this has had flow-on effects on the TV drama market. Censorship allows the Chinese government to check ideological pluralism and the free flow of information and entertainment. Ironically, the state policies on market access destabilize its control over expression. Current restriction on foreign film imports under China's WTO agreements limits audience access to foreign cinema; these restrictions have had the effect of unwittingly promoting the popularity of Hollywood commercial films among Chinese viewers. Lacking legal channels, many turn to piracy for gratification.[48] While movie piracy is driven by profit and cannot be simply attributed to government intervention to shape and manage popular desire, it is nonetheless true that piracy weakens the state's ideological control, "allow[ing] its subjects to experience the world without any filtering."[49]

TV drama consumption presents a similar case. As market research proves, the Chinese TV drama market is not entirely driven by demand. For example, to protect the domestic TV industry and curb foreign influence, the State Administration of Radio, Film and Television (SARFT) has issued a number of decrees to restrict foreign-made TV drama on Chinese television. Regulations issued in 1994 limit foreign TV drama to less than 25 percent of a station's total daily broadcast of TV drama and film. In contrast, all other imported television is limited to 15 percent of daily transmissions.[50] The regulations published in 2000 also reiterate the ban on overseas TV drama during prime time (7–10 p.m.) without SARFT permission. In addition, the decrees stipulate that any given imported TV drama should not be aired on more than three provincial satellite channels. Certain topics are also regulated. Palace drama and martial arts drama cannot exceed 25 percent of a station's yearly quota of imported drama.[51] Domestically made TV drama is subject to restrictions as well. When the so-called costume drama set in pre-modern China became popular in the late 1990s and at the beginning of the new century, SARFT decided to rein in the trend. Benefiting from the curb, police drama and crime stories flourished in 2003 (see Chapter 3, this volume). Alarmed that drama on crime and violence might produce a negative influence on the viewing public, SARFT subsequently reduced production permits by 40 percent and prohibited broadcasting of the genre between 7 and 11 p.m. This in turn led to a renaissance of costume drama.[52] Admittedly, thanks to market competition and media reforms that compelled television stations to come up with innovative programs to create channel loyalty, viewers now had more choices than before. Nonetheless, government policies could still structure the audience and limit the consumption of TV drama. Consuming TV drama through the use of video technologies bypasses government censorship in several ways. First, it overcomes the policing over content, whereby consumers are denied access to many dramas. Bernard Cohen's comments on the role of press some four decades ago are still highly pertinent. The media, Cohen argues, "may not be successful much of the time in telling people what to think, but it is stunningly successful in telling its readers what to think about."[53] Video viewing subverts state restrictions, allowing viewers to choose "what to think about." Many titles on "restricted topics" were readily available in the video market. Official quotas apparently had no effect. For example, about 40 percent of TV drama available on the video market was produced outside Mainland China, while the broadcast ratio of foreign-made drama, as I have mentioned above, was restricted to 25 percent.[54] Similarly, there is no enforceable limit on the amount of police drama and crime stories people can watch on video. As a result, government regulations no longer retain the power to regulate viewer intake and modes of consumption. Their illegality notwithstanding, cheap pirated HDVDs made TV drama of all varieties accessible and affordable to even the less well-off, offering viewers an opportunity to breach the ideological and cultural boundaries that the state wished to install over leisure entertainment.

Second, video viewing frustrates the policing of meanings in a more serious manner. Beyond satisfying individual tastes and allowing personal convenience, it releases viewers from broadcast programming and institutional controls. It provides users with an alternative circulation system, thus creating possibilities for social intervention. As in many countries, censorship is part of media practice in China. Commercialization of the cultural industry, however, has made government oversight a more tricky business. Although quite strict regulations remain on sensitive topics, reforms and marketization have led to more relaxed policies and greater autonomy for media producers. The desire to be competitive, together with increasing tolerance for expression by television producers, sometimes results in unconventional creations falling through the cracks of censorship. The controversy surrounding the drama *March toward the Republic* (*Zou xiang gonghe*), a drama focusing on China's tumultuous modern revolution, is a good case to illustrate this point. Encouraged by highly positive responses from test audiences at previews, CCTV-1 began to air the series in early April 2003. A month into the program, without preannouncement, the station increased the pace to three episodes per evening, before suddenly pulling it off the air. It became clear later that unexpected controversies over the interpretation of the republican revolution and the portrayals of well-known historical figures such as Li Hongzhang, Yuan Shikai, and Sun Yat-Sen had compelled the station to conclude the transmission ahead of schedule. After its first appearance on CCTV-1, *March* was never rerun on any TV channel in China — a standard commercial strategy to use reruns to maximize revenues. But the ban apparently had no impact on the video market. Months after *March* was taken off air, the series could still be found on shelves in video stores. In fact, word of the government ban prompted those (many of them college professors and scholars) who normally did not watch TV drama to buy the video to see what the fuss was about and participate in the debates. In cases that involve re-imagining of national history and collective identity — issues of vital importance to the current regime facing constant challenges to its legitimacy to lead — the subversive effects of video viewing cuts closer to home than the consumption of pirated Hollywood movies. As Pang points out, piracy of Hollywood movies provides amusement and expresses viewers' desire for Western cultural products.[55] Video thus fosters a certain democratic tendency discouraged by regulated broadcast television. The video market can be a vehicle for disseminating polemical ideas, a channel outside television where censored information can flow and where unorthodox positions germinate and grow.

In conclusion, I want to turn to the issue of time-shifting, another important way of using video to construct agency among Chinese viewers. Media specialists point out that communication technologies such as telephone, radio, and television help structure social as well as private space and time; consequently these technologies are powerful mechanisms in creating public identities. Scannell argues that broadcasting provides individual and institutional contexts for people to locate their daily routines. Through its schedule, broadcasting connects public and private spheres, ensuring the participation of the whole population in national life. The task of broadcasting is therefore "the normalization of the public sphere and socialization of the private sphere."[56] The dominant national mass medium with constant streaming of images and fixed and calculated programming to attract and retain audiences, television possesses a power to frame people's leisure time and activity on a scale that film does not enjoy. Television engages viewers on a daily basis, whereas a trip to a movie theater is only an occasional indulgence for most people in China. The significance of using centralized broadcasting to standardize citizenship can be seen very clearly in the tight control exercised by the Chinese government over CCTV and the privilege and supremacy accorded the national network. CCTV's prime-time news program, *Headline News*, has a powerful grip on public schedule and national imagination, and has remained the major source of news for Chinese audiences.[57] Given the stringent media control in China, time-shifting helps subvert the organization of private time and space that broadcast imposes on the public, allowing the viewer to redefine his or her relationship with television. It must also be pointed out that viewing TV drama on video or DVD is not the same as using remote control. While remote control gives the audience a freedom to zip and zap (zipping commercials and zapping channels) — a freedom of choice that video viewing also affords — remote control does not dislodge the user from the broadcast schedule. To track a TV drama on television, the viewer has to follow pre-decided programs and submit to the prescribed pace. Thus broadcasting systemizes the pattern and rhythm of viewers' private time and activities, bringing individual leisure into unison with a national and collective schedule. This is especially true in the case of TV drama. With multiple television sets common in most households nowadays, communal family viewing — a common mode of TV reception in the early 1980s — has become rare.[58] Watching TV drama — unlike watching sport competitions and national events, such as the winning of the bid for the 2008

Olympic Games — therefore tends to be an intensely individual activity carried out in the privacy of the home for personal pleasure. In addition, as TV drama by definition provides an ongoing narrative (serial or series) punctuated by climactic events, consuming regularly requires commitment and daily planning. It involves a more sustained and concentrated gaze than the "momentary" and "casual" glance from the TV watcher described by John Ellis in his comparative study of cinema and broadcast TV.[59] The infiltration into the personal space of TV drama viewing and the control over the viewer's daily agenda make the regulatory function of a fixed schedule even more notable. The video — whether cassette or DVD format — detaches the audience from a public timetable, returning the power to structure their leisure space and time to viewers. Time-shifting facilitated by video viewing frustrates the distribution of individual time and space by public television, disrupting the pattern established by broadcasting and making leisure activities and consumption of TV drama less synchronized. As Miss Sun's case shows, having a personal copy of the drama puts her in control of when and how she chooses to consume it.

The establishment of the audio-visual market has been a notable development in China's cultural industry since the late 1970s. The variety of audio-visual products has expanded from gramophone and audio and video cassettes in the 1980s to all kinds of optical discs in recent years. Production capacity and sales volume have likewise increased dramatically. Piracy, unfortunately, developed concurrently with the growth of the audio-visual sector. In spite of repeated efforts by the state and audio-visual publishers and producers to combat it, piracy continues to plague the industry and the market. Consumption of piracy has far surpassed legitimate trades, as the latest battle against illegal HDVDs discloses. HDVD piracy has affected the TV drama market more than any other sector, for the decline of magnetic video tapes and introduction of digital technology since the late 1990s have made the digital disk a major recording medium for television drama. But piracy does have a productive use in an environment where mass media is subject to rigorous official intervention. Despite being illegal in many cases, extensive use of VCD and DVD as viewing options — especially among the more educated and more wealthy in the populace — has reshaped home viewing, and consequently produced alternative modes of circulation of TV drama among Chinese consumers. Viewing TV drama on video disk not only frees people from the control by broadcast schedule, it also creates fragmented audiences, individualized consumption, and undisciplined reception outside the frames and patterns prescribed by the official networks. The widespread practice of video viewing offers audiences a chance to resist the organization of cultural life and the incursion into private leisure and space by broadcast television. A centrifugal force, it helps diffuse the centralized production of knowledge and social coherence, giving viewers the power to structure their private time and leisure activities to define their own meaning.

10

From National Preoccupation to Overseas Aspiration

Michael Keane

Dramatic content, including imported drama, comprises almost half of the broadcast time on Chinese television.[1] The considerable viewer appetite for TV drama on the Mainland, however, does not necessarily translate into high quality output that captures export markets. In fact, the apparent advantage of large numbers is undermined by market fragmentation and lack of rights-consciousness. As I will suggest, these institutional imbroglios lead to cost-cutting in so far as producers are unwilling to take risks. Censorship at the pre-production stage further weakens the vitality of Chinese dramas. When finished dramas look for audiences in overseas markets, ideological emphasis militates against reception. Due to the pedagogical role of Chinese TV drama within the nation-state, moreover, there has until recently been no concerted push to internationalize. In turn, the predisposition to concentrate on the domestic market, combined with a lack of export consciousness among producers, has impeded innovation. As Taiwan, Hong Kong, and Korea have found out, selling content in multiple markets pushes producers to create new trends and genres, in this way taking more risks.

While some dramas have done well, the track record in regional and international markets is patchy when compared with the achievements of Hong Kong, Korean and Taiwanese drama. At the moment little reliable

I would like to thank Weihong Zhang, Tingting Song, Ran Ruxue, Lu Hong and Bonnie Liu for their assistance in this chapter.

evidence exists to quantify overseas sales, although national statistics are willing to acknowledge that China remains a net importer of cultural products, and television drama in particular. On April 15, 2005, a report in the *People's Daily* lamented China's "cultural trade deficit," noting that in 2004 China imported nearly 1.2 million audio-visual products — the same amount as it exported.[2] However, the value of exports was significantly lower. In the television sector the trade deficit was stark. Since then, Korean dramas have captured an even greater share of the Mainland market.

In this chapter I look at some of the export successes of China's television drama industry. In recognizing dramas that have registered sales in international markets, it becomes apparent that classic and historical tales have been the mainstay. Other evidence, often anecdotal, suggests that the influence of Chinese dramas overseas has been considerable, mainly assisted by video distribution networks in Chinese communities and informal piracy channels (see Chapter 9). There is a sense, however, that Chinese producers may be on the verge of breaking out of the national mindset, either by selectively targeting the tastes of audiences in East Asia, or by co-producing dramas with Taiwanese and Korean partners. Achieving these objectives aligns with a broader national aspiration, for China to become recognized as a "creative nation."[3]

Limitations and Great Expectations

In many cases, national success anticipates export success: that is, it is easier to sell a TV product abroad once it has conquered the home market, assuming of course there is a degree of cultural proximity in the targeted market.[4] Furthermore, the sale of product abroad is subject to competition from other international destinations. As I will discuss, Mainland TV drama had begun to establish a market presence in the Taiwanese market from 2000 to 2005. Within a year, however, the impact of the Korean Wave — a term used to describe the surge in Korean popular culture from the late 1990s — had washed away much of the gains. Assisted by the Korean government cultural export agency, Korean TV drama first colonized the Japanese market before moving into Chinese-language markets. Korean producers were quick to realize that cross-border trade in finished programs observes a fundamental economic logic of television industries — namely, that once initial production costs were met, further profits can be attained in secondary markets, even taking into account translation costs of subtitling.[5]

To understand the value of TV serial exports it is worth considering other regions of international trade. Undoubtedly, the most successful international drama export, aside from US cop or investigative genres, is the Latin American telenovela. This serial format constitutes approximately 70–80 percent of TV exports from Latin America. Mexican telenovelas in particular have consistently garnered home success as well as strong sales in Spain. Despite what one writer sees as a limited set of social situations and stereotypes: "poor and beautiful but tender women, rich men, bad stepmothers, good priests, incidental doctors, faithful servants, decadent aristocrats . . ." — these narratives are sought after by international audiences.[6] Thematic limitation, together with huge overseas language markets, also reflects the Mainland Chinese experience. However, unlike Latin American telenovelas Mainland Chinese TV drama has not transcended its limitations. When dealing with modern themes, Chinese TV drama scriptwriters have consistently struggled to fashion silk purses out of pig's ears; in other words, restrictions imposed by zealous officials on the thematic content of TV drama have led to a glut of dramas featuring good characters wronged by unscrupulous authorities, tragic characters molded from the clay of socialist realism. While some dramas have used partisan themes to excellent effect, such elements have reinforced perceptions of Mainland content as excessively ideological.

In effect, the national preoccupation with pedagogy has a dual impact: it impedes the confidence of the local industry and it opens the door for imports, whether these are consumed through broadcast channels or through video disk sales. During a presentation in Guangzhou in 2003 at the seventh annual Feitian Awards for TV drama excellence, China's Propaganda Department Arts Bureau director Li Baoshan lamented that only 20 percent of television dramas in China experienced significant sales, that another 20 percent barely covered costs or made narrow profits, while 60 percent were unable to cover their costs of investment. Such complaints about market failure might appear somewhat incongruous coming from a spokesperson for a regulatory body that has relentlessly stifled the creativity of Chinese artists and writers over the past fifty years. Without wishing to cast blame on this government "spiritual civilization" protection agency, Liu Junjie, the vice-general manager of China International Television Corporation Company, weighed into the quality debate, suggesting that the reasons for the huge waste of resources in television drama were low levels of creativity, mediocrity, slipshod production, and an inability to adapt to the demands of the market.[7] In 2005, Zhang Xinjian, the deputy director of the Cultural Market Department within the Ministry of Culture, explained the root causes of China's inability to correct the TV drama trade deficit as follows: "Most exported Chinese TV dramas are old-fashioned and poorly packaged by international standards, which dooms them to failure."[8]

In effect, these criticisms were directed at the inward-looking media production mentality. Under the media system that operated up until the late 1990s, TV production and distribution were co-linked. In other words, television stations had drama production units that produced dramas according to the decisions of stations chiefs who were obliged to churn out a requisite percentage of political stories each year. These might then be sold or exchanged with other stations, in effect a limited distribution model. There was no great need for quality, supply of dramas regularly exceeded demand, and the preoccupation was the national audience. If overseas broadcast was countenanced, it was invariably framed as sending out politically correct accounts of Chinese history and society.

On a national policy level, the extension of the number of TV channels for the sake of ensuring propaganda delivery was deemed more important than content. This "channel-before-content" model of Chinese media production was neither a long-term growth model, nor an export-enhancement model. Fortunately for the growth of the industry, China's World Trade Organization (WTO) accession in 2001 heralded a sea change. While not liberalizing the television market to the same extent as the telecommunications sectors, the WTO accession alerted industry regulators to the challenge of internationalization. The key proposition that emerged was: China had to make better TV programs if the industry was to prosper in the face of new competition. One of China's leading TV executives, Bruno Wu, made this point at an international forum in 2006. When asked the reason for China's "cultural trade deficit," he neatly summarized the solution and the problem in two words: "good content."[9]

From National Propaganda to Export Aspiration

The turn from national propaganda to export success provides a number of challenges. Part of the solution is to strengthen the quality of domestic production, which is blighted by over-production and wastage of resources. Many dramas never make it to the small screen, and only a minority has a chance of finding a prime-time audience. In 2007, 13,840 episodes were produced in China, of which only 7,000 were actually broadcast.[10] Many of the 6,840 episodes that failed to make the small screen were undoubtedly of dubious quality; however, many are not broadcast because they are deemed too risky, despite having received clearance. Problems of conservatism at the point of sale persist, although the recent outbreak of pink dramas (see Chapter 7) signals greater receptivity from viewers to issues of sexuality and personal freedom. During the 1980s and 1990s, state censors had ruled such themes to be too "foreign" and too "unhealthy." However, internationalization inevitably brings with it a degree of liberalization. As China's accession to the WTO approached during the late 1990s, many critics expressed fears that Western culture would impact upon the Chinese national audience; producers, however, were more worried about the next wave of competition for the Chinese TV drama industry. Fears of Western imperialism proved to be largely unfounded. By 2001, Chinese audiences had turned in large numbers to Korean dramas.

As mentioned in the introduction, several factors have impeded the successful export of Chinese TV dramas. The fundamental constraints are financial limitations on production, censorship, and cultural specificity.[11] The first is fairly self-explanatory: most of the television stations in China that produce narrative content are under-resourced and unable to invest substantially in high-quality production. The second indicator has already been mentioned: the heavy hand of politics in China irrevocably stifles innovation and risk-taking. It reinforces a culture of mediocrity.[12] The first two factors combine with the third, which is perhaps more significant, and arguably more representative of China than elsewhere in Asia. Media analysts have coined the term "cultural discount" to describe impediments to the sale of audio-visual cultural content.[13] In other words, Chinese drama is often embedded with cultural nuances particular to a region (Beijing, Shanghai), or is weighed down with the language of political reform. These ingredients do not translate well into regional and international markets. In short, specificity detracts from wider market success.

Success leads to cross-territorial and inter-regional demand in most international media markets. During the late 1980s and early 1990s a spate of modern popular serials written by Wang Shuo and others reshaped the perceptions of Chinese TV drama.[14] At that time television dramas of foreign origin were offering alternative pleasures to stories fashioned from the plain cloth of socialist realism, stories that celebrated China's socialist reforms or retold the past in accordance with Chinese Communist Party historiography.[15] The success of "popular" dramas came with an upsurge of mass cultural forms, and in particular urban-style (*shimin*) culture, during the late 1980s and early 1990s.[16] The literary talents of writers who could reproduce the witty dialogue of Wang Shuo were in demand from directors who sensed growing disillusionment with model characters. However, few could deliver the goods in the same way.[17]

Contemporary serials such as *Beijingers in New York* (*Beijing ren zai Niuyue*, 1993) and *Stories from an Editorial Office* (*Bianjibu de gushi*, 1991) found success in overseas communities in the early 1990s. The twenty-one episode serial *Beijingers in New York*, directed by Feng Xiaogang and Zheng Xiaolong in 1993 chronicled cross-cultural confusions (language, lack of strong family relations, clash of social values, etc.) experienced by Chinese immigrants and scholars in foreign lands. In Diasporic Chinese communities worldwide it was one of the most talked-about media products of the early 1990s.[18] Similarly, the 1991 serial *Stories from an Editorial Office*, starring the enigmatic Ge You, an actor whose film career was then on the rise, challenged the limits to expression by satirizing the media reforms of the day. For a short time it seemed that the commercial media market might liberate artists and writers from the gravitas of performing as "engineers of the soul." For many Chinese living overseas these serials signaled a mood of optimism, of openness and positive change. Despite the acclaim of overseas compatriots, however, the earnings achieved by these, and several other contemporary narratives in overseas markets, were marginal. One of the problems at the time was that the mode of distribution through video shops encouraged piracy. However, distribution through informal channels gave exposure to these works that was not reflected in economic returns.

Tapping the overseas market through legitimate channels provides a much more difficult challenge and the most successful genre remains historical dramas. Indeed, the supply of historical costume dramas would appear to be almost unlimited, taking into account the many dynasties of Chinese history. Compared with contemporary dramas, historical dramas are more easily green-lighted by the State Administration of Radio, Film and TV's Censorship and Review Committees. In an environment of entrenched conservatism, it is hardly surprising that Hengdian World Studios in Zhejiang, the imagined center of China's television drama industry, has based its entire business model on producing historical dramas.[19] In fact, not only are historical dramas being written, they are being remade from earlier versions with greater production values and special effects, all possible because of the ready-made production backlots at locations such as Hengdian.

Mainland China's earliest successes in exporting historical dramas began during the 1980s. Productions of *Dream of the Red Chamber* (*Honglou meng*, 1986) by CCTV and *The Water Margin*[20] (*Shuihu zhuan*, 1981) by Shandong TV achieved moderate success in Taiwan and Hong Kong. By the mid-1990s a number of long-form historical dramas based on traditional stories emerged. In 1994, Hong Kong's Asia Television purchased the broadcast right of CCTV's *The Romance of the Three Kingdoms* (*Sanguo yanyi*) for US$8,000 per episode while Taiwan's China Television (CTV) paid US$12,000 per episode. The success of *The Romance of the Three Kingdoms* for ATV in Hong Kong created a surge in value, following which rival station TVB Jade outlaid US$12,000 per episode for a remake of *The Water Margin*, which was then still in production. By the first decade of the twenty-first century, Chinese historical dramas were attracting higher fees in Taiwan. By 2003, dramas including *Swordsmen* (*Xiaoao jianghu*), *Kangxi Dynasty* (*Kangxi wangchao*, 2001), *Yongzheng Dynasty* (*Yongzheng wangchao*, 1999) and *Grand Mansion Gate* (*Dazhaimen*, 2001) had recorded strong sales in Taiwan.

At the same time, however, competition was emerging from elsewhere. The rising popularity of Korean popular culture in East Asia since 2000 is well documented, although little has so far been said about its flow-on effects on the TV drama market.[21] The first point to note is that the attractiveness of Korean drama for viewers has impacted upon the market value of other nations' drama. Korean dramas made inroads into the Taiwanese market from 2001. Offered at much cheaper prices than Japanese dramas, and with a distinctive affective dimension that embraces Confucian morality, they soon established a following among Chinese audiences. The surge in Korean drama in Taiwan in turn impacted on the value and market share of Mainland Chinese drama. By that time Taiwan had become the prime market for Mainland China drama, absorbing between 60 and 70 percent of Mainland sales. According to a Chinese producer, Zhang Jizhong, after the peak of the Korean wave in 2005 the sale price of his dramas in Taiwan dropped from an average of US$15,000 to US$10,000 an episode.[22]

Korean dramas were at the time being marketed aggressively in TV trade shows in China. By 2002, Korean dramas had surpassed Taiwanese dramas in Mainland sales (see Chapter 12). Meanwhile, stations like Hunan Satellite TV sought to tap into the Korean Wave, in 2004 broadcasting *The Jewel in the Palace* (*Da changjin*). By 2006, however, the surge of interest in Korean drama had begun to wane, some viewers finding the pace of Korean drama too slow and the narratives too predictable. In that year the four most popular dramas purchased by provincial stations were *My Rude Old Lady* (*Wode yeman popo*); *The Dance of Passion* (*Huowu huangsha*); *The Charm Beneath* (*Yanzhi shuifen*) and *Always Ready* (*Suishi houming*). All of these were Hong Kong dramas.

Nevertheless the Korean Wave had unleashed an undercurrent of export ambition. Chinese drama began to change its tactics in order to tap into Asian markets. Hunan Satellite TV's own production, *Princess Huanzhu* (*Huanzhu gege*, 1998), a serial that took the domestic market by storm, was the first Mainland Chinese drama to achieve success in Korea, although broadcast after 11 p.m. on SBS due to Korean Broadcasting Commission's foreign content restrictions. Apart from *Princess Huanzhu*, the success of Chinese TV dramas in Korea was limited. However, from 2005 and 2007 more than 700 hours of Chinese drama were sold to Korea broadcasters, the most tradable category being military offerings such as *The Eighth Army* (*Balu jun*), *The Long March* (*Changzheng*), *The DA Regiment* (*DA shi*) and *Peaceful Times* (*Heping niandai*), the last two purchased by KBS. These dramas signaled a new stage in China's aspirations to achieve export status. Whereas previously, the operating principle of cultural exports was the greater good of the nation: in other words, all content directed internationally was regarded as serving a propaganda function, the strategy nowadays is more incremental. Building on small successes and in some cases, large successes such as *The Romance of the Three Kingdoms* and *Princess Huanzhu*, Mainland Chinese producers have established a foothold and in some way broken down stereotypes of Chinese drama as being boring and ideological.

However, making Chinese TV drama more fashionable for overseas consumption has presented an unprecedented challenge. In the past Taiwanese and Hong Kong dramas established the fashion benchmarks, the former learning much from the success of Japanese trendy dramas in Taiwan and then establishing its own idol dramas (*ouxiangju*: see Chapter 12).[23] China's attempts to make and export its own trendy dramas have met with a mixed response. The 2005 serial *Falling in Love* (*Haoxiang haoxiang tan lianai*) (see Chapter 7), with its muted sexual tension and implicit bed-hopping by its four female protagonists met with some bemusement in Taiwan where viewers deemed there was a discernable mismatch between text and characterization.[24] A copy of HBO's *Sex and the City*, incidentally available in video stores in China, *Falling in Love* appeared to overcompensate for its lack of onscreen intimacy with excessive dialogue in the form of gossip and complaints about women's lives.

The question confronting producers thus becomes: how do you make drama that sits well with Chinese censors while retaining appeal for overseas audiences? As Chen (Chapter 12) points out, these are issues that regularly confront Mainland-Taiwan co-productions. Other strategies adopted by Chinese producers include trying to imitate the contemporary Korean style with its emphasis on emotive sensibility, replacing the literary language of many historical dramas with the vernacular, and using actors that have cross-border appeal. In addition, the format of serial drama, which is so popular in East Asia, provides an obstacle to distribution in many international markets. In general, the international format for drama favors soap opera or series, which are constructed around a self-contained story rather a continuing narrative. In order to facilitate distribution in Western markets a certain amount of cosmetic surgery is often required to reduce the content and insert elements that appeal to non-Mainland audiences.

Marketing Chinese TV Drama: The New Imperative

While capturing niche markets in Korea and Taiwan is a step forward for Chinese TV drama, aspirations to play in the global arena are constrained by distribution limitations. While it is undoubtedly true that the imagined community of Greater China extends globally, and compares favorably in numbers with the thriving Indian and Spanish-speaking media markets, the availability of platforms for Chinese TV drama are limited. China Central Television (CCTV) operates three overseas satellite television channels that purport to service 67 million viewers. According to SARFT, this breaks down approximately into 50 million for CCTV-9, 15 million for CCTV-4 and 2 million for CCTV's Spanish and French language channel.[25] These state-sponsored channels are received around the world in more than 100 countries via direct satellite reception, cable networks, IPTV and terrestrial broadcasting. However, despite the spin often associated with reciprocal landing rights, for instance deals between US networks such as News Corporation and CCTV, the latter's overseas offering are still predominantly focused on information about China rather than entertainment content.

The answer would appear to be a unified approach rather than a state-dominated one. In February 2005, the China International TV Corp. (CITVC) — a subsidiary of CCTV — was launched. Branded as "The Great Wall satellite platform," this initiative delivers a suite of Mandarin-language channels to Vietnam, Thailand, South Korea, Myanmar, Hong Kong, Macao, and Taiwan, as well as to US cable networks. The platform brings together seven of China's leading provincial television stations along with Hong Kong-based Phoenix Television, Asia Television (ATV), and the US Huaxia Television station under the broad leadership of CCTV.[26] Chinese TV channels are also accessible via satellite subscription in many countries.[27] A good example of success in this marketplace was the serial *Song of Eternal Regret* (*Changhen ge* 2005), Based on a novel by Wang Anyi, it was first released in Hong Kong as a film directed by Guan Jinpeng. Chronicling life in Shanghai from 1940 to 1970, its refined and elegant style inspired a TV drama version which was successfully distributed in US cable networks, finding an audience in the Chinese diaspora.

During the next few years, the pan-Asian market for drama will necessitate a rethink of strategies. The formation of media conglomerates from

1998 was an attempt to develop economies of scale and compete with the transnationals; the benefits of agglomeration include linking with independent production units. In effect, the Chinese media market is entering into a more mature stage. I have argued elsewhere that China is moving up the creative industries value chain. In this transition imitation is replaced by innovation. Part of this process is exploiting co-productions, formats and licenses. Producers are attempting to break out of the low-value domestic market and move toward marketing more in East and Southeast Asian markets. As the example of the Korean Wave demonstrates, export competitiveness builds on strengths in domestic production. Breaking out of local markets requires a shedding of local nuance and a rethinking of strategy. The market is beginning to respond to cross-regional diversification. Until a few years ago, television fairs in Sichuan, Shanghai and Beijing were the primary means for trading television dramas. Most dramas were exchanged between broadcasters, not for cash but for other dramas. The emergence of independents is bringing forward new business models, including the production of promotional footage that can be made available to prospective buyers or distributed on websites such as the Beijing Television Entertainment Exchange Network (Beijing Dianshi Yule Jiemu Jiaoyi Wang). Currently 70 percent of sales of TV drama are conducted through either TV industry fairs or by agents or companies specializing in the field.

Larger networks such as CCTV and Shanghai TV are increasing the value of their cable and pay TV channels, not only by buying more diverse offerings, but by investing in co-productions, made-for-television movies, and new dramas. In 2004, CCTV established a new initiative for the production of television drama: four producers — Yu Shengli, Lian Zhenhua, Zhang Lujie, and Wu Zhaolong — were assigned a "studio" (*gongzuoshi*) under the umbrella of the Television Cultural Development Company.[28] This enterprise was designed to incubate and produce new and interesting quality television drama, with an emphasis on independence from existing marketplace practices such as bartering content for advertising space, the constraints of trading exclusive rights to CCTV, or having to include product placements for a range of sponsors.

The clarification of rights management issues, particularly in the context of co-production deals, has now emerged as a key issue in the next stage of expansion.[29] Pressure has come from other sources. Korean, Hong Kong, and Taiwanese television producers are insisting on negotiating rights deals in order to ensure that they recoup some of their costs (see Chapters 12 and 13). In some instances, these include the rights to broadcast for several years, in contrast to the international model of extremely limited broadcast scheduling — for instance, a free-to-air and cable deal. The development of competition is an important theme within segments of the industry. Pay TV platforms that offer a buffet of specialized niche channels — a feature of contemporary multi-channel environments — represent a new business model for large provincial and city stations within China. This emerging "post-broadcasting" landscape is having an impact upon the producer–viewer relationship, with the latter demanding more specialized fare. Nevertheless, despite a cornucopia of programming options and formats emerging from the reshaping of the market in China, television drama production is likely to remain the wellspring of economic viability.

Conclusion: Good Content and the Pan-Asian Marketplace

Can China become a leader in regional television drama production? In targeting the East Asian region and the international Mandarin-speaking community, Chinese film, TV and animation can reach a potential audience exceeding that of the Indian film and TV industry. In addition to commercial considerations there are national aspirations: the idea that China has been colonized by international media, more recently Korean drama, does not sit well with many Chinese nationalists, particularly in an era when China is making international gains on other economic battlefields. But there are far deeper problems than getting the content right. China's cultural trade deficit is not a quick fix. How do China's TV drama producers become competitive? The key point is that, rather than following the pattern of the past of producing programs that placate cultural officials, China needs to become more innovative. Can this happen within the current politicized production environment? Rather than just churning out seemingly endless and often predictable historical television dramas, Chinese producers need to acknowledge that popular modern stories are the most lucrative model, particularly with regard to attracting advertising.

What, therefore, is good content? From one perspective it is content that has appeal to certain valued demographics — for instance, "pink dramas." These trendy dramas are both a response to competition and a step forward in thinking about audience niches. As I have mentioned, the current phase of internationalization is taking localization strategies seriously, incorporating themes that have more cross-territorial appeal, along with the use of actors that are familiar to regional audiences. According to the TV Program Marketing Department of the China International TV Corporation, good Chinese content first and foremost reflects national culture and socialist ideology. However, this does not necessarily entail proceeding as before, simply producing much of the same. For Chinese TV drama-makers, the ultimatum is clear: producing better content is a learning process; it also entails a certain amount of un-learning; that is, breaking free of the pedagogical straightjacket that has to date restricted the market success of Mainland drama. For many, the world of Chinese TV drama is on the verge of a new dawn.

11

A Trip Down Memory Lane:
Remaking and Rereading the Red Classics

Gong Qian

In the late 1990s, the term "Red Classics" (*hongse jingdian*) began to appear with increasing regularity in the Chinese media. The concept comes from an earlier age, and was an invention of Chinese Communist Party (CCP) historiography. The term "classics" normally refers to works that have attained canonical status over a long period of time. In this case, the classics were created in the modern era — a conscious endeavor by the Chinese state to create a revolutionary culture which would mold the socialist subject. The word "red" is directly associated with revolution in modern Chinese history. The Red Classics defined themselves against traditional classics by criticizing and negating the latter, but at the same time they needed the resources of traditional folk culture.[1] A short list of the Red Classics includes *Tracks in the Snowy Mountain* (*Linhai xueyuan*), *The Red Detachment of Women* (*Hongse niangzijun*), *Shajiabang* (*Shajiabang*), and *Struggles in the Old-line City* (*Yehuo chunfeng dou gucheng*).

The changing social and political environment ushered in by the passing of Mao Zedong led to a repudiation of the Cultural Revolution (1966–76). From the late 1970s, the emphasis shifted to economic development. Emerging from the cataclysms of political upheavals, post-socialist China sought a complete break from the Maoist era and its revolutionary discourse. However, the widespread belief in what economic reform could deliver was soon replaced with anger and disillusion in the face of growing social disparity, corruption, and daily anxiety. A public dissatisfied with the competition of economic society looked back to the past with a sense of nostalgia and a longing for strong leadership, idealism, and egalitarianism.

Revolutionary texts, signs, and objects, which were shunned in the 1970s, gradually regained popularity. Totalitarian nostalgia[2] peaked in a "Mao Zedong fever" (*Mao Zedong re*), in which this god-like "savoir" was reimagined, repackaged, and narrated as a humanistic figure in numerous popular novels, TV dramas, and films. Revolutionary-themed blockbusters and TV dramas were produced, backed by huge government investment; dozens of biographies, as well as numerous audio and video productions, enjoyed phenomenal success. As Dai Jinhua astutely points out, the "Mao fever" constitutes a successful ideological operation as well as an act to consume ideology.[3]

The repackaging of the Red Classics as popular entertainment and a nostalgic artefact creates an interesting cultural phenomenon. Why would a highly ideological genre, lying dormant for two decades, come back so strongly? How is the genre, which was used to addressing viewers as socialist citizens, reframed and resold as a commodity? What are the roles of the state and the public in redefining the genre? How is the preferred reading of the state and the TV production company received at the individual level? To unravel the process of production and consumption, we need to trace major changes in the ways in which revolutionary characters, events, and themes are represented. In this chapter, I will start off by briefly setting the cultural backdrop against which the interest in the Red Classics was rekindled. I will then identify television's main narrative strategies to capture audiences. I will also consider the role of the state in regulating the production and influencing the reception of the genre. Finally, I will engage with the experience of some viewers in order to understand the complexity and unpredictability, which, as I will demonstrate, marks the process of reading the Red Classics.

The Politics of Rewriting the Red Classics: Tapping a Cultural Reserve

The Mao Zedong fever of the 1990s was a precursor to the revival of the Red Classics. Nowadays, it is not uncommon to see images from different periods juxtaposed in visual spectacles.[4] In this "post-revolutionary age," advertisements, TV dramas, and even restaurant signs utilize the resources of the Red Classics. Created to answer the political needs of the 1950s and 1960s, they are now a national cultural heritage, and a fashion to be exploited for commercial gain. The production of the Red Classics is a conscious act on the part of the market to cash in on audience nostalgia for a collective cultural memory.[5]

In 1998, Vanke Film and Television Co. Ltd., a sibling company of the multi-million-dollar business Vanke Group,[6] proposed a television drama to commemorate the fiftieth anniversary of the founding of the People's Republic of China. After much deliberation, the producer chose to adapt a novel penned by Nicholas Ostravski in 1929. *The Making of a Hero* (*Gangtie shi zenyang lianchengde*, 2000) was an autobiographic account of a legendary young communist from his childhood in a working-class family to his role in the Russian Civil War (1918–20), and in the subsequent reconstruction of the Soviet Union after the First World War. Even though the protagonist suffered from rheumatism and typhoid fever, and became blind and bedridden later in his life, he managed to write his life story by dictating it. The novel had been popular with Chinese youth in the 1950s, when Soviet cultural works were the only legitimate foreign art. It remained on the list of books recommended to youth by government ideological organizations after the Cultural Revolution, and continued to be a bestseller over several decades.

The popularity of *The Making of a Hero* signaled the beginning of the "adaptation craze." TV producers quickly jumped onto the Red Classics bandwagon. The works had quickly become the primary focus of many aspiring investors. Revolutionary and heroic stories were transformed into products for consumers. The TV versions reduced the didactic dimensions of the original works, and focused more on entertainment appeal. Several narrative strategies were adopted, notably subversive representations of the heroes and reconstruction of love relationships. The outcomes were controversial. The key players involved in the production and reception — including the state, viewers, media commentators, and intellectual elites — all joined in the debate over the canonical status of the Red Classics, their historical truth and the value of patriotism in contemporary society.

Two main narrative strategies were deployed in the rewriting of these texts: humanizing the heroes and the enemy; and reconstructing romantic relationships between the heroes and heroines. The former subverts the hero/enemy binary, an important organizing principle in the meta-narrative of revolutionary texts; the latter engages with taboo themes in the socialist era, such as personal relationships, sexuality, and desire.

Humanizing the Heroes and the Enemy

Tracks in the Snowy Mountain (*Linhai xueyuan*, 2004), written by Qu Bo in the 1950s, is a story about the eradication of defeated Kuomintang bandits who had joined professional brigands and landlord tyrants in northeast China during the 1940s. The hero, Yang Zirong, was modeled after the life experiences of a real person who slipped into the bandits' den and won the trust of the enemy leader. Based on the intelligence Yang provided, the communist army was able to eliminate the bandit den. In 1967, a Beijing Opera about this legendary figure was commissioned and became one of the eight Model Revolutionary Works (*yangbanxi*) widely performed during the Cultural Revolution. Yang Zirong became a household name. Nearly everybody growing up in that era could sing the famous aria sung by Yang Zirong during his first encounter with the bandit head.

The TV drama made significant alterations to Yang's character. There was controversy concerning the representation of Yang Zirong. On the small screen, he is portrayed as a cook in the army and is not particularly disciplined. In fact, he is quite foul-mouthed. He only becomes a scout squad leader because somebody taunts him. Not only that, his former fiancée has married a bandit due to a bizarre combination of circumstances. Part of the story revolves around the ambiguous feelings that Yang and his former lover have for each other when they meet again after living a world apart.

Similar devices are used to demystify heroes who seemed to possess God-like perfection in earlier stories. For example, in the film *The Red Detachment of Women* (*Hongse niangzijun*), the heroine, Wu Qionghua, is the daughter of a poor peasant who suffers as a slave girl of Nan Batian, a landlord despot in a village on south China's Hainan Island. She is rescued from a water dungeon where Nan Batian has incarcerated her by Hong Changqing, the Communist Party representative. Wu then joins the revolutionary corps to seek personal revenge and, under the influence and education of Hong Changqing, she gradually becomes a conscientious revolutionary fighter. The leading character Wu Qionghua is portrayed with a fiery temper; there are many close-up shots of her eyes burning with indignation.

Wu Qionghua's feisty personality is downplayed in the TV drama, however. During a press conference before shooting started, Yuan Jun, the director of the television version, claimed that the new "Qionghua should outgrow the old one; she should above all be cute, delicate and charming, so that everybody has the urge to help and protect her. This will make it easier for the audience to relate to her."[7] The TV version (2005) was refashioned into a "teenage idol" show — a genre that portrays glamorous teens as protagonists, and is melodramatic in style and set in urban locations. Qionghua is played by the delicate "feminine" actress Yin Tao; the women soldiers wear neat clothes, change their hairstyles at will, and invariably seem to have a crush on Hong Changqing. Nan Batian, the landlord ogre in the original, becomes a bookish literati, who is adept at using a typewriter.

The TV version of *The Red Detachment of Women* downplays the didactic content of "class struggle" represented by the feud between Wu Qionghua and Nan Bantian in both the film and ballet. According to interviews with the film director Xie Jin, scenes depicting love between Wu Qionghua and Hong Changqing were shot but later censored.[8] The TV rendering brings the love relationship between Qionghua and Hong Changqing to the fore.

Romanticizing the Relationships

There have been criticisms of "unfaithful" adaptations of the Red Classics; many of which are focused on the amorous relationships in television dramas. The socialist era was marked by near-total erasure of the private sphere in cultural works. When love and marriage were touched upon in the Red Classics, they had to be reordered as serving the revolutionary cause, the Communist Party, and the state. Artistic works created during the Cultural Revolution allowed even less depiction of love and marriage: gender differences were de-emphasized and androgyny was regarded as the norm.[9]

Two decades after the Cultural Revolution, the love interest returned with a vengeance; it was promoted and publicized as "the selling point" (*kan dian*). In the modern Beijing Opera production *Shajiabang*, for instance, the leading female character, Sister A Qing, is the leader of the underground communist cell that runs the teahouse as a cover for a liaison station. By the way she is addressed — as *sao*, literally sister — we know she is married. This is apparently a deliberate device. A young, pretty, unmarried woman running a public teahouse would inspire too much erotic imagination. There is just one line in the opera which vaguely suggests that her husband is in Shanghai doing business. In the novelized version of *Shajiabang,* the "chaste" Sister A Qing is now a licentious woman, who is sexually involved with both the communist guerrilla leader and the Kuomintang commander-in-chief at the same time. Meanwhile, her incompetent and chicken-hearted husband secretly provides for a woman who has given birth to his child in the countryside.

The TV drama did not go that far, but the sensuality of Sister A Qing is emphasized. Indeed, the actress in the role looks so young and beautiful that her ability to maintain her "honor" among a group of powerful men has to be plainly defended. In one scene, a few customers chatting in her teahouse raised the issue of why no man has yet laid his hand on Sister A Qing. One of them offers an explanation: "Sister A Qing's popularity comes from her capability." The scene and the line are obviously used to contain the "danger" of Sister A Qing's sex appeal. But the statement ends just there.

Critical Reception and State Regulation

In spite of the fact that consumerism and commercialization are now readily embraced as global ethos, the attempt to rewrite and reinterpret a cultural memory remains a highly sensitive matter. The exploitation of the Red Classics as a cultural reserve contests cultural memory, established social values, and the authority of official history. To maintain its custodial role, the government has resorted to two means: direct administrative intervention, and motivation of public opinions to rein in the reproduction of revolutionary texts and influence their reception.

In May 2004, when the re-adaptation craze was in its heyday, the State Administration of Radio, Film, and Television (SARFT) issued a circular to the administrative departments concerned, stipulating that all Red Classics TV dramas had to be submitted to the Censorship Committee of the SARFT for final approval after passing the initial censorship at the provincial level. The document stressed that current adaptations of the Red Classics invariably demonstrated a tendency toward "misreading of the original work," and were "based on a misinterpretation of the market," eventually "misleading the audiences."[10] According to the circular, the specific problem with adaptations included imposing complicated love relations on the main characters, representing the heroes and the villains with multiple personalities so that the ideological intention of the original work was distorted, and diluting content because of the length required for the TV genre. Underlying the circular are two assumptions. The first is that the original creations of the Red Classics are "sacred," as they represent the collective memory and the spiritual wealth commonly owned by the public. The second is that the viewing public is easily offended by overt displays of sensual pleasure, the "disrespect" shown for the historical "truth," and the sacred feelings people hold for the heroes in the original works.

Corresponding to the official rhetoric, public debates on the canonical status of the original works and public morality were lively. Newspapers ran opinion letters; critics wrote reviews and published interviews with the writers or creators of the original works. Unlike many other debates about artistic productions, however, this genre is more emotionally charged. News headlines reacted with strong wording: "Chinese Art Circle Defends 'Red Classics' " and "*The Red Detachment of Women* has nothing to do with the 'Red.' "[11] In several cases, bickering broke out between the original authors (or their offspring) and TV producers over the prototypes of the heroes or heroines, sometimes escalating into legal battles. For example, the adopted son of the man upon whose experience the character of Yang Zirong was created filed a defamation case against the TV producers, claiming that the drama series tarnished his father's image.[12]

The remakes have also drawn criticism from artistic circles and audiences. Some critics argue that, although many of the Red Classics were produced to suit the ideological needs of the time, most were fine artistic works. The commercial rewriting subverts the revolutionary sublime — the authoritative archetypes in the original works — to cater to popular or even hedonistic consumer tastes.[13] It is clear, however, that the state adopts a "stick and carrot" policy toward the TV adaptation. While condemning the untruthfulness of many reproductions, it has no intention of imposing a ban. Amid the heightened tension induced by the two circulars issued in April and May, China Central Television (hereafter, CCTV) organized a seminar in June 2004 on *Little Soldier Zhang Ga* (*Xiaobing Zhang Ga*, 2004) and the adaptation of the Red Classics, sending out a message that adaptations would not be pulled as long as they were done in the "right way." Meanwhile, the SARFT granted licenses for another four adaptations in 2004, soon after it had issued the circular on more control over reproduction.

The Red Classics provide the opportunity to promote nationalism and collectivism — rare commodities in a society that has become increasingly materialistic and individualistic. The bottom line is not whether the Red Classics are sacred and untouchable, but how to adapt the stories within the genre so that they serve official ideology. This translates into the fundamental question of who has the right to speak, and for whom — a question that had simple and definite answers in the Mao era. Now it has become complicated by other factors, one of the most important of which is the market. The "adaptation craze" is, after all, mainly driven by profit.

While revisions of revolutionary texts aim to demythologize heroes, restore historicity and humanism, and subvert the overtly lofty image of the revolutionaries, the main objective for reformulating the original work is to appeal to maximum audience segments. The co-producers for *Tracks in the Snowy Mountain* (*Linhai xueyuan*, 2004), for example, had different opinions on how to define the niche. One of the producers, Zheng Kainan, believed that the drama should target the middle-aged to elderly — those who were familiar with the original plot. Moreover, due to its military theme, it should also target viewers serving in the military sectors. However, another producer, Zhou Qiyue, wanted to attract teens and urban youth through its romantic content.[14] It is not altogether surprising that the final product was a hybrid.

The strategies used in rewriting Red Classics TV drama is most telling of the ways in which revolutionary culture is transmogrified in many other forms of popular arts. Since the early 1990s the nation's market-savvy popular art sector has been busy packaging the "Red" by taking advantage of its official canonical status while transforming it in a fashion that was in keeping with the demands of the marketplace. The Red Sun cassette published in 1993, for example, featured 30 revolutionary lyrics sung by popular singers in a sexy breathy style, with modern electronic accompaniment.[15]

The Audience for the Red Classics

The Red Classics arise at the right moment — the public is looking back to the past with a sense of nostalgia and a longing for the collective demands of socialism; the state has been searching for new ways to enhance its representational pedagogy; popular media such as TV have become a symbolic resource for the general public to make sense of reality and history and the "Red" culture can now be more safely appropriated for commercial entertainment. The double bind of the Party-state and the marketplace serves as the major influence over the reconfiguration of the Red Classics. However, neither the ideological control nor the market manipulation is fully capable of defining the ways in which the revolutionary culture is evoked in the reproduction. The exchange between politics and money is exceedingly complex. Ideology and market coincide, contest, compromise and intertwine, producing a muddy cultural scene.

One important dimension of these tensions and the mediations involves the audience. The producers of the TV remake follow the logic of consumer society and the market to re-imagine and reconstruct the original state of revolutionary life while the state, still eager to claim its legitimacy as the speaker for the people and history and maintain its relevance in the cultural market, manipulates and intervenes through policies, censorship and public opinions. However, fathoming the needs of the audiences or framing their interpretations of the text proves to be a formidable task for both the market and the state. Through a few case studies discussed below, I want to show that audiences are not fixed in one viewing position and that their reading of the remake is inflected with their gender, age, class, educational background, socio-economic status and in relation to a range of cultural repertoires that the audiences possess. The murkiness of production is thus further complicated at the reception level.

The reinvention of the revolutionary mass culture for popular entertainment has generated much anxiety, fear, hope, criticism, praise and mixed feelings among various sectors in the Chinese society. Unfavourable comments on the representations of heroes appeared after the first run of *Tracks in the Snowy Mountain* (*Linhai xueyuan*) on Beijing Television (BTV) in March 2004. In the two circulars mentioned above, the SARFT had emphasized the public anger at the remake. The official sanction was followed by a wide variety of articles and viewer letters in mainstream newspapers highlighting audience dissatisfaction — even indignation — about the "unfaithful" revisions of the original work. Public figures, including the celebrated CCTV program host Cui Yongyuan, admitted that they dare not watch the remake for fear that the familiar images in their minds would be changed beyond recognition.[16]

Zhao Yong has provided a useful analysis of the role of the audience in reception of such remake.[17] Relying on Althusser's theory of interpellation, Zhao has argued that viewers' negative responses to remakes are, in fact, genuine. He contends that the Red Classics were created and popularized under very special circumstances when such cultural works functioned as a part of a powerful state ideological apparatus. He believes that "negotiated" or "oppositional readings" of cultural products were virtually impossible in that highly political atmosphere.[18] Viewers were forced to adopt the dominant-hegemonic position of the creators; over time, they internalized the feelings and ideologies encoded in these works. In other words, the individuals were "hailed" into a subject position by the state.

Some of the strong feelings invested in the criticisms of the remake certainly point to the normalizing effects of the Red Classics. However, Althusser's thesis suggests a subjectivity always predetermined by the ruling ideology. Such a position overlooks two important factors in the construction of subjectivity: first, there might be a number of discursive practices at play at the same time, including everyday practices; and second, the process is ongoing — subjectivity is constantly renewing itself and antagonism to a collective subjectivity is possible when a collective subject "finds its subjectivity negated by other discourse or practices."[19] Recent studies of the genre have shown that, even in highly politicized eras such as that of the Cultural Revolution, negotiated or subversive readings of the Red Classics were still possible.[20]

My own finding is that there is a continuum of responses. Some viewers are highly critical of the imagery in the remake; others deliberately look for how the original representations are subverted; still others watch purely for pleasure; and some do not care to watch at all. The fact that only complaints and criticism are reported in the media is due to the government's attempts to influence public opinion. This result is indeed curious: on one hand, the so-called "public" seems to find the revisions of revolutionary texts distasteful; on the other, these texts continue to enjoy reasonable ratings. Without further exploration of audience response, it is hard to give a satisfactory answer to this complex phenomenon. In the following brief analysis, I will demonstrate the complicated process of how audiences negotiate subject positions in reading the Red Classics.

I conducted a focus group discussion and follow-up interviews based on the viewing of *Struggles in the Old-line City* (*Yehuo chunfeng dou gucheng* 2005), one of the seminal works in the genre. Although no single reason emerged from the discussion to explain the revival of interest in the Red Classics, what does become clear is that the viewing process involves a relationship with the past, and this relationship varies according to experience. Furthermore, it is entwined with viewers' specific social, class, gender, and educational backgrounds. The respondents' critique of the revised TV drama is a discursive construction of their own past, present, and future. Their responses to revised revolutionary texts are shot through with a concern with public morality and historical truth. They are also imbued with an anxiety for China's modernity project as well as their uncertain place in this project. The story of Zhang Yunhong, as I recount below, demonstrates powerfully that very often readings of these revolutionary texts are neither governed by the preferred reading suggested by the state, nor dictated by the dominant reading encouraged by commercial rewriting.

Love and Marriage: A Personal Story

Few know better about change than my interviewee Zhang Yunhong.[21] A fifty-five-year-old retired woman who worked for a film project team in the medium-sized city of Hengyang in central China's Hunan Province from 1970 to 1977, Zhang worked as a ticket-seller in a local cinema during the Cultural Revolution when the film versions of the Red Classics were in their heyday. As part of her work, she screened and watched the eight Model Revolutionary Works (*yangbanxi*) hundreds of times.

Throughout the interviews, she showed considerable discomfort when asked about her opinion on the *yangbanxi* and other Red Classics. She did not dismiss the *yangbanxi* as pure political propaganda, but rather justified their existence as a matter of fact — because the "focus of the government at that time was on politics." She mentioned several times that "society is always progressing," and that the focus of the government is on the economy now. Zhang's assertion of the progress of society shows that she is aware of the modernity discourse and the danger of being viewed as "unmodern" if she shows too much nostalgia for the revolutionary past. She is anxious not to turn into what Lisa Rofel — talking about Chinese factory workers in the socialist era — describes as a "parodic figure."[22] Anxious that she might be perceived as living in the past, Zhang claims that the shift to the new economy is good: "We can't hang on to the past." But she emphasizes that she still misses the lost innocence of the old days.

Zhang's account of the 1970s runs counter to the common discursive narrative of the period as inhumane, chaotic, and violent. Her stories could be taken as what Rofel calls "memory-practice"[23] — selective memories re-created against a feeling of irrelevance, antagonism, and marginalization in the current commercial society. This kind of narrative about an idealized past is constantly reinvoked to comment on the present. At one point, Zhang told me: "At that time there was no corruption, no bribery whatsoever. The leaders were fair and upright. I once lived in the same compound with a county magistrate. His furniture was a desk and a bed, same as what was in my room. Nothing more. Nowadays, a county magistrate would even have security guards in the gate of his house." I tried to get her to talk about the adaptations of TV dramas. Her answer was simple: "I don't like them. The love stories are way too amorous and forcing."

Her descriptions of the revolutionary utopia, her indignation toward corruption and disparity, and her marriage to a military commander suggested to me that she might have belonged to the politically privileged during the Cultural Revolution. However, as we discussed the topic of love and marriage further, I discovered that the socialist utopia, as she saw it, was vehemently negotiated in the first place. Zhang's husband-to-be served in the army in Vietnam during the 1960s. In 1969, when he was twenty-six, he came back to his home village for about a month to see his parents. Part of the duty of his trip was also to find a wife, which the local commune Party Secretary happily took on as a political task. Zhang, only seventeen and a high school student, went on an "arranged" blind date. In this way, she met her future spouse and he told the Party Secretary that he had chosen her. Persuaded by her mother and the authorities of the commune, Zhang agreed to write to him but soon decided she did not feel anything toward him. However, when she wanted to end the relationship, the army sent representatives to investigate whether there was a "third person." Scared of getting into serious political trouble, she married him. She described the ensuing years as "a dumb person tasting bitter herbs" — a Chinese idiom for someone who is forced to suffer in silence. She followed her husband across half the country as he was transferred here and there, looking after the children while doing all sorts of work regarded as fit for her. Even though she never developed feelings toward him, she was powerless to take any initiative to leave the relationship, as this would risk her being given a three-year sentence in prison for sabotaging "marriage with one in military service."

Forced to give up her dreams of love or a career, Zhang suffered greatly in the overtly politicized society. It is therefore surprising to hear that she is nostalgic about the past. As she explained: "Life was simple then." Our further discussions revealed that she was faring even worse now. In the new society, money is God. Her husband, demobilized from the army, was assigned by the government to manage a cigarette company in China's southern port city of Shenzhen. Taking advantage of his power in this enviable position, he quickly became rich and powerful and lived a raunchy lifestyle while she, already forced into passivity in the relationship, found it hard to regain the initiative. At forty-five, she opted for early retirement.

The freedom of the post-Mao era did not liberate her from political confinement or provide her with opportunities to live a more meaningful and richer life. In fact, she realized that the material society had granted her husband freedom, but not her. Her overview of the society is in a way reflected in her critiques on the Red Classics TV dramas. She sees the rendering of love and relationships in the TV adaptations not as restoring humanity from the hero role model myth, but as overcompensation for the lack of humanity in the revolutionary society. What the TV producers and directors construe as attracting audiences, Zhang finds distasteful: "I don't know whether it's the problem of the scriptwriter or the director, nowadays films and TV drama can't seem to function without messing up the family relationships depicted."

She even attributes her son's reluctance to enter into matrimony to anxiety created by watching too many TV dramas, invariably with dysfunctional relationships. Zhang's narrative of her past and present underscores the complexity of an individual viewer's reception of a TV product. It is a response which neither the triumph of commercial logic nor revolutionary hegemony can adequately explain. Zhang is nostalgic for the revolutionary past, in spite of the fact that she is not a beneficiary. In fact, her narrative runs contra to the state projects of socialist modernity: the free choice of partners, the heroic worker as the active political actor, and gender transgression. She is indignant about commercial realism and TV's contaminating effects, but not because she treats the revolutionary realism as sacred, like the state. She idealizes the lived experience of the past because of its absence in the present.

While Zhang's reading of the TV drama is closely related to her life story, some other interviewees stressed their viewing experience as purely pleasure seeking. Gao Ming, the owner of a small business in his mid-forties, said he liked the remake of *Struggles in the Old-line City* (*Yehuo chunfeng dou gucheng*) because the actors did a superb job of portraying the romance between the hero and the heroine: "What else makes people watch a TV drama but to enjoy the acting? There has to be a reason why the Hollywood stars are paid that much money — because people are there to see their acting." Gao also insisted that the success of the original film versions to a large degree depended on the attractiveness of the leading actors and actresses. The attitude Gao displayed toward the remake was that he was disinterested in the ideological message of the TV drama. He was more willing to accept the remake as a commercial product and judge its degree of success in commercial and aesthetic terms.

His opinion was shared by a much younger Jie, who claimed that he quite enjoyed both the old and the new versions of the Red Classics, but he treated the genre more as Chinese versions of Hollywood action or thriller shows, as many involved scenes of battles and conflict.

Gao and Jie's reactions prove that there are different aspects to the reception of the remake than simply "offended public." It is over-simplistic, however, to conclude that Gao and Jie totally embrace the terms of commercial media discourse and ignore or resist the revolutionary ideology in the story; but their reactions indicate that the Red Classics are open to competing interpretations and that TV producers have not entirely miscalculated their audience.

For most other informants, television is not only a technology for entertainment, but also a source of education. Such viewers often express anxiety over the representation of history in films and TV, and are quick to challenge its "authenticity." One informant, Zhang Zhengyu, commented that the romances developed in the remake failed to attract him as it was just "not real." He seemed to believe that explicit romance in the cruel environment of war was rare; he backed up this view with stories he drew from relatives such as his parents-in-law, both of whom were army officials and were married during the Korean War (1950–53). He is offended by the commercial tricks in the remake, but it is not because he takes the original works as sacred. In fact, in his reading of both the old and new versions, he makes an attempt to verify the historical narratives by applying the standard of realism. In his spare time, Zhang Zhengyu helps edit his father-in-law's memoirs and admits that he is even tempted to write "more realistic" revolutionary fictions based on his own knowledge of historical events. He maintains a cautious distance toward the socialist state ideology and the urban consumerism, and tries to assume agency in his reading of the genre.

Conclusion: Remaking the Past, Making Ratings in the Present

Initially created to construct the revolutionary hegemony of the Chinese Communist Party during the 1950s and 1960s, the works collectively referred to as the Red Classics have been given a new lease of life. The recent trend of producing TV drama series based on classics capitalizes on nostalgia and cultural memory in a post-revolutionary age. This cultural phenomenon is not without tensions and contradictions, however. Different camps demonstrate varied interests in the production and reception of these remakes. The state, the TV production companies, the press, and the TV audience all weigh in according to their own investment in the remake.

The TV production companies and scriptwriters mine the Red Classics, hoping to feed off the past and grab ratings. The state treats the revival of the genre as an opportunity to reinstate socialist values by means of willing participation. The common interest in exploiting Red Classics as a cultural resource does not rule out conflicts and struggles between the state and the market over the content of the remakes, nor does it preclude the state from exercising tight control over production companies, producers or scriptwriters when their reinvention transgresses official boundaries. The remakes play down ideological questions such as class struggle, nationalism, power, and patriotism, and stress romantic or divergent portrayal of heroes to appeal to the audiences' desire for novelty. This commercial vision, however, is very much at odds with that of the state. Officials are agitated when certain characterizations of the remakes dissipate, challenge, or even subvert the legitimacy of the past and institutionalized definitions of the revolution. What the TV producers see as potential audience-pleasers is quite often what the state wants to avoid. The process of how politics make room for the market is extremely complicated.

Once created as part of the official culture aiming to politicize socialist citizens, the Red Classics are now transmogrified to appeal to the increasingly sophisticated, demanding audience in the form of TV drama. Its transformation embodies the transition from an era dominated by mass production and consumption for ideological control in the socialist period to an era in which political indoctrination and market differentiation jostle for audiences in contemporary China. The differences, conflicts and compromises between the state and the commercial segments with reference to reproducing the TV remakes are further complicated at the reception level. TV consumption is complex and unpredictable. TV dramas are charged with ambiguities and open to interpretation. A few case studies show that neither the regulatory discourse of the state nor the commercial rewriting according to the capitalist logic is capable of totally framing audience readings of the TV remakes. And it is precisely these ambiguous moments and diverse ways of interpreting the Red Classics that have provided an important discursive space, where a range of new social identities can be constructed and contested. The consumption of the Red Classics provides a fine example of the contemporary identity constantly forming and reforming amid the remnant of utopian socialist values and the rising material reality of consumerism.

IV

Co-productions and Pan-Asian Markets

12

Looking for Taiwan's Competitive Edge: The Production and Circulation of Taiwanese TV Drama

Yi-Hsiang Chen

In 1998, the most popular drama in Mainland China was *Princess Huanzhu* (*Huanzhu gege*), first broadcast by Beijing TV Station (BTV) in November of the same year. Based on a novel by Qiong Yao, a famous female romance writer in Taiwan, *Princess Huanzhu* was produced by Hunan Satellite Television. The director, Sun Shu-Pei, was also Taiwanese. The story of *Princess Huanzhu* is about a peculiar girl who mistakenly became a princess during the Qing dynasty. In spite of the historical context, the characters' dialogue reflects present-day values and attitudes. *Princess Huanzhu* thus transcends the stereotype of historical costume drama. According to one critic, it was as if modern people were wearing ancient costumes.[1]

Taiwanese TV dramas and co-productions have achieved great success in Mainland China since the mid-1980s. In 2005, one of the most popular serials in China was *Pink Ladies* (*Hongfen nülang*) (see Chapter 7), a story set in Shanghai but based on the cartoon series by Taiwanese artist Zhu Deyong. Again, the serial was co-produced with a Taiwanese media company.

In this chapter I will discuss why China has become a fertile market for Taiwan television drama and show how Taiwan has exploited its Chinese connections to respond to the market challenges presented by Japanese and Korean drama. One success enjoyed by Taiwan productions in recent years has been the idol drama genre, best illustrated by the serial *Meteor Garden* (Liuxing huayuan) (2001). Although the serial was eventually banned in Mainland China, *Meteor Garden* provided a template for other productions which have subsequently captured a slice of the Chinese market. Dramas adopting the same formula are now produced in the Mainland. But in addition to adaptation and rights-selling to Chinese television stations, dramas like *Meteor Garden* are now reformatted for distribution on mobile phones, a platform which facilitates a range of ancillary cultural products and services.

The Local Environment and the Lure of China-based Production

In order to account for Taiwan's cultural exports in television drama, and particularly the appeal of Taiwanese drama in the Mainland, it is helpful to understand how the local production environment has interacted with neighboring Asian cultures. The Taiwanese TV drama genres and formats that made an impact in China during the early 1990s have themselves evolved, and have taken in influences from Japan and Korea.

Television drama in Taiwan is generally categorized according to type, for instance, Amoy drama, idol drama, costume drama, historical drama, literary drama, and religious drama. Dramas imported into Taiwan have come mainly from Japan, Korea, Hong Kong, and Mainland China. In the early 1980s, TV drama production was dominated by three terrestrial stations, Taiwan Television Enterprise (hereafter, TTV), China Television Co. (hereafter, CTV) and Chinese Television System (hereafter, CTS). The Taiwan market was then considered large enough to allow these three stations to produce prime-time dramas. During the past few decades the most popular dramas were *Judge Bao* (*Bao Qing Tian*) and *China Armed Escort* (*Baobiao*). *Judge Bao*, more popularly known as Bao Gong, recounts tales of court trials in which the venerable judge administers justice and fairness. *China Armed Escort* describes a military escort that overcomes many difficulties and setbacks to complete a series of missions. Both dramas portray faithfulness, dedication and honor — values that were popular with the mass audience at the time. *Judge Bao* was the blockbuster hit of 1974, setting a Taiwanese broadcasting record of 350 episodes.[2]

The popularity of these dramas attracted interest in Southeast Asia, including broadcasters in China, Singapore, Malaysia and the Philippines. However, costume drama production in Taiwan lost ground in the 1990s. Cable TV expanded and as a result audiences are now fragmented. (There are 5 terrestrial commercial stations, including 1 public television service, 63 cable TV systems, and 135 satellite channels in Taiwan.)[3] Escalating costs are the major concern in producing drama in Taiwan, and this applies particularly to costume drama. In 2006 it cost US$70,000 to produce an episode of a high-end costume drama, while other genres such as idol drama cost US$20,000 to US$30,000.[4] Costume drama requires specific resources such as scenery, casting, costume and stage props.

During the 1990s, knight-errant tales (*wuxia*) and romantic stories were the dominant TV drama exports. Hong Kong writer Jin Yong and Taiwanese writer Qiong Yao were responsible for many dramas, which were made in either Taiwan or Hong Kong. Television producers took an active role in the process. Qiong Yao's romantic serials and producer Yang Pei-Pei's knight-errant tales circulated in Mandarin-speaking markets. However, the majority of sales in the Chinese market during the past few years have been from Hong Kong and Korea, with Taiwan occupying the third position. In 2002, 327 drama programs were sold to major TV channels in China: 133 were from Hong Kong (40.7 percent), 67 from Korea (20.5 percent), and 42 from Taiwan (12.9 percent).[5] Dramas from Hong Kong and Taiwan together occupied 53.6 percent of the Mainland's drama imports.

The Refashioning of Taiwanese TV Drama

During the 1990s, Japanese dramas became extremely fashionable in Taiwan, particularly among female audiences. Koichi Iwabuchi notes that the term "idol drama" (alternatively rendered as "trendy drama" in Japan), was first used by Star TV Taiwan (StarTV) in 1992.[6] These modern narratives of romance and friendship among young urban professionals invariably featured handsome male leads and beautiful women. Their appeal to youth precipitated a Japanese wave. Iwabuchi argues that Taiwanese youth tend to view Japanese television and music as culturally proximate; and that they share a sense of "Asian modernity," despite language differences.[7] Chua Beng-Huat suggests that the popularity of idol dramas in Taiwan is attributable to "coevalness" between Taiwanese audiences and the Japanese represented in the dramas — in other words, "the feeling that Taiwanese share a modern temporality with the Japanese."[8]

Japanese idol dramas are essentially very different from the "traditional" Taiwanese prime-time drama, the key conventions of which are local flavor, historical anguish, and moral exhortation. Following the success of Japanese trendy drama, Taiwanese producers borrowed and incorporated ideas from the genre in order to create a distinctive local idol drama format. It is generally agreed that this cultural borrowing provided Taiwanese drama with a fresh look and a new feel. In 2000, Taiwanese producer Angie Chai adapted a Japanese manga into a television series. *Meteor Garden* (*Liuxing huayuan*) was an instant success throughout East Asia. In Taiwan it served as a template for others to emulate; soon after *Meteor Garden* other television stations followed suit, hoping to replicate the success at home and abroad.

The reception of *Meteor Garden* in the Mainland, however, was a different story. *Meteor Garden* was jointly introduced into China by Beijing Jiyang Communication Inc. and Harbin TV HRBTV.[9] The Chinese media responded to the success of this popular show and the leading characters, known collectively as F4, quickly became idols of the young generation. The success of the drama was subsequently correlated with a moral panic. Children running away from home or from school were serious problems at the time and the Chinese government deemed that the *Meteor Garden* narrative had a negative impact on the young generation. Inevitably, the government used its television content guidelines to suppress the broadcast. From the censors' point of view *Meteor Garden* was "misleading the young generation". It was banned in China.[10]

The market for Japanese trendy drama lapsed after 2000; production declined and sales in Taiwan fell. Due to limited budgets, Taiwan's cable channels looked to Korea for cheaper program alternatives.[11] In 2001, the cable channel Gala Television Co. (hereafter, GTV) imported *Falling in Love with the Anchorwoman* (*Aishang nüzhubo*) and *Autumn in My Heart* (*Lanse shengsi lian*) from Korea. Following this, FTV, a terrestrial station, broadcast a Korean drama *Sparkle* (*Huohua*) in their evening schedule. Soon afterwards, TTV decided to air Korean drama during prime time. The new Korean wave swamped the diminishing Japanese wave, and had an important role in helping to transform domestic drama. The themes, characterization, and even settings of Korean drama were similar to those of Japanese drama, but Taiwanese audiences are more familiar with the Korean style, as it reflects family life in Taiwan more so than Japanese drama. The success of Korean drama in Taiwan is not solely based on its affective dimension and proximity to Chinese culture. As Dong-Hoo Lee argues in Chapter 13, Korean television drama producers have been supported by government in exporting their dramas. Leading actors and actresses have visited Taiwan. Almost all Korean dramas are dubbed into Mandarin.

Exportable and Profitable Drama

The domestic market for television drama remains buoyant and the current strategy of Taiwanese TV drama production remains strongly focused on local demand. Overseas broadcasting rights are merely regarded as an added value. Although domestic audiences constitute the first market, Taiwanese television dramas have, for some time, had a presence in Singapore, Malaysia and China. A good example is Amoy drama, which is produced in the local dialect called Hokkien (or *minnan hua*). While Amoy drama is primarily traditional family drama made for local consumption, it has achieved substantial export sales in Southeast Asia and China. *Flying Dragon in the Sky* (*Feilong zaitian*), produced by FTV, combines costume drama with a Chinese knight-errant style and creates a pioneering Taiwanese style. The ratings were surprisingly high in Taiwan, and generated much interest among younger viewers. It was also dubbed into Mandarin and subsequently garnered high ratings in China.[12]

Since the success of *Meteor Garden*, the attitudes toward export markets have changed. In particular, idol drama is now regarded as an exportable format. Some television stations and producers have begun to export idol drama series to the Mainland market. According to the analysis of local producers,[13] idol drama producers often incorporate "de-localization" when creating an idol drama. De-localization is the deliberate removal of local characteristics in order to make the product more acceptable to audiences in China and the global Mandarin market. Another critical factor for success in entering overseas markets is the choice of leading actors or actresses. Having a big name in the leading roles helps boost sales as well as ratings. This celebrity phenomenon seems to be more evident in the Mainland market, where audiences seem to judge idol dramas mainly by the impression of the leading actor or actress.

Since 2000, a new business model has appeared whereby television stations control the production and overseas marketing of drama programs. Sanlih E-Television Co. (SETTV) produces a twenty-episode idol drama every three months. According to Robert Xue of SETTV,[14] the average production cost of an idol drama is comparatively high, which is about US$20,000 to $30,000 each episode. However, selling idol dramas overseas is relatively profitable. The sale price of a one-hour episode to local agents in China can range from US$5,000 to US$8,000. GTV, a cable TV station which formerly broadcast Korean idol drama, is aggressively producing four or five idol dramas annually and targeting the ethnic Chinese market. If we take into account co-productions with China, the number is even higher.

Cultural proximity assists in the marketing of these dramas.[15] Production is largely based on geo-linguistic similarity. In the East Asian region, however, in addition to common languages, there are other affinities embodied in transborder productions: ethnicities, body language, humor, story ideas, plots, pace, music and religion. Lai Tsung-Pi, vice president of the Planning Department of GTV, contends that due to fierce channel competition in Taiwan, as well as the diversity of imported drama, viewer uptake in Taiwan provides an index to test marketability in ethnic Chinese regions. Put in another way, if a drama is popular in Taiwan, it will definitely be popular in other ethnic Chinese areas. The popularity of a drama broadcast in Taiwan is therefore an important guide for Asian agents in purchasing products.

Recently, more independent production companies with an export focus have been established, such as the TV-Comic Production Co., the Yang Ming Channel Film and Video Co., the Hon To Production Co., and the Fu Long Production Co. When developing programs, these companies do not only consider the taste of the domestic audience, but also factor in demands from overseas markets.[16] This is the so-called "programming as marketing" principle; in other words, production and broadcasting are based on the principle of "marketing-orientation" in order to expand the market and gain more profit from the programs.

Television stations will attempt to diversify their distribution windows to extend the life-cycle of their dramas. In other words, programs are not released simultaneously in all markets. The export focus is primarily on Mandarin-speaking areas, such as Southeast Asia, Mainland China, the western US, and parts of Canada. In addition to having direct contact with TV stations in these respective locations, most production companies and TV stations in Taiwan work with agents to promote overseas business. In Mainland China, all of SETTV's idol dramas are sold with the help of local agents whose major asset is their ability to steer their way through the complex content reviewing process and the regulations on time slots for offshore programs in Mainland China. Another serious issue is pirating. Pirated copies of idol drama often circulate in the market before the official product is broadcast on TV channels. All these factors add to the transaction costs and operational risks. The business model for the Chinese market is therefore to sell rights at the right time, so that the risks are transferred to the local agent. Although China is a huge market, the lack of reliable local contacts and the severe piracy problem make it difficult for Taiwanese TV stations to develop a long term program distribution strategy.

Idol drama has generated a unique value chain. In addition to the high license fees associated with ratings, marketing and merchandising of the idols also helps to create ancillary value. According to Vincent Chiang,[17] deputy director of the International Affairs and Program Department of FTV, the overseas program broadcasting rights issued by most Taiwanese television stations include rights on terrestrial TV, cable TV stations, satellite TV, home-entertainment products (such as VCD and DVD), the Internet, video-on-demand (VOD), and any new communication technology such as mobile TV and cellular phone. Home-entertainment products (VCD and DVD), while generating good sales in Japan, find their markets extremely restricted in China due to piracy. With revenue lost through piracy and a decrease in the value of spot advertising in mainstream programming, idol dramas provide new business streams, primarily through branded web-sites. Merchandising and derivative royalties have become essential to success.

The cost of the TV drama for overseas sale is largely the reproduction cost of the program itself. The reproduction cost includes the revision of the length of each episode and any necessary adjustment to the number of episodes. Drama exported from Taiwan is in Mandarin. There are no subtitles. The buyers dub the drama into their native language or add appropriate subtitles. Since the language used in the drama, the length of each episode and the number of episodes all have impact on narrative continuity, the post-production units in the TV stations will endeavor to maintain the quality of the original when they format the shows for overseas markets.

Integration of Resources through Digital Technology

With advances in mobile communication, media channels can exchange content rapidly and this in turn brings new business opportunities. The integration of telecommunication, media, and information technology has created a new information platform where mobile phone communication has gone beyond pure speech and transformed into multimedia formats. Through the mobile platform, traditional media content broadcasters can provide various content to end users and benefit directly from the usage fee; that is, they earn whenever users retrieve the information.

Hand-held devices have added a new dimension to how people experience audio-visual entertainment. Mobile phones are branded as fun products and new applications are pushing the interactive experience in new directions. Furthermore, these features have a direct impact on the development of media content. Issues of "size," "entertainment" and "interactivity" have to be considered altogether, so that users can read and walk at the same time, and can search information for fun or for specific purposes. In Taiwan, content providers within the TV industry are cooperating with telecommunication companies to deliver drama and entertainment through mobile devices. The "pocket idol drama" now provides content about idols, fashion and entertainment narrowcast over mobile phones. It provides consumers with a new interactive experience of TV drama.

SETTV was the first TV station in Taiwan to provide "pocket idol drama" over mobile phones. Its first multinational program was *The Boy Who Lost His Memory* (*Shiqu jiyi di nanhai*). The concept originated during the production process of an idol drama called *The Prince Turns into a Frog* (*Wangzi bian qingwa*) — a prime-time drama broadcast by TTV. Since the ratings were impressive, the station decided to produce a spin-off program using interesting behind-the-scenes stories. Meanwhile, SETTV also sold the rights of *The Boy Who Lost His Memory* to SingTel and China Mobile — the two leading telecommunication companies in Singapore and China respectively. The pocket drama is formatted to meet market requirements in different areas; in Singapore each episode runs three minutes and in China currently one minute, due to the bandwidth limitation. Simultaneously, the idol drama is broadcast on the local TV station.

Another customized mobile drama product is *The Photo Diary of Green Forest, My Home* (*Lüguang senlin cepai riji*), which shows behind-the-scene clips of *Green Forest, My Home* (*Lüguang senlin*). Giving mobile phone subscribers a window to view the creation, construction, and production of an idol drama, as well as incidents occurring during shooting, the application was first used on the 3G cellular channel by Far Eastone, a mobile communications provider in Taiwan. It was subsequently licensed to the Singapore-based SingTel.

Love Hairdresser (*Aiqing mofa shi*), another popular idol drama, also provided its pocket drama, called *The Show of Love Hairdresser* (*Aiqing mofa xiu*), together with beauty-related information for mobile users. The major added-value components here relate to fashion: users of these mobile devices have access to the latest fashion trends as modeled by the actors or actresses. The multi-platform media content and extensions of popular TV dramas focus on entertainment and do not involve any political or ideological issues that might restrict delivery in Mainland China.

Co-productions between Taiwan and PR China

China is the motherland of ethnic Chinese culture. With reference to the historical drama genre, China possesses an advantage of interpretative power in ethnic Chinese regions. Historical costume dramas have scored high ratings in Mandarin-speaking areas. However, in contrast to China's huge consumer market for imports, the presence of China as a drama production location in East Asia is still marginal. With reference to fashionable drama — those featuring contemporary themes of middle-class affluence and conspicuous consumption — China is still at its exploratory stage (see Chapter 7). Since consumerism is a relatively new phenomenon in China, fashionable drama is yet to achieve the quality and style of other Asian productions. Fashionable drama in China is now drawing on material from Taiwan to create a contemporary urban style. Taiwanese material include comics, such as *City Ladies* (*Se nülang*) and *Double-Bang Firecracker* (*Shuangxiangpao*); popular fiction, such as *Protein Girl* (*Danbaizhi nühai*); and illustrated books like *Turn Left, Turn Right* (*Xiangzuozou xiangyouzou*) by the famous illustrator Gimmy Liao. These local cultural resources provide opportunities for Taiwanese producers to develop contemporary dramas that take advantage of the linguistic and cultural affinities in order to meet the needs of the Chinese-speaking world, especially within greater China.

Increasingly, Taiwan television producers are leaving their home base to look for opportunities within larger spaces defined by linguistic and cultural similarities or proximities. Due to the demands and opportunities of the China market, numerous drama producers who formerly worked with the three Taiwanese terrestrial stations have relocated in China. Since Taiwan cannot directly enter the China market or open its channels to the Mainland, transnational cooperation in program and content development is an alternative. At present, TV drama cooperation between Taiwan and China is limited by politics; up till now, there is no official cooperation allowed. For that reason, the funding, technical support, and communication among agents are often achieved through non-governmental production companies.

The objective of cooperation with China for Taiwanese drama producers is to explore the Mainland market and to share more production resources. Therefore, if both parties find the appropriate story for the Greater China market, it is possible to generate quality profitable dramas which conform to the taste of the ethnic Chinese market. For example, the literary drama *April Rhapsody* (*Renjian siyue tian*) was co-produced by Zoom Hunt International Productions Co. in Taiwan and ROSAT (Beijing Rosat Film and Production Co.). The producer, Xu Ligong, is not only a famous producer in Taiwan, but also a well-known figure in China. The rights for this drama were purchased in advance by Public Television Service (PTS) in Taiwan. The business model of pre-purchasing covered the concept and project of the drama, but not the final product.[18] The script of *April Rhapsody* was original — the life story of an early twentieth-century Chinese poet Xu Zhimo who is well-known in Greater China (the Chinese Mainland, Hong Kong and Taiwan). Both the screenwriter and the director are from Taiwan. Two of the leading players are from China, and the other two from Taiwan.

The development cost of each episode was about US$70,000 and production companies in Taiwan and China apportioned the costs equally. The party in China (ROSAT) owns the broadcasting rights in China, and

Zoom Hunt maintains the broadcasting rights in Taiwan and other areas except China. According to Claire Young,[19] planning manager of Zoom Hunt, due to the production quality and positive response from the audience, international sales and licensing have continued to grow since its launch in 2000. *Orange is Red (Juzi hongle)* and *She is from the Sea (Ta cong haishanglai)* are two other literary dramas which have been co-produced between China and Taiwan.

However, *Moment in Beijing (Jinghua yanyun)* — a story about a large Chinese family — produced by China Central Television (hereafter, CCTV) and Phoenix Talent Company (the subsidary of FTV in Taiwan), did not go smoothly. This joint production was dominated by the Mainland side; the screenwriting and the direction were both led by CCTV. While the drama was reasonably well received in China, it was far less successful in Taiwan. Pre-production accounted for almost three years. The casting of actors, apportioning of costs, and division of shooting script in each episode was difficult and tedious. Furthermore, scheduling conflicts of actors during the shooting severely delayed development, and the dubbing and other post-production work devoured more time. By the time the drama was finally available, this type of drama had become less popular in Taiwan and other overseas markets. One objective of developing this drama through cooperation with China was to reduce costs and to manage overseas rights. But due to disruptions in the production schedule, the opportunity to sell rights had long disappeared. As a result the production failed to deliver its promise, except for some success in the Mainland Chinese market.

GTV has cooperated with a Mainland company to produce their first idol drama, *Don't Love Me (Bie ai wo)*. GTV plans to maintain their collaboration with the Chinese media company in order to achieve an output of two to three dramas each year. Technical and financial cooperation with the China party can also help GTV take advantage of the popularity of fashionable drama in ethnic Chinese markets, and at the same time gain more experience from co-production projects such as this one. In order to jump on the bandwagon of the Beijing 2008 Summer Olympics, GTV has developed an idol drama on the subject of sport with a production company in China.

When developing a drama between Taiwan and China, the subject matter needs to be mutually accepted by both parties. Different interpretations of the characters require compromise. For example, *She is from the Sea*, a literary drama based on the autobiography of novelist Eileen Chang, could not attain approval for broadcast due to controversial and different interpretations of Eileen Chang's work in China. As for the aforementioned *April Rhapsody*, audiences from Taiwan and China have different interpretations of Xu Zhimo; the ending of the drama was altered in order to facilitate its broadcast in China.

Examination of subject matter is demanding and many taboos exist in Mainland China; it is therefore very important to choose the right subject for a drama. For example, *Evil Son* (*Niezi*), a drama adapted from the novel of the same name by famous writer Bai Xianyong (Pai Hsien-yung) touched on the subject of homosexuality and for this reason cannot be broadcast in China. *Fighting Fish* (*Douyu*), an idol drama produced by GTV, although very popular in Taiwan and Japan, cannot be shown in China, because the Chinese government contends that it is a gangster drama. It is interesting to note that while some programs are very popular in the pirate DVD market, they are not allowed to be shown on TV.

Co-production between Taiwan and China provides a mix of opportunity and risk. The critical factors for a successful co-produced TV drama are themes and scripts. However, the main risks are policy regulations and political considerations. The regulations set by the State Administration of Radio, Film and Television (SARFT) in China place excessive restrictions on co-production, such as percentage limits on the number of overseas actors/ actresses, restrictions on time slots for broadcast, restrictions on episode length, quotas of co-produced programs — in addition to the complexity of content examination. For Taiwanese producers and TV stations, the inducement of drama co-production is the sharing of funds and the China market. The risk of co-production, apart from the limitation of content, is the uncertainty of China's reviewing system, which is deeply rooted in authoritarianism and is ideologically determined.

Conclusion

Until recently the expansion of the Taiwanese TV industry has been limited by the scale and resources of its domestic market. The financial benefits of cheaper production, together with the potentially massive Chinese market, are attractions for Taiwan in pursuing internationalization strategies. However, due to restrictions of the broadcasting law in China and the conflicting political ideologies between the two sides, the Chinese market remains difficult to penetrate.

It has become obvious that television drama is moving into a new stage of development, which is an inevitable outcome of keen competition in the television drama market within Asia. The trend toward diversification means that drama needs more financial investment, more market segmentation, and more effective management of production, including topics, scripts, shooting, and talent.

Taiwan has the largest ethnic Chinese population outside Mainland China and is the second largest consumer market for Mandarin cultural products. It has advantages of cultural resources and experience of running sophisticated entertainment businesses. In linking up with funding, market, and talent in China, and benefiting from an inevitable relaxation of policy restrictions on the Mainland, Taiwan will have greater opportunities to play a key role as a Mandarin drama provider in the Great China market.

13

From the Margins to the Middle Kingdom:
Korean TV Drama's Role in Linking Local and Transnational Production

Dong-Hoo Lee

In 1998, China Central Television (CCTV) broadcast a Korean drama, *What is Love All About?* (*Aiqing shi shenme?*) The result was a 4.3 percent audience share — the second highest audience share among all imported TV programs in China to that time. Since then, a succession of Korean television dramas have captured the imagination of Chinese audiences and made successful inroads into other Asian markets.

The creation of *hanliu* (*hallyu* in Korean) — sometimes known as the Korean Wave — is a complex phenomenon.[1] In fact, the sudden surge in popularity of Korean television dramas and other popular cultural products in Asia was not fleeting and accidental. As demonstrated by the positive reviews for *Winter Sonata* (*Dongri liange*, 2002) and *Jewel in the Palace* (*Da changjin*, 2003) — and the increase in Korean TV program exports throughout Asia in recent years — *hanliu* has maintained its momentum and now represents one of the largest transnational cultural flows within Asia.

The transnational circulation of Korean pop culture products within Asia has brought about a fundamental transformation in Asian television industries, whose cultural territories have traditionally been defined by the nation-state. Until the 1980s, domestically produced programs occupied a far greater proportion of local prime-time scheduling relative to imported global programs. TV program exchange among neighboring Asian countries was practically non-existent.[2] However, the 1990s saw the introduction of new media outlets, notably cable and satellite TV channels, and the expansion of Asian media markets. The combined effect of this was greater demand for media products.³ While the United States was the most dominant international TV program provider for Asian media markets during the formative years of television,⁴ by the 1990s Japan — and later Korea — had become major providers of programs directly targeted at Asian audiences' cultural demands.⁵

The origin of the *hanliu* phenomenon cannot simply be ascribed to the attraction of a specific media product. Mediascapes within Asia are now interlocked and integrated as the globalization of local and regional media industries moves to new levels. More importantly, *hanliu* exemplifies an intercultural traffic beyond national boundaries, drawing on the fact that many Asian audiences share common cultural tastes and sensibilities.⁶ As a part of this inter-East Asian cultural traffic, *hanliu* has added another dimension to transnational media flows in Asia. It has contributed to increasing the layers of transnational popular cultural flows in Asia through complex production practices and sites, methods of circulation, and consumption.

This chapter outlines the inflow of Korean TV dramas into China and the effects of this traffic on media industries in both countries. In particular, I demonstrate the important role of *hanliu* in the recent transformation of Korean TV drama industries. My examples are drama co-productions between Korean and Chinese TV producers. The rapid diffusion and growing popularity of Korean cultural products across Asia have affected the structure of domestic TV drama productions not only in Korea, but also within East Asia. Whereas previously production was restricted by national boundaries, the success of Korean drama has encouraged greater trans-border collaboration.

Korean TV Program Exports

Since the late 1990s, exports of Korean TV programs have vastly increased due to their popularity in other Asian markets. During this time, the total economic value of Korean television program exports has jumped by an average of 42 percent per year. According to the Korean Ministry of Culture and Tourism, since 2002 total television program exports exceeded imports in Korea's television market (see Figure 13.1).⁷ As of 2005, exports of Korean TV programs brought in US$123 million — more than the amount spent on imports of foreign TV programs, which accounted for just US$30 million. This notable growth in program exports can be explained by the increased market value (the sale price) of Korean TV dramas as well as the expansion of export markets due to the increasing popularity of Korean dramas. In 2002,

TV dramas accounted for 76.8 percent of Korean TV program exports. By 2005, this percentage had jumped to 92.0 percent. Furthermore, the average sale price per episode of exported programs rose from $2,198 in 2003 to $4,046 in 2004 and $4,921 in 2005.

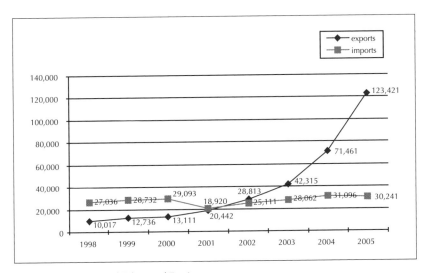

Source: Korean Ministry of Culture and Tourism

Figure 13.1   TV Program Exports versus Imports in Korea (US$1,000)

Exports of Korean TV programs have greatly depended upon demand in Asian markets, with 95.3 percent of total television exports going to other Asian countries in 2005. In 2001, China was the second largest importer of Korean television programs, accounting for 20.1 percent of Korean television programming sales, closely following Taiwan (20.2 percent). China and Taiwan remained the leading importers of Korean television programs until 2003, when *Winter Sonata* broke through in Japan. Since then, Japan has rapidly emerged as the biggest buyer of Korean TV programs. Program exports to Japan accounted for just 19.0 percent of total Korean television program exports in 2003, but increased to 60.1 percent in 2005. While the overall amount of Korean programs exported to China and Taiwan has continued to increase, their share of the total export market has declined.

Table 13.1   Major Importing Countries of Korean TV programs (US$1,000)

	China	Hong Kong	Indonesia	Japan	Singapore	Taiwan	Others	Total*
2001	2,487 (20.1%)	1,161 (9.4%)	–	1,186 (9.6%)	974 (7.9%)	2,494 (20.2%)	4,054 (32.8%)	12,356
2002	3,663 (17.2%)	2,001 (9.4%)	875 (4.1%)	2,311 (10.8%)	945 (4.4%)	7,085 (33.2%)	4,462 (20.9%)	21,342
2003	6,149 (18.6%)	1,080 (3.3%)	412 (1.2%)	6,276 (19.0%)	1,089 (3.3%)	8,100 (24.5%)	9,970 (30.1%)	33,076
2004	6,803 (10.8%)	1,496 (2.4%)	591 (0.9%)	36,084 (57.4%)	951 (1.5%)	9,616 (15.3%)	7,326 (11.6%)	62,867
2005	10,962 (9.9%)	3,685 (3.3%)	1,176 (1.1%)	66,367 (60.1%)	1,166 (1.1%)	12,538 (11.4%)	14,714 (3.3%)	110,428

*Amounts of exports (TV programs and video sales) for overseas Koreans are excluded.
Source: Korean Ministry of Culture and Tourism

Korean Television Drama Industry in Transition: The Rise of Independent TV Drama Productions

The unprecedented growth of Korean TV program exports has facilitated the transformation of Korean TV's industrial landscape. In 1990, the Korean government amended the existing broadcasting law, which for the previous decade had banned commercial television. It granted a license to the Seoul Broadcasting System (SBS), a commercial broadcasting company. Since its inception in 1991, SBS has competed with the two public broadcasting companies, the Korean Broadcasting System (KBS) and the Munhwa Broadcasting Corporation (MBC). In addition, the Cable Television Act was passed in 1991 to foster and develop multi-channel cable television services. Most importantly, however, the government also enacted the Broadcasting Act Enforcement Ordinance in 1991. This legislation provided annual notification of the compulsory programming quota of "outsourced programs." This term refers to programs produced by local independent production companies for terrestrial television (that is, in comparison to studio programs produced by terrestrial broadcasters). This ordinance was intended to reform the structure of the Korean television industry, which had up until then favored an oligopolistic model of television broadcasting. It activated competition within the television market with the objective of ensuring demand for programs in the coming multi-channel television era.[8] The compulsory outsourcing quota was initially 3 percent. However, by 2006 it had expanded to 35 percent.

The expansion of the required quota of outsourced programs in turn provided momentum to increase the number of outsourced television dramas on terrestrial television channels. All terrestrial television dramas had been in-house products; however, soon after the policy was legislated, most dramas were being produced by independent production companies. From this brief history, it can be seen that the Korean government's outsourcing policy drastically altered the environment for television drama production in Korea.

In addition, broadcasting efficiency provided another reason for the rapid growth of these outsourced dramas. Although terrestrial broadcasters have wanted to invest heavily in order to make competitive dramas, their budgets are limited and regulated by laws that restrict commercial sponsorship, such as product placement (hereafter, PPL). In contrast, independent production companies have been allowed more freedom to pursue commercial sponsorship and have hired celebrated actresses, actors, and writers in the hope of scoring high ratings. As a result of this government intervention into the market, the broadcasters have been compelled to form strategic alliances with independent production companies in order to produce a marketable drama.

As of March 2006, three Korean broadcasters were airing twenty-five drama serials every week, including eleven serials on KBS, six on MBC, and eight on SBS.[9] While about 50 percent of KBS dramas are produced by the independent production companies, more than 90 percent of those shown on MBC and SBS are produced by such companies.

Transformation of the Production System

There are currently two methods to produce dramas in Korea. The first is called "complete production"; that is, an independent production company plans, casts, and produces a drama, then sells the end product to a broadcasting channel. The second method refers to a case in which an independent production company is commissioned to produce a drama based on the synopsis and casting given by the broadcasting channel. The production company then uses the broadcaster's facilities to produce the drama, or sometimes an in-house director produces the outsourced drama. Most of the outsourced dramas in Korea have been produced using the latter method. Since the complete production system is not a common practice, dramas are usually produced as they air. This allows for incremental adjustments, depending on audience reception. Moreover, there are few independent production companies who can afford to take a risk to produce a drama without securing a broadcaster's commission and televising rights. Although the independent production sector actually produces most of the television dramas seen on the terrestrial stations, the broadcasters usually exercise power over the independent production companies, the majority of which were founded by former broadcasting television producers and employees.[10]

However, production costs and revenues from subsidiary enterprises, such as original soundtrack (hereafter, OST) sales, celebrity and character merchandising rights, rights for cable and satellite channels, video, DVD, and international programming sales have continued to increase. These increases have contributed to a conflict over copyright between broadcasters and independent production companies. In particular, in response to the increased popularity and export of Korean TV dramas throughout Asia, both broadcasters and production companies have shown a greater interest in copyright. Both sides have started to consider an enlarged reproduction model with international implications beyond the limits of the domestic television market. For example, *Super Rookie* (*Xinjin zhiyuan*, 2005) was a sixteen-episode serial that cost an average of US $89,600 per episode to produce. When exported to Asian countries, it earned US $144,200 per episode, a total of US$2,883,040, over and above its local profits. *Jewel in the Palace*, a fifty-four episode serial, cost US $137,000 per episode, and was sold for an average of US$76,000 per episode to Asian as well as Middle Eastern countries. In addition to its huge commercial successes in the local television market, its earnings from international television sales amounted to US$4,105,101.[11] Since the profit from exporting some popular dramas commonly exceeds 60 percent of the total production cost, independent production companies have predictably started to insist on maintaining copyright privileges while the broadcasters try to defend their copyrights more vigorously.

In the early 2000s, the three major Korean broadcasters had created departments to oversee copyright and international program sales. KBS launched the "Global Strategy Team" under its Division of Global Affairs; MBC organized the "Overseas Business Operations Team"; and SBS started the "Content Business and Strategy Team." From the broadcasters' perspective, the copyrights of outsourced programs should belong to them because most of the programs are dependent on their financial contribution, personnel, and facilities. A personal interview with a "content producer" at KBS, who deals with program marketing abroad, suggests that the unprecedented success of *Winter Sonata* and other dramas in Asia — especially in Japan — has made the broadcasters more alert to the value of copyright and marketing strategies.[12] Indeed, the popularity of Korean dramas abroad has made domestic television drama production a higher value-added business. Expansion of markets across Asia adds more emphasis to this value proposition.

As a result, while the number of outsourced dramas has increased, the broadcasters are insisting on maintaining tighter control over copyright.

Recently, the broadcasters' monopoly over the terms of copyright ownership has begun to change. Many independent production companies have attempted to break from their traditionally subordinate relationship with the broadcasters by developing their own fundraising and investment plans. This changing paradigm is best described by Jonghak Kim, a representative of the independent Kimjonghak Production Company:

> Now, it is a transitional period because there's a conflict of interest with the broadcasters. In fact, there's no clear criterion to deal with this conflict. Until now, we have to give our copyrights to the broadcasters who sponsor our production costs in advance. The production companies have endured with PPL or sponsorship. As we are marketing *Sad Love Story*, we realize that we can earn two or three times more by selling it abroad than to the domestic broadcasters. For me, the production companies can create more profits by actively and persistently entering into marketing.[13]

At present, capital from the non-broadcasting sector is beginning to flow into independent drama productions. Additionally, *hanliu* stars are exerting greater influence upon drama productions, and independent drama production companies are increasingly striving to secure copyrights. These factors have clearly affected the relationship between producers and broadcasters. For example, *Taewangsashingi*, a drama starring Yong Jun Bae, a star of *Winter Sonata*, was produced in 2006, utilizing a $10 million drama fund raised by the Seoul Asset Management Company and the Kimjonghak Production Company. Olive 9, an independent production company, and Gold Bridge Asset Management Company also raised a $10 million drama production fund. These resources are used to produce dramas and generate profits for investors through a variety of sources, such as PPL, OST, ancillary merchandising, and international sales of copyrights, including the licensing of celebrity portraits. These funding mechanisms have reduced the independent drama production companies' reliance on broadcasters for production funds. Furthermore, they increase the likelihood and expectation of additional sources of revenue from sales to cable channels, the Internet, and wireless broadband as well as international circulation.[14] By raising drama funds and creating revenues from exports, major independent drama production companies endeavor to establish a viable business base in the Korean media industry. In the process, they are exploring new revenue sources beyond the domestic television drama market which is currently dominated by the broadcasters.

Television dramas have come to be regarded as cultural products with market value rather than a domestic public service. The surge in the overseas drama market is a key factor for local drama producers to consider when they propose and produce dramas. The expanding market has contributed to the concurrent transformation of the local drama production structure, which used to be dominated by the domestic broadcasting industry. In short, Korean drama producers are increasingly concerned about international marketing, investment, and co-production.

Trans-border Collaboration: Co-production in Cultural Industries

Since 2000, Korean drama producers have tried to market their products in China by pursuing collaborative efforts with Chinese broadcasters. While there have been several attempts at co-production by broadcasters in both countries, it is important to point out the barriers that impact on the trans-border flow of television programs. Some are cultural, while others are political — for instance, the Chinese government's restraint on the inflow of foreign programs. Co-production can be an effective way to overcome these barriers and maximize a drama's market value. Before discussing co-production practices between Korea and China, however, I will briefly consider the concept of co-production in cultural industries.

The international co-production of cultural products can be approached from a number of different perspectives. Co-production can be considered as an internationalizing strategy. John Sinclair has examined how STAR TV uses co-production agreements to create programming acceptable to viewers in different parts of Asia.[15] Co-production can be also viewed as a cost-effective strategy. For instance, Renaud and Litman have identified co-productions as "the most effective response strategy to the new economic pressures reshaping the television programming environment, in the USA and abroad."[16] Several studies have examined co-productions to assess their cost-effectiveness. Hoskins, McFayden, and Finn examined television and film co-productions in several countries and concluded that the benefits include pooling of financial resources and cheaper production inputs (e.g. labor) in the partner's country.[17] In addition, there are a number of important access opportunities. These include incentives and subsidies provided by the foreign government (national or local), access to the partner's market, access to third-country markets via better distribution agreements, and access to desired foreign locations. Another advantage is mutual learning effects — partners discover new ways of adding value and creativity (see Chapters 10 and 14). On the other hand, possible drawbacks include greater coordination costs, increased shooting costs, loss of control and cultural specificity, increased costs of dealing with government, and opportunistic behavior by the foreign partner. In addition to the mutual learning effects mentioned above, there is the possibility of creating a more formidable competitor in the future. Hoskins et al.'s studies of co-productions in Canada, Australia, and Japan found that the most important co-production benefit is usually the pooling of financial resources, while the greatest drawback is increased coordination costs. However, while co-production partners in different countries experience benefits and drawbacks, the extent of the cultural differences that exist between the partners does affect their experiences. There is considerable evidence that cultural distance affects the process of internationally co-producing television programs and feature films, and thus conditions the participant's perception of benefits and drawbacks.[18]

The *hanliu* phenomenon has inspired drama producers in Korea and China to consider the potential for co-producing dramas in both local and transnational television markets. One of the early forms of co-production involved Chinese drama producers simply casting Korean stars. These Korean actors and actresses became celebrities in China, and their transnational stardom was exploited in order to boost the profile of the dramas, mainly for Chinese audiences. Many Korean actors and actresses, including Jae Wook Ahn and Na Ra Jang have been cast in Chinese domestic dramas. This represents a highly limited form of collaboration in that the program is produced entirely with Chinese capital and personnel; the Korean counterpart participates only as the protagonist in the drama. Other forms of collaboration involve more extensive use of Korean investment and personnel, in addition to Korean actors and actresses. *The Hundred and First Proposal (Di 101 ci qiuhun,* 2004) is an example of this expanded form of collaboration. A Chinese remake of a Japanese drama of the same title starring Ji Woo Choe, the Korean heroine of *Winter Sonata*, *The Hundred and First Proposal* was made by a Chinese production staff working with a Korean scriptwriter Wan Gyu Choe, who was famous for *Hu Joon* (1999), *All In* (2003), and *Love in Harvard* (2004). This project also involved a number of Korean investors.

The number of co-production projects involving Korean actors or actresses, directors, scriptwriters, production staff, and investors who collaborate in the production of Chinese dramas has increased in recent years. In 2006, MBC, a Korean broadcaster, and E&B Stars, an independent production company based in China, raised a private equity fund worth more than US$6 million. This fund is to be used to finance Korean–Chinese drama co-productions. With this fund, three dramas are to be produced and distributed in both countries. Another co-production project is funded by China HealthCare Holdings Limited (CHC), a health care service company in China, and Olive 9, an independent drama production company in Korea. They are co-producing a sixteen-part medical drama, set in a general hospital in Beijing. While CHC provides financial support totaling more than $2 million, Olive 9 takes charge of production planning, production, and distribution. This drama will also be used to promote additional health and beauty care-related products. This kind of co-production project will continue as long as there is a viable market for it.

These types of co-production projects exist for several reasons. For the Chinese co-producers, Korean co-production boosts the profile of dramas. For the Korean co-producers, these projects represent a way to access audiences not only in Mainland China, Hong Kong, and Taiwan, but also in Malaysia, Singapore, and other countries where a large Chinese diaspora lives. These vast Chinese media markets offer a way for the co-producers to maximize financial resources and ensure large returns on their investments.

Second, co-production overcomes foreign content constraints on terrestrial television in each national territory. This represents an especially useful way for Korean co-producers to bypass the restrictions on the time allowed for foreign programming and to deal with the problem of pre-censorship of television programs imposed by the Chinese government (see Chapter 12). Recently, China's State Administration of Radio Film and Television (SARFT) announced that it would cut the quota of Korean dramas and hold back the review processes of imported Korean TV dramas.[19] The Taiwanese government is also considering a ban on the broadcast of foreign dramas during prime time, a measure that seems to be directed against popular Korean dramas. These policies are intended to address the concerns of local drama producers related to the influx of Korean television dramas. However, these defensive measures against Korean drama exports will ultimately serve to facilitate more co-production projects rather than imports of end-products. Co-production would be a way to avoid the risk from governmental restrictions and cultural barriers and, importantly, reduce "cultural discount" — the problem of programs being misunderstood and undervalued due to cultural nuances. Third, co-production can utilize "desired foreign locations" and other cultural resources. Korean drama producers are fascinated with China's spacious and graceful landscapes, as well as martial arts and sword techniques.

Co-production is an ongoing process with great potential value. Drama producers in both Korea and China anticipate synergetic effects through collaboration in the areas of marketing, finance, and access to production resources and know-how. Co-productions reduce the financial risk assumed by participants and enable access to wider television markets. However, these collaborative efforts are currently limited primarily to the production of TV dramas that appeal to Chinese audiences. Co-produced dramas have yet to appeal to Korean broadcasters or audiences. *Apartment (Bailing gongyu,* 2002), starring Jae Wook Ahn, was aired by a local Korean independent broadcaster, as well as a cable channel called China TV in Korea. This program received little public attention. *The Hundred and First Proposal* also failed to find a timeslot in a major television network in Korea. Co-producers have recently become more conscious about differences between Asian audiences, including those in Korea and China. The next step is that co-producing parties must now figure out how to better deal with cultural distance and differences, and how to best use each partner's symbolic resources, and determine what kinds of narrative strategies will attract a positive reception for their projects across Asia.

Two Cases: *Beijing, My Love* and *Bichunmu*

In 2004, KBS co-produced the twenty-part serial *Beijing, My Love* (*Beijing, wode ai*), with China's CCTV. First proposed in 2002 to celebrate the tenth anniversary of the establishment of diplomatic relationship between Korea and China, and to help foster understanding between cultures, this co-produced drama was one of the few that was ultimately broadcast on Korean terrestrial television. This production was unusual from the Korean perspective since it was intended to be completed before it was broadcast.[20] This project cost $3.7 million, and 80 percent of its content was shot in China. Koreans took charge of directing and scriptwriting while the Chinese participated as the production staff. Leading and supporting roles went to both Korean and Chinese actresses and actors.

Beijing, My Love is a romance in which the Korean hero, Minkook, and the Chinese heroine, Yang Xues, overcome misunderstandings and difficulties to finally realize their "true love" across national borders. The production of cultural products is always accompanied by financial risks and considerable uncertainties. Therefore, the producers and directors made every effort to mitigate these problems by consciously and unconsciously following conventions.[21] *Bejing, My Love* repeats the same love theme deployed in the three previous co-produced dramas by Korean and Japanese broadcasting companies: a Chinese (Japanese) woman and a Korean man accidentally meet, fall in love, split up because of trivial misunderstandings, and meet again. This story also follows conventional narrative strategies that employ double love-triangles: the heroine and the hero are both loved by someone else in their respective native countries. The cultural barrier, the foremost element to trouble these heroines and heroes, is often expressed in the form of love triangles.

Although the production of this drama overcame significant obstacles related to the SARS outbreak at the time, as well as cultural barriers and coordination costs, it ultimately did not appeal to Korean audiences. When *Beijing, My Love* aired in 2004, it earned an average 4.9 percent audience share in Korea, one of the lowest among dramas. Audiences complained that its main theme was neither innovative nor entertaining, and that the narrative depicting cultural differences was not realistic and sophisticated enough. Korean subtitles were also said to reduce the drama's appeal. Korean audiences also took exception to a statement offered by the Chinese heroine in the third episode. The Chinese protagonist stated: "Korea used to be our dependency, and now, it is a small country divided by two. However, this small country is now affecting a big country with a population of 1.3 billion. I want to know what the power is."

The expression that "Korea used to be our dependency" aroused bitter criticism in Korea. Audience members framed this statement within an additional political context. At the time, China was attempting to incorporate the ancient Korean kingdom of Goguryeo into its own national history. Ultimately, the Korean director and writer apologized to the public, saying that the statement was intended to express the power of *hanliu* and caution against Sinocentrism rather than insinuate the superiority of a specific country. They hoped that this "well-intended" drama would not stimulate nationalist sentiments.[22]

Beijing, My Love was intended to portray a love fantasy beyond national borders in order to cater to audiences in both countries. But its failure to present its subject matter in a culturally sensitive way suitable to viewers with differing viewpoints illustrates the limits that must be intentionally imposed upon co-produced dramas in order to gratify transnational audiences.

On the other hand, *Bichunmu (Feitian wu)*[23] was a twenty-part drama co-produced by Korea's Eight Peaks, an independent production company, and China's Shanghai Film Studio. *Bichunmu* was shot in China and was completed before being televised. While the Korean director was in charge of drama production, the Chinese director took responsibility for the drama's action sequences. The director of photography was Korean and the director of production design was Chinese. Although the hero and heroine were played by Koreans, Chinese actresses and actors played significant roles in the drama.

Bichunmu tells an ill-fated love story involving the illegitimate daughter of a Han Chinese family and a Korean swordsman during the Yuan dynasty. It was based on the best-selling Korean comic book written by Hyelin Kim, previously adapted for a Korean movie in 2000. According to Byungjun Song, a representative of Eight Peaks, it was co-produced in order to be faithful to the original story's setting in China and to give life to the original's martial art fantasy.[24] With help from the Chinese martial arts team and production design team, this drama realistically portrays the original setting and provides spectacular action sequences. This project was an attempt by the Korean independent production company to complete a drama before its airing and to meet production costs by pre-sales in China, Japan, and other countries, rather than depending on a domestic broadcaster. With this co-production, the Korean independent production company tried to establish new connections with several domestic broadcasters and to be more actively involved in its distribution throughout Asia.

The Korean co-producers were unable to contract with a Korean broadcaster for television rights, and to date this drama has not been broadcast. Although China's television industry typically completes all production before televising, Korea's television industry is oriented toward the pre-programming system. In contrast to China's television industry, whose main clients are television programmers and distributors, Korea's television industry responds directly to the television audience. In the latter, dramas are typically produced while being televised in order to respond to audience tastes. By completing its production, *Bichunmu* attempted to secure its copyrights in domestic and international markets. However, this drama has considerable difficulties finding a timeslot in local terrestrial television. The domestic broadcasters have shown little interest in the pre-produced drama with a copyright that belongs to an independent production company. Moreover, they have not been assured of the value of the complete production system in terms of ratings. Compared to domestic television dramas which strive to please public sentiment and emotional tempos, this pre-produced drama model represents a substantial risk.

Although *Bichunmu* challenged the existing domestic production system with its co-production model, it failed to build a strong relationship with the Korean broadcaster. The local production culture has motivated the local independent production company to consider co-production as an opportunity, and at the same time, has conditioned its cultural effect.

Conclusion

The transformation of the Korean television drama industry has been facilitated by the ascendancy of *hanliu* throughout Asia. *Hanliu* has encouraged local broadcasters and independent producers to attempt novel strategies aimed at the transnational market. *Hanliu* has also contributed to recent developments within the Korean television industry. As local television markets expand, they are affected by capitalist logic. Television drama is regarded as a cultural product with increasing market value, and drama producers have become more concerned about the distribution, copyright, and marketing of their products.

The trans-border co-production of television dramas between Korea and China has been driven by emerging markets. These co-productions were initially intended to boost the profile of Chinese dramas by employing Korean *hanliu* stars. More recently, co-productions have been used to pool financial resources, to reach wider audiences in the region, and to reduce cultural discount. Co-produced dramas aim to attract pan-Asian audiences and to develop a regional market. The television industry's pursuit of capital beyond national boundaries has driven producers to strategically plan dramas with transnational narratives. However, the market-oriented dramas co-produced by Korean and Chinese producers have shown limited imagination. They tend to reproduce the already-verified characters and plots, install popular stars, and rely upon well-known formats, genres and cultural codes in order to reduce risk and uncertainty in production and distribution.

To co-produce cultural products such as television programs represents a significant challenge for participants with different cultural resources and industrial capacities, different conventions or shared understandings, and from different organizations. Those products usually embody cultural elements that reflect interests and values within the national boundary as well as locally specific cultural conditions. The co-production of television programs means more than working and funding a project together; it makes participants realize and accept degrees of cultural distance between partners.

Co-production of television dramas by Korean and Chinese producers can be considered a part of the globalization process in the Asian media industry. Such transnational projects will continue as long as there is a profitable regional market. The potential for these market-oriented projects to foster cross-cultural understandings and trans-border dialogues should also be questioned. Further research into how trans-border co-production and other media projects for pan-Asian markets affect the formation of cultural regionalization would help us understand the characteristics of transnational "Asian" popular culture.

14

Rescaling the Local and the National: Trans-border Production of Hong Kong TV Dramas in Mainland China

Carol Chow and Eric Ma

New media technologies enable a rapid flow of media materials across national borders. In recent years, studies have examined the processes, forms, difficulties, and impacts of these media flows, especially on the influence of foreign media on audiences and industries in the recipient countries.[1] This chapter focuses on a particular aspect of trans-border media flow. It looks at the career histories and productions of two prominent Hong Kong TV workers: executive director Chik Kei-yi and script-supervisor Chow Yuk-Ming. We also trace the transformation of media representations of China together with changes in the production practices of Hong Kong television dramas. In the 1980s and 1990s, Hong Kong television dramas were very popular in South China, while Mainland dramas made no impact in Hong Kong schedules. This unidirectional flow of media content from Hong Kong to the Mainland has become more complex recently. A significant amount of Hong Kong production has relocated to the Mainland, and this has facilitated a concomitant flow of national geography and historical imageries into the Hong Kong mediascape. The consequence of these flows is what we call the rescaling of Hong Kong's TV drama production.

The term "trans-border production" used in this chapter is unique to geo-cultural politics of the Hong Kong Special Administrative Region (SAR). As everyone knows, Hong Kong is now constitutionally part of the People's Republic of China, albeit under a different administrative system known as "one country, two systems" (*yiguo liangzhi*). Elsewhere in the world, on-location shooting in diverse parts of a nation is standard practice, and would not be considered "trans-border." However, Hong Kong's colonial history and sovereignty transfer add a distinctive cultural and political hue. In short, production in the Mainland becomes a unique *trans*-border practice. This will become clearer in the ensuing discussion of how the early TV drama output of Chik Kei-yi and Chow Yuk-Ming engaged with the formation of Hong Kong's identity and its differentiation from Mainland China.

In effect, the 1997 reunification brought with it a discursive shift from "border" to "boundary" in describing cultural and geographical differentiations between the former colony and the motherland.[2] After 1997 it became less a physical "border," and more an intangible "boundary." However, the atypical combination of "two systems within a single country" creates an inherent contradiction, engendering a disjuncture between Hong Kong and the Mainland that is concomitantly administrative, physical and psychological. The continual existence of a boundary, while more tacit than real, also defines a duality (the local and national) which operates in all political, economic and cultural domains in Hong Kong. In this particular social context, on-location shooting of Hong Kong dramas in the Mainland becomes a complex trans-border process in which negotiations are culturally and politically framed, much more so than in other sites of offshore production.

Through life history interviews, participant observation of location shooting in the Mainland, and a historical comparison of televisual content produced by our two informants Chik and Chow, we examine three issues: first, the economic and historical conditions for the emergence and development of Hong Kong's trans-border production in the Mainland; second, the impact of trans-border production on the rescaling of Hong Kong's identity; and third, the influence of such practices on the creative outputs of the producers. We believe our approach of examining the cultural through the personal illustrates the subtle relations between TV production, geographic specificities, and producers' cultural imagination. Our thesis is that trans-border production of Hong Kong drama is characterized by a paradoxical combination of de-territorialization of production and re-territorialization of national imaginations, whereby inherent tensions enable and engender a dialectic between the local and the national.

Formation of a Flexible and Mobile Trans-border Production Network

In September 2004, we flew to Yinchuan, a remote village in the north-western border of China, to visit Chik Kei-Yi and Chow Yuk-Ming, who were making their new drama serial *The Dance of Passion* (*Huowu huangsha*). These two producers have been producing highly successful TV dramas for fifteen years. During the 1990s, they primarily targeted local audiences, but have included the Mainland audiences in recent years. *The Dance of Passion* is the third trans-border production made by Chik and Chow together, after *Blade Heart* (*Xuezhan xuanyuan,* 2004) and *War and Beauty* (*Jinzhiyunie,* 2004).[3]

A taxi took us to a two-storey hotel where the crew lived. Shooting rundowns were posted on the whiteboard in the hotel lobby, with large Chinese characters of the title of the TV drama, *The Dance of Passion,* written on posters. Huge metal boxes with TVB logo stickers were piled up against the wall of the corridors (see Photos 14.1 and 14.2). These boxes are used for carrying wardrobe, props, and production equipments. A few rooms were transformed into make-up rooms, fitting rooms, an editing room, storage rooms for wardrobes and props, and so on. TVB staff were busily preparing for the following day's shooting in their corresponding "divisions." If the situation required, there were two filming units working twenty-four hours around the clock. The hotel was "colonized" into a place resembling the TVB City in Hong Kong. While the production process was just as routinized as in Hong Kong, the assemblies of the production units were much more mobile and flexible.[4]

A major difference in this colonized TV city, however, implicates a new division of labor in trans-border production. A Mainland production team was employed by TVB on project-based activities. A chief producer and a group of assistants were responsible for coordinating on-location shooting, managing extras and casual artists, and arranging meals, accommodation, transport, and props. They performed an intermediary role between the local social networks of production support and the Hong Kong crew, who were unfamiliar with how things operated in Mainland China. The Mainland team served as an essential component of an emergent network facilitating smooth, flexible, and efficient production.

We followed the crew to their shooting location at Chenbeibao (north side fortress) Western District Movie TV City (hereafter, CBB), where Zhang Yimou made his award-winning film *Red Sorghum.* CBB is famous for its desolate geographic features and historical relics of two deserted fortresses in the wilderness of the north-western frontier of China. About two-thirds of the filming of *The Dance of Passion* was done during this particular production trip. Similar to Hengdian World Studios in Zhejiang Province where Chik made *War and Beauty,* CBB combines TV/film production and cultural tourism.[5] TV and film companies shoot for free, while CCB charges tourists an admission fee to see some of the behind-the-scenes production.

Photo 14.1 Metal boxes in the hotel corridor

Photo 14.2 Chik (right) is explaining the scene to the mainland
production manager (right) and the leading actor (the middle)

With China now actively encouraging trans-national productions, many support services have been routinized. On-location shooting in China provides new production possibilities for Hong Kong TV drama producers who previously were restricted to locations in Hong Kong. In addition to shooting in China's huge studio complexes, Hong Kong producers can also exploit stunning cityscapes in big Mainland cities, which contribute a tantalizing mix of the old and the new. Grand natural landscapes in the vast national territory provide previously unimaginable production sites for Hong Kong producers. Chik's first two on-location shootings in Mainland China, *Fight for Love* (*Tantanqing lianlianwu*, 2001) and *Blade Heart* were shot in Beijing and Chengdu respectively, where the producer could exploit the cityscape and the natural landscape as exotic and scenic backdrops.

In addition to a wide range of choices available for on-location shooting, low production costs in the Mainland are another compelling advantage. During the week of our visit, the production crew was shooting the ending of *The Dance of Passion*. The sequence was somehow ironic: the female protagonist went back to her home town, which was once a rural village in the 1930s, and was now turned into a studio complex for tourists and movie producers. The sequence was designed to be a surreal treatment of the old lady revisiting her past. To achieve this, the director had to intercut the story in the past with the scene in the present. This required a large number of extras or casual artists dressed in costumes of different historical periods. In contrast to Hong Kong, where an extra costs HK$180 for nine hours of shooting, the cost is only RMB 30–50 in the Mainland. Cost advantage allows the production team to hire their desired number of extras for production. Considerable production support is also available. During the shooting of the sequence, many workers were assisting with the set-up of a camera crane. This was rented at almost one-tenth of the cost of the same equipment in Hong Kong. Extra helpers were hired to assist the production team on site. From the production point of view, these resources enabled the Hong Kong team to overcome the financial constraints of producing more serious and grand projects.

In summary, the flexibly aligned Mainland production team, mobile experts and labor, grand studio complexes, exotic locations, natural landscapes, and cheap production support in Mainland China constitute a web of "alliances of talents and resources" upon which a post-Fordist mode of trans-border production is developed.[6] By post-Fordist mode, we refer to a flexible division of labor and sharing of resources which are not common in a factory mode of in-house studio production.[7] With these alliances, Hong Kong TV production is no longer confined to its own territory; it can organize productions in various ways which suit different production needs,[8] thus rendering a flexible yet routinized mode of trans-border production possible.

The nature of the post-Fordist networks that facilitate Hong Kong's trans-border production in Mainland China cannot simply be explained by what Toby Miller calls "the new international division of cultural labor" (NICL).[9] Miller argues that NICL underpins global Hollywood, and suggests that peripheral locations compete on low production costs. Trans-border production in Hong Kong is different. There are two major factors that are unique to the Hong Kong case: China's media reform; and the political-economic transformation of Hong Kong brought about by the sovereignty change in 1997.

As mentioned above, on-location shooting in Mainland China can help alleviate the problems of the shortage of location choices and high production costs. This does accord with the NICL thesis. It also makes available a more diversified range of dramas. But this trend toward trans-border production cannot be realized without the endorsement of the PRC government. China's economic reform and media decentralization policy are fundamental to the emergence of trans-border networks, particularly in regard to what can broadly be termed the joint venture model.[10] Since the "open door policy" of the late 1970s, the Chinese media have undergone gradual reform. Asia Television Limited (ATV) was granted permission to jointly produce dramas with Mainland TV stations in 1983. In 1984, TVB broadcast *Guangdong tieqiaosan*,[11] co-produced with Guangdong Province Television Limited.

The first large-scale trans-border TV drama production was TVB's *The Grand Canal* (*Da yunhe*, 1987). It was shot in Xi'an and assisted by Xi'an Television Station.[12] However, according to Liu Shi-yu, the executive producer of the serial, the assistance offered by the Mainland team was very limited. In fact, trans-border productions before 1997 were mostly concentrated in locations near Guangdong Province where Hong Kongers had better socio-cultural connections.[13] Since the emergence of commercial studios in the 1990s, pools of mobile production talents and labor (the main constituents of trans-border networks) have steadily developed and nested around major studios. In this regard, media commercialization[14] in the PRC is a major factor leading to the formation of the post-Fordist networks that have facilitated dispersed trans-border Hong Kong TV productions in the Mainland. From Guangdong Province to Xinjiang, and from Beijing to Zhejiang, the territorial trajectory of Hong Kong TV production underscores the unique and shifting geo-political position of Hong Kong in relation to the PRC.

Apart from the chain reactions triggered by media commercialization in Mainland China, the changing political-economy in the Hong Kong TV industry since 1997 has also accelerated the normalization and routinization of trans-border production. Chik and Chow's career histories reflect this transformation. They were originally producers whose major works were locally based (in terms of both production and textual content). Chik's first Mainland drama was *Fight for Love* — a co-production between TVB and China Central Television (CCTV) produced in 2001. Chik is renowned for, and experienced in, grand productions. His assignment to this joint project was an indication that TVB was serious about production collaborations with the Mainland. Chik argues: "The local market has been saturated. Everyone is looking to the Mainland market." Since then, Chik and Chow have produced three major productions in the Mainland.

Indeed, the timing of the co-production between TVB and CCTV coincided with the expansion of TVB's market in Mainland China. A month before China acceded to the World Trade Organization (WTO) in December 2001, TVB and CCTV formed a joint venture for the buying, selling, and distribution of global and Greater China TV programs.[15] This move shows the privileged position of Hong Kong, later illustrated by the signing of the Closer Economic Partnership Arrangement (CEPA) that has granted Hong Kong easier access to the Mainland China market for its products and services.[16]

Rescaling the Local and the National

Trans-border productions provide fresh visual treatments for Hong Kong audiences and hybridized content which is more sensitive to Mainland audiences. There is no doubt that the massive China market is attractive to media institutions from all over the world. The description of post-Fordist production in the above section is applicable to many institutions which seek to exploit China's rising market and abundant resources. The Hong Kong TV industry is one of these institutions, but it is unique in the sense that it is a cultural industry sensitive to the historical, economic, and political conditions of its production. As a Special Administration Region of China, Hong Kong has the competitive advantage of geo-cultural proximity. Both in terms of content and market projection, the Hong Kong TV industry is actively negotiating and rescaling its strategies from local to the national scale of operations. This illustrates the cultural politics of trans-border production.

Chik Kei-yi's career history and his collaborations with Chow Yuk-Ming illustrate how TV dramas were influential in the formation of a Hong Kong cultural identity. In 1976, Chik began working as a log-keeper in the Film Unit in TVB. He then transferred to work for Kam Kwok-leung as his production and administrative assistant. Kam was one of TVB's founding executive producers, renowned for making avant-garde dramas. As Chik recalls, "Kam is very demanding. He pays attention to details, loves brand products and expresses his preferences in his productions. He is sensitive to the brands of props and fashions used and worn by the characters. He knows how different brand products work and what the audiences want. Working with him is very pleasurable. You enjoy the process and learn lots of things other than merely the basics of television production." Through his dramas, Kam introduced the lifestyles of people living in big cities in other parts of the world. Television producers at that time served as cultural intermediaries for Hong Kong people who yearned for modern urban living. Chik contends that what he learned from Kam has been important throughout his career. He has been quite conscious in seeing his works not as mere entertainment but as a cultural form which can mediate his own interpretations of what modern and sophisticated living should be for the people of Hong Kong.

In the early 1990s, ATV tried to compete with the dominant TVB for ratings and talent. Chik left TVB and began to produce his own works at ATV, where he teamed up with his creative partner Chow Yuk-Ming. At that time, ATV was eager to reposition itself through innovative works. Chik and Chow were provided with strong production support and the freedom to produce experimental works such as *The Butcher School Master I & II*.[17] However, ATV failed to compete successfully with TVB, and Chik and Chow finally returned to TVB. Capitalizing on their ATV experiments, the team produced some successful action and epic series at TVB.[18] Featuring a wide range of characters — tycoons, professionals and grassroots workers — their dramas during this period were embedded with values of commercialism, professionalism, law and order, and a belief in social mobility. These are considered to be some of the core values shared by the people of Hong Kong. In their dramas, Hong Kong was a liberal, modern, and civilized society.

Nationalistic historical themes did exist in some period dramas before 1997. For instance, *Qiu Jin: A Woman to Remember* (*Qiu Jin*, 1984) and *Shanghai Conspiracy* (*Shanghai da fengbao*, 1986) were staged respectively in the Qing dynasty and the New China period (*minguo*). However, these early productions with nationalistic themes were produced in artificial studio settings in Hong Kong, and the nation was represented in an abstract manner. Without a coherent narrative of the nation in schools and in popular media during the 1980s, Hong Kong people generally positioned the Chinese nation in remote histories, vague geographic representations, and ambiguous imaginations. In short, the vivid representation of Hong Kong and the obscure representation of the nation in the dramas produced in the colonial era fostered a strong cultural boundary between Hong Kong and the Mainland.

"Mundane spatiality" constitutes "ordinary national politics"[19] and facilitates what Billig called "banal nationalism."[20] It is the space within everyday life where a sense of collectivity is played out. In the colonial years, mundane spatiality for Hong Kong viewers was largely confined to the territory of Hong Kong. In the media, Hong Kong was an international city without a nation. In everyday life, the territory of Hong Kong was the stage for the "people." Crossing the border into the Mainland was even considered a venture into the space of otherness. However, since the 1990s, when trans-border traveling has become more frequent, mundane spatiality has gradually been rescaled from the local to the national. Hong Kong people travel frequently to the Mainland and integrate their trans-border experiences into their imagination of the national collective, which is spatially expanding the Special Administrative Region. This shifting mundane spatiality is evident in both the trans-border experiences of TV producers and the concrete representations of national history and geography in the texts.

When Hong Kong producers explore new possibilities of shooting on Mainland sites, they become more aware of the complex and pluralistic social situations in Mainland China. Many start to revise their stereotypical imaginations of the nation. As Chik said in our interview, for a very long time he did not like China. To him, China was a primitive and corrupt country. However, following a few production trips to the Mainland, he now realizes that China is much bigger than what he had previously imagined. When he visited Beijing in the production trip of *Fight for Love*, he was inspired and enchanted by the compassion of the people, the peculiar cityscape which juxtaposes traditional style with modern style, and the swift progress made. Yet he was also distressed by the lack of an established system of regulations, Mainlanders' reliance on social capital (*guanxi*) to get things done, and the perpetuation of conservative ideas that restrict the creativity of the people.

When he made *Blade Heart* in Chengdu and *The Dance of Passion* in the hilly district of Xianxi, he came to the realization that the majority of people in these less developed districts are still living below the poverty line. Several times, Chik was forced to give up his original shooting plan because of the restrictive conditions of these places. Sometimes local peasants demanded unreasonable prices for on-location shooting. Once, in a drastic move some people in a village cut off the flow of a small river halfway through a shooting session and demanded more money. In another case, Chik was forced to abandon his shooting in a *yaodong* because of the same reason. Despite all these issues, Chik thinks that the spectacular landscapes in the Mainland are good for TV productions. With mixed emotions of excitement and frustration, these trans-border experiences have changed Chik from a typical Hong Konger who dislikes and avoids China to someone who acknowledges the complexity — the problems as well as the opportunities — of producing drama in the Mainland.

Another aspect of these trans-border experiences is the cultivation of an historical consciousness that is rooted in the physical sites of on-location shooting. Admitting that he had only weak knowledge of Chinese history before, Chik has become interested in the history of the sites he visits — although it is an interest instrumentally tied up with the motivation of producing popular dramas. Chik recalls, "The CCB studio is a historical heritage (two fortresses built in the Ming and Qing dynasties), the site is a piece of history before our eyes. It saves much of our effort in creating and producing a believable set. Because there are historical relics on the spot, we can just shoot everything there, and we have a believable drama." (see Photos 14.3 and 14.4).

Photo 14.3 A scene taken in the desolate landscape of CCB studio

Photo 14.4   The ending sequence shot on the fortress of CCB studio

Awareness of the geographical distinctiveness and place-bound historical specificity are then transformed into symbolic resources of the creative team and are visualized in the drama texts.[21] The visualization portrays the place as an ethnoscape of everyday life instead of exotic landscapes such as those represented in the fictional drama produced in the earlier stage of trans-border production. By "an ethnoscape of everyday life," we refer to the life-world of people, encompassing a specific set of rituals, habits, customs, norms, and everyday routines. On location, shooting in the Mainland sensitizes producers to pick up those details and insert them into the dramas they produce.

The Dance of Passion is a drama set in the 1930s which revolves around the rivalries within and between two big families in a northern village in China. Chik and Chow deliberately chose more strongly built actors and asked the make-up stylist to darken their skin so as to match the images of northern people. The habits and routines of northern people are integrated into the plots, thus inscribing regional specificities into the televisual texts. *The Dance of Passion* is just one example of a more general trend of the concretization of national geographical space in Hong Kong TV dramas.

Besides period dramas, other trans-border drama productions in modern settings, such as *Fight for Love* (staged in Beijing) by Chik, depict the trans-border experiences of Hong Kongers and Mainlanders, and various everyday practices in different parts of China. These dramas have similarly contributed to the reconfiguration of the Hong Kong television landscape. They are crucial vehicles reconnecting Hong Kong into the collective imagination of the nation.[22]

Visualizations of the nation in concrete time and space in trans-border televisual texts — whether urban or rural, historical or contemporary — have been reconfiguring the mundane spatiality in the local mediascape of Hong Kong. This mundane spatiality blurs the boundary between Hong Kong and the Mainland, and renationalizes Hong Kong's imagined community to include historical and geographic specificities. This reconfiguration is in fact a rescaling of a once very strong Hong Kong identity from the local to the national scale. The process is non-linear: producers' personal psychological responses toward the nation and its history acquired via trans-border productions are crucial to the reconfiguration of the televisual map. Yet it is not a simple erasure of cultural boundary. There are subtle and complicated negotiations between the local and national scales in trans-border productions. In the following section, we examine these negotiations in the rescaling process.

The Local–national Dialectics in Trans-border Productions

It is important to consider the changing dynamics of reception in this trans-border picture we are describing, particularly the changing composition of the Hong Kong television audience. In the 1970s and 1980s, Hong Kong audiences were regarded as somewhat homogenous. But local audiences are no longer a group of people with relatively similar socio-cultural backgrounds. Hong Kong TV audiences are a very diverse group of locals and migrants. And added to this mix are the potential audiences of the Mainland. The relations between TV producers, their outputs, and audiences have shifted from a relatively synchronic to a disjunctive mode.

The synchronic mode refers to a convergence of expectations among producers and audiences. Chik explains this convergence of expectations in the 1970s and 1980s. First, a group of visionary producers played a leading role in cultivating new trends for commercial TV programs. Kam Kwok-leung, Chik's mentor, was one such producer who tried to introduce new lifestyles to Hong Kong people through TV productions. Second, the TV industry in its early years had not yet been fully institutionalized, and TV producers had license to experiment with creative formats. Lastly, at that time television was relatively new to local audiences, who were less demanding and eager to seek new information and entertainment in various television programs. Because of these contextual factors, there was a wider range of TV drama formats — from mainstream works such as martial arts series modified from Jin Yong's novels to modern melodramatic serials and a few experimental dramas.

Since the 1990s, what constitutes a "good" TV drama has become a rather complicated question. Producers, broadcasters, and audiences may have different expectations, and sometimes these expectations diverge. In order to maintain control in a period of financial crisis, broadcasters are seeking out standardized production practices. Meanwhile, audiences have become more demanding and discriminating. "They complain a lot," says Chik. These changes have led to a more conservative and restrictive production environment, which discourages innovative, adventurous, and risky productions. It creates problems for experienced and visionary producers like Chik and Chow, who try to be innovative.

There are new tensions, as well as opportunities for change. As Chik observes, new production sites and creative ideas have been developed in various trans-border projects. At the same time, broadcasters are struggling to understand the expanding markets in China which are more complicated and diverse. Some audiences in urban centres are more sophisticated, but others are more conservative and may be less receptive to innovative works. As Chik argues, "if we move too fast, there is a danger of audiences turning away." In fact, Chik's second trans-border production, *Blade Heart* — a non-traditional martial arts drama — performed poorly in both Hong Kong and the Mainland.

Since the mid-1990s, Hong Kong drama productions have been engaged in the process of rescaling and negotiation between the local and the national. Apart from the sharing of production resources, producers have become more aware of the creative potential of "mutual referencing" of cultural and media texts from both sides of the border. The idea for Chik's latest production, *The Dance of Passion,* is a modified version of a Mainland novel, *Bailuyuan.* TVB had tried to purchase the copyright for production but failed.

War and Beauty (2004) is about the lives of the concubines of a Qing Emperor. The story involves internecine squabbles and power struggle by secret alliances and conspiracies. It is a nice blend of the local and the national, the contemporary and the historical. Instead of presenting an ordinary Qing drama, Chik and Chow used a concrete historical setting — the Forbidden City — and mixed it with office politics in the contemporary business world. A local and modern theme is represented in a national and historical context. Many previous TVB dramas were staged in the Qing Dynasty, but *War and*

Beauty was the first to be partly shot in Beijing's Forbidden City, where emperors and concubines lived. The confined space in the palace builds up tensions. Shooting in the authentic Forbidden City and the replica palace in Zhejiang's Hengdian World Studios offered spacious and realistic locations. This was also a selling point of the drama.

On-location shooting does not only increase the marketing value of the drama, but also enhances viewers' involvements and gives them a realist sense of history. Despite the usual criticisms concerning Hong Kong period dramas' negligence of historical details, some Mainland netizens praised the production as an "historical drama" — a rare compliment for a Hong Kong production. These compliments from Mainland audiences might not be accurate evaluations of the drama, but they do indicate a reterritorialization of national history in the mediascape of Hong Kong.

Chik recalls that the idea of the story, picked up from everyday observations, is just about women's squabbles. "When you read local newspapers, you will find news about women quareling with each other almost every day," he said. Textual displacement of local tastes by national market expectations will often alienate the Hong Kong audience. Just how did they circumvent this problem? Chik and Chow purposely preserved some local elements in the design of characters, the costumes, and the cinematography. For instance, instead of creating characters in a binary distinction of good or evil, they featured characters which were neither wicked nor virtuous. The producers were well aware of the fact that this treatment may not be welcomed by Mainland audiences. However, they knew that Hong Kong audiences would be fond of the subtleties because they have been veteran viewers of local TV dramas and are dissatisfied with stereotypical representations of heroes and villains. For them, local audiences come first, Mainland resources are the added value.

This negotiation of cultural boundaries eventually renders the text a crossover between the local and the national. Their strategy has proved to be a success. Reviewers found the delicate costumes appealing and the plots intriguing. More interestingly, this period drama was read as a story about contemporary office politics by both Hong Kong and Mainland audiences. Interviews with Chik and Chow, the mastermind of the drama, appeared in popular as well as elite media in both Hong Kong and Mainland China.[23] This unusual credit to the producers — as well as the obvious success of the drama — suggests that trans-border productions can provide new creative possibilities for cutting-edge dramas that are capable of meeting the demand of broadcaster, while reaching out to the Mainland market, and revitalizing the domestic TV industry.

Conclusion

By drawing on the field trip data and the career history of two successful producers, we have demonstrated how trans-border production of Hong Kong TV dramas in the Mainland has been routinized and normalized within flexible and mobile production networks; how it has transformed mediated mundane spatiality from a local to the national scale; and how it has provided new creative opportunities for drama production.

We proposed to investigate three issues at the beginning of the chapter. With reference to the first on trans-border production, we have described the emergence of the post-Fordist production mode which advocates a flexible division of labor and promotes sharing of resources not found in in-house studio production. De-territorializing and relocating TVB's production routines in trans-border production networks, trans-border TV producers combine the efficiency of the TVB production format and the flexibility and mobility of trans-border support to enhance creativity and production possibilities.

As for the ideology of trans-border television dramas, we have illustrated how the once denationalized Hong Kong TV drama has been injected with vivid representations of national histories and geographies. The contextual changes in the political economy of TV production after 1997 have allowed for this new cultural (re)mapping. Deterritorialized production thus paradoxically leads to reterritorialization of cultural texts. It is a process of complex rescaling of the local to the national in TV dramas produced trans-borderly — that is, in Mainland China. The changing perception of the nation by individual producers is one of the key factors contributing to the reconfiguration of the imagined boundary.

Finally, we have illustrated, through examining the career history of two producers, the impact of concrete geographic and historical sites on their conceptualization of TV dramas. The creative mind is the product of specific historical conditions. The local-centricity of Hong Kong producers bears the mark of Hong Kong's colonial history. Our case study gives a concrete example of how rediscovery of the national territory is revising the cultural maps of TV dramas created by Hong Kong producers. Their interpretations of the geographic and historical "texts" embedded in specific sites permeate the televisual texts they produce, and this trend is likely to continue. A dual tension between the local and the national is operating in the production of televisual texts. This is the new landscape of production which we have observed.

Notes

Introduction

1. See *China Television Drama Report, 2002–2003* (Beijing: CSM Publishing, 2003).
2. For diasporic use of media, including TV drama, see John Sinclair, Audrey Yue, Gay Hawkins, Kee Pookong and Josephin Fox, "Chinese cosmopolitanism and media use," in Stuart Cunningham and John Sinclair (eds.), *Floating Lives: The Media and Asian Diasporas* (Lanham: Rowman and Littlefield, 2001). Discussions of Chinese TV drama serials have appeared periodically. For a selection, see James Lull, *China Turned On: Television, Reform and Resistance* (London: Routledge, 1991); Lisa Rofel, " 'Yearnings': Televisual love and melodramatic politics in contemporary China," *American Ethnologist* (1994) 21 (4): 700–722; Yin Hong, "Meaning, production, consumption: The history and reality of television drama in China," in Stephanie Hemelryk Donald, Michael Keane and Yin Hong (eds.), *Media in China: Consumption, Content and Crisis* (London: RoutledgeCurzon, 2002), pp. 28–40; Michael Keane, "Television drama in China: Engineering souls for the market," in Timothy J. Craig and Richard King (eds.), *Global Goes Local: Popular Culture in Asia* (Vancouver: UBC Press, 2002), pp. 120–137; Geremie Barmé, "The graying of Chinese culture," in Kuan Hsin-chi and Maurice Brosseau (eds.), *China Review 1992* (Hong Kong: Chinese University Press, 1992) (13): 1–51. See also Sheldon Lu, "Soap opera in China: The transnational politics of visuality, sexuality, and masculinity," *Cinema Journal* (2000) 40 (1): 25–47 and Wanning Sun, "A Chinese in the new world:

Television dramas, global cities and travels to modernity," *Inter-Asia Cultural Studies* (2001) 2 (1): 81–94.

3.   Ying Zhu, "*Yongzheng Dynasty* and Chinese primetime television drama," *Cinema Journal* (2005) 44 (4): 3–17.

4.   For a discussion, see Ien Ang, *Watching Dallas: Soap Opera and the Melodramatic Imagination* (London: Methuen, 1985); Robert C. Allen (ed.), *To Be Continued . . . : Soap Operas Around the World* (London: Routledge, 1995).

5.   Ana Lopez, "The melodrama in Latin America," in Marcia Landy (ed.), *Imitations of Life: A Reader on Film and Television Drama* (Detroit, MC: Wayne State University Press, 1991); John Sinclair, "Mexico, Brazil and the Latin World," in John Sinclair, Elizabeth Jacka and Stuart Cunningham (eds.), *New Patterns in Global Television: Peripheral Vision* (Oxford: Oxford University Press, 1996); Nico Vink, *The Telenovela and Emancipation: A Study of Television and Social Change in Brazil* (Amsterdam: Royal Tropical Institute 1988); Robert C. Allen (ed.), *To Be Continued . . . : Soap Operas Around the World.*

6.   John Corner, "Framing the new," in Su Holmes and Deborah Jermyn (eds.), *Understanding Reality Television* (London: Routledge, 2004); Jon Dovey, "Confession and the unbearable lightness of factual," *Media International Australia* (2002) 104: 101–119.

7.   Koichi Iwabuchi (ed.), *Feeling Asian Modernities: Transnational Consumption of Japanese TV Dramas* (Hong Kong: Hong Kong University Press, 2004).

8.   Qu Chunjing and Ying Zhu, *Zhongmei dianshi bijiao yanjiu* (A comparative anthology of Chinese and US television research) (Shanghai: Sanlian Press, 2005).

9.   Ying Zhu's *Television in Post-Reform China: Serial Dramas, Confucian Leadership, and Global Television Market* (London: Routledge, 2008) explores the political, economic, and cultural forces, locally and globally, which have shaped the evolution of Chinese prime-time television dramas, and the way that these dramas have actively been engaged in the major intellectual and policy debates concerning the path, steps, and speed of China's economic and political modernization during the post-Deng Xiaoping era. The book also provides cross-cultural comparisons that parallel the textual and institutional strategies of transnational Chinese-language TV dramas with dramas from the three leading centers of transnational television production, the US, Brazil and Mexico in Latin America, and the Korean-led East Asia region.

10.   Zhong Yibin and Huang Wangnan, *Zhongguo dianshi yishu fazhanshi* (The history of television arts) (Zhejiang: Zhejiang renmin chubanshe, 1994), p. 8.

11.   Zhong Yibin and Huang Wangnan, *Zhongguo dianshi yishu fazhanshi*, p. 7.

12.   In 1982, CCTV broadcast a total of 220 episodes of television drama: 14 percent of these focused on rural life, 8 percent portrayed the work style of CCP cadres, 31 percent concerned topics such as young workers, love, marriage, and criticism of society, while 16 percent were about children's

lives. See Yu Jinglu, "The structure and function of Chinese television 1978–89," in Chin-Chuan Lee (ed.), *Voices of China: The Interplay of Politics and Journalism* (New York: Guildford Press, 1990), p. 80.

13. James Lull, *China Turned On: Television, Reform and Resistance*.

14. Zhang Jiabing, "Strike up the music of the times: On the main melody and television drama," *Chinese Television* (1994) 9: 2–5.

15. Cai Xiang, "1982–1992: Woguo tongsu dianshiju de huigu yu qianzhan" (1982–1992: Chinese television drama — looking back and to the future), *Dianshi yishu* (Television Drama Art) (1993) 4: 7.

16. For a discussion of the making of *Kewang*, see Jianying Zha, *China Pop: How Soap Operas, Tabloids, and Bestsellers Are Transforming a Culture* (New York: New Press, 1995); also Geremie Barmé, "The graying of Chinese culture," p. 2.

17. See Feng Yingbing, "Li Ruihuan deng lingdao tongzhi yu Kewang juzu tan fanrong wenyi zhi lu" (Li Ruihuan and other leaders talk with the production team of Kewang about the road for the flourishing of literature and art), *Renmin Ribao* (People's Daily), overseas edition, January 9, 1991, p. 1.

18. Yang Wenyong and Xie Xizhang (eds.), *Kewang chongjibo* (The shockwave of Yearning) (Beijing: Guangming ribao chubanshe, 1991).

19. Zhong Yibin and Huang Wangnan, *Zhongguo dianshi yishu fazhan shi* (The history of the development of Chinese television arts) (Zhejiang: Zhejiang People's Publishing, 1995), p. 370, quote translated by author.

20. The following survey of the dominant Chinese drama genres is taken from Ruoyun Bai's dissertation, *Anticorruption Television Drama: Between Propaganda and Popular Culture in Globalizing China* (2007).

21. Lijuan Wang, "Thoughts on the popularity of historical dramas" (Guanyu lishiju zouhong de sikao), *Zhongguo dianshi* (Chinese Television) (2002) 10: 18–24.

22. Jianmin Gao, "Several issues concerning domestic television drama production" (Guanyu guochan dianshiju zhizuo de jige wenti), *Zhongguo guangbo yingshi* (Chinese Radio, Film and Television) (2000) 24: 62–65.

23. Yuanyuan Luo, "*Draw your sword* drew the highest ratings of all CCTV television dramas" (Yangshi daxi shoushilü Liangjian duokui), *Huashang bao* (Chinese Business News), December 9, 2005.

24. John Fiske and John Hartley, *Reading Television* (London: Methuen, 1978), reproduced in Horace Newcomb (ed.), *Television: The Critical View*, third edition (New York: Oxford University Press, 1982), p. 496.

25. Raymond Williams, *The Long Revolution* (London: Chatto and Windus, 1961).

26. Horace Newcomb and Paul Hirsch, "Television as a cultural forum," in Horace Newcomb (ed.), *Television: The Critical View*, sixth edition (New York: Oxford University Press, 2000).

27. Newcomb and Hirsch, "Television as a cultural forum," p. 564.

28. "Lack of savvy behind cultural trade deficit," *China Daily*, April 19, 2005.
29. See, for example, Michael Keane, "Facing off on the final frontier: China, the WTO and national sovereignty," *Media International Australia* (2002) 105: 130–146.

Chapter 1   *Yongzheng Dynasty* and Authoritarian Nostalgia

1. Dramas with an anti-corruption theme set in contemporary times appeared in the early 2000s, with endorsement from the CCP leadership. For detailed discussion, see Chapter 3 in this volume.
2. The book is adapted from Eryue He's 1998 novel, *Yongzheng Dynasty*.
3. For detailed discussion, see Joseph Fewsmith, "The emergence of neo-conservatism," in Joseph Fewsmith (ed.), *China Since Tiananmen: The Politics of Transition* (Cambridge: Cambridge University Press, 2001), pp. 75–100.
4. See Wang Chaohua's introductory chapter to his edited book, *One China, Many Paths* (London: Verso, 2003), p. 11.
5. Ibid., pp. 16–17.
6. Joseph Fewsmith, "The emergence of neo-conservatism," in Joseph Fewsmith (ed.), *China Since Tiananmen: The Politics of Transition* (Cambridge: Cambridge University Press, 2001), p. 87.
7. Ibid., p. 93. He Xin attended the conference.
8. His view on late Qing's Kang-Liang Reformation was endorsed in another drama series, *Marching towards the Republic* (*Zouxiang gonghe,* 2003).
9. Wang Chaohua, 2003.
10. Wang Hui is now a political science professor at Tsinghua University.
11. See Wang Hui's essay, "Dangdai zhongguo de sixiang zhuangkuang yu xiandaixing wenti" (The circumstance of contemporary Chinese thought and the problem of modernity), *Wenyi zhengming* No. 11 (1998): 20.
12. Wang's own work draws on a wide range of Western thinkers, from the French historian Fernand Braudel to the globalization theorist Immanuel Wallerstein.
13. See the English translation of Wang Hui's essay, "The 1989 social movement and the historical roots of China's neoliberalism," in Hui Wang, Theodore Huters and R. Karl (ed.), *China's New Order: Society, Politics, and Economy in Transition* (Cambridge, MA: Harvard University, 2003), pp. 112–114.
14. Joseph Fewsmith, "The emergence of neo-conservatism," pp. 75–100.
15. It is the bill that both foreign investors in China and Chinese businessmen had been lobbying for. The bill was eventually passed in March, 2007 at the National People's Congress, the annual two-week gathering of the Communist Party-controlled legislative body.
16. See Pankaj Mishra, "China's new leftist," *New York Times*, December 15,

2006. Available: http://www.nytimes.com/2006/10/15/magazine/
15leftist.html [accessed April 15, 2007].

17. Intellectuals advising the state have been part of an old Chinese tradition.

18. See Pankaj Mishra, "China's new leftist."

19. Joseph Fewsmith, "The emergence of neo-conservatism," pp. 125–126.

20. Hu Mei, "Yige mingzu de shengsheng sisi" [Life and death of a nation],
    Dianying dianshi yishu yianjou (1999) 3: 83–86.

21. His alliance with the government earned him the lasting enmity of the
    Chinese intellectual circle. Hu's desire to disassociate herself with He is
    understandable.

22. Zhu himself is reportedly an ardent follower of the show. See Alexandra A.
    Seno, "High-ranking hit," *Asiaweek Online*. Available: www.asiaweek.com/
    asiaweek/99/0226/feat8.html [accessed February 26, 1999].

23. See an interview with the actor published in *China TV* (*Zhongguo dianshi*),
    December 25–28, 2001.

Chapter 2   Family Saga Serial Dramas and Reinterpretation of Cultural Traditions

1. David Thorburn, "Television melodrama", in Horace Newcomb (ed.),
   Television: The Critical View, 7th edition (New York: Oxford University
   Press, 2006), pp. 438–450.

2. Robert C. Allen, *Speaking of Soap Operas* (Chapel Hill: University of North
   Carolina Press, 1985).

3. David Thorburn, "Television melodrama", pp. 438–450; p. 439.

4. Horace Newcomb, " 'This is not Al Dente': Sopranos and the new meaning
   of 'television'," in Horace Newcomb (ed.), *Television: The Critical View*,
   pp. 561–578.

5. Arvind Rajagopal, "Mediating modernity: Theorizing reception in a non-
   Western society," in James Curran and Myung-Jin Park (eds.), *De-Westernizing
   Media Studies* (New York: Taylor and Francis, Inc., 2000), pp. 293–304;
   p. 293.

6. Anne McLaren, "Chinese cultural revivalism: Changing gender constructions
   in the Yangtze River delta," in Krishna Sen and Maila Stivens (eds.), *Gender
   and Power in Affluent Asia* (London and New York: Routledge, 1998), pp. 195–
   221.

7. Sheldon H. Lu, "Postmodernity, popular culture, and the intellectual: A
   report on post-Tiananmen China," *Boundary 2*, 23, no. 2 (summer 1996):
   139–169.

8. Guo played a significant role in the birth of Chinese New Wave films as the
   Art Supervisor of Guangxi Film Studio in the early 1980s. He encouraged
   new film school graduates like Zhang Yimou and Zhang Junzhao to explore

new filmmaking methods and guided their "youth production team," facilitating the creation of a groundbreaking work of the fifth generation, *One and Eight*. It is no coincidence that *Grand Mansion Gate* managed to gather many Chinese film celebrities to play supporting roles, among them, Zhang Yimou, Chen Kaige, Tian Zhuangzhuang, and He Qun.

9. The focus of this school was romance and urban life. These writers were widely denigrated as commercial and ideologically backward during an age when literature in China was dominated by the leftist politics and European aesthetics of the New Culture Movement in the 1920s. Writers of the "Mandarin Duck and Butterfly" never accepted the belittling label themselves.

10. Lin Yutang, *Moment in Peking: A Novel of Contemporary Chinese Life* (New York: The John Day Company, 1939).

11. David Thorburn, "Television melodrama," p. 440.

12. John Fiske, *Television Culture* (London: Routledge, 1987).

13. Other serial dramas with Chinese entrepreneurs as heroes include: *The Big Dye-House (Da ranfang)*, a rags-to-riches story about the dyeing industry in Shandong Province in the Republican era; *White Silver Valley (Bai yin gu)*, which depicts the Shanxi banking industry in the late Qing dynasty; *Top Restaurant under Heaven (Tianxia diyi lou)*, about the history of Quanjude Restaurant, which is famous for its Beijing Roast Duck; and *Shattered Jade (Yu sui)*, about an antique dealer during the Japanese expansion in China in the 1930s.

14. For a study of contemporary representations of masculinity in Chinese cultural industry, see Sheldon H. Lu, "Soap opera in China: The transnational politics of visuality, sexuality, and masculinity," *Cinema Journal* (2000) 40:1, 25–47.

15. Chris Berry reviews Kam Louie's *Theorising Chinese Masculinity: Society and Gender in China* (Cambridge: Cambridge University Press, 2002), in *Intersections: Gender, History and Culture in the Asian Context*, Issue 8, October 2002. Available: http://wwwsshe.murdoch.edu.au/intersections/issue8/berry_review.html [accessed May 22, 2006].

16. David Ownby, "Approximations of Chinese bandits: Perverse rebels, romantic heroes, or frustrated bachelors?", in Susan Brownell and Jeffrey N. Wasserstrom (eds.), *Chinese Femininities, Chinese Masculinities: A Reader* (Berkeley/Los Angeles: University of California Press, 2002), pp. 226–250.

17. The Boxers were a late nineteenth-century Chinese secret society rebelling against foreign influence in China during the final years of the Qing dynasty. In June 1900, thousands of Boxers occupied Beijing and besieged the foreigners and the Chinese Christians there. Hundreds died in the chaos. The siege was lifted in August by an international force of about 20,000 troops, consisting mainly of British, French, Russian, American, German, and Japanese, which occupied Beijing and ended the uprising. See Jonathan Spence, *The Search for Modern China* (New York: W.W. Norton and Co. 1990), pp. 231–235.

18. An article in *Beijing Youth Daily* on May 19, 2001 called *Grand Mansion Gate* "a museum of schemes," attributing the high ratings partly to the variety of tactics and schemes demonstrated in the show. The article also warned of "the dangerous tendency" of admiring and beautifying these schemes through the creation of the drama. See Yu Jia'Ao, "Yifenwei'er kan Dazhaimen" (Divide one to two to look at *Grand Mansion Gate*). Available: http://www.people.com.cn/GB/wenyu/64/130/20010519/468831.html [accessed June 16, 2006].

19. Liu Jianghua, "Zhang Henshui's descendent comment on *The Story of a Noble Family*: Idol actors hard to make either side happy." Jin Yang Net. Available: http://ent.sina.com.cn/m/2003-04-11/1239144362.html [accessed July 24, 2007].

20. Ren Yan, "*Moment in Peking* is on, comparison of new and old versions causes controversies." Beijing Entertainment Newsletter. Available: http://ent.sina.com.cn/v/m/2005-10-31/0144880460.html [accessed July 24, 2007].

21. Michael Schudson, "Culture and the integration of national societies," *International Social Science Journal* (1994) 46: 63–81.

Chapter 3   "Clean Officials," Emotional Moral Community, and Anti-corruption Television Dramas

1. See Xueliang Ding, "The illicit asset stripping of Chinese state firms," *The China Journal*, 43 (2000): 1–28; Ting Gong, "Dangerous collusion: Corruption as a collective venture in contemporary China," *Communist and Post-Communist Studies*, 35, no. 1 (2002): 85–103; Hilton Root, "Corruption in China: Has it become systemic?" *Asian Survey*, 36, no. 8 (1996): 741–757; Andrew Wedeman, "The intensification of corruption in China," *The China Quarterly*, no. 180 (2004): 895–921; Yan Sun, *Corruption and Market in Contemporary China* (Ithaca, NY: Cornell University Press, 2004).

2. "The Chinese Communist Party Center starts to investigate into the serious discipline violation of Comrade Chen Liangyu," *People's Daily* [online version, September 25, 2006]. Available: http://www.people.com.cn.

3. For the notion of hegemony, see Todd Gitlin, "Prime-time ideology: The hegemonic process in television entertainment," *Social Problems,* 26 (1979): 251–266; Stuart Hall, "Culture, media, and the 'ideological effect'," in James Curran, Michael Gurevitch and Janet Woollacott (eds.), *Mass Communication and Society* (London: Edward Arnold, 1977), 315-345; James Lull, *Media, Communication, Culture: A Global Approach* (New York: Columbia University Press, 1995).

4. Benedict Anderson, *Imagined Communities: Reflections on the Origin and Spread of Nationalism* (London and New York: Verso, 1991).

5. George A. Hayden, *Crime and Punishment in Medieval Chinese Drama: Three Judge Pao Plays* (Cambridge, MA: Harvard University Press, 1978), p. 15.

6. Quoted in Hayden, p. 18.

7. See Ding Zhaoqin, *Suwenxue zhong de baogong* (Lord Bao in Popular Culture) (Taipei: Weijin Publishing House, 2000).

8. Ibid.

9. Wang Yi, "Mingdai tongsu xiaoshuo zhong qingguan gushi de xingsheng jiqi wenhua yiyi" (Qing guan stories in popular novels of the Ming period and their cultural meanings), in *Wenxue yichan* (Literary Legacy) no. 5 (2000): 67–80.

10. Guan Lianhai, " 'Pure as Snow' won critical acclaim," *Beijing Evening News,* February 20, 2001.

11. In imperial China, an official of the seventh grade was among the lowest levels of bureaucracy.

12. Episode 11, *Pure as Snow.*

13. Episode 2, *Pure as Snow.*

14. Episode 12, *Pure as Snow.*

15. Simon Cottle, "Mediatized rituals: Beyond manufacturing consent," in *Media, Culture and Society* 48, no. 3 (2006): 411–432; 414.

16. Ibid, p. 422.

17. Ien Ang, *Watching Dallas: Soap Opera and the Melodramatic Imagination* (London: Methuen, 1985), p. 45.

18. Lawrence Grossberg, *We Gotta Get out of This Place: Popular Conservatism and Postmodern Culture* (New York: Routledge, 1992), p. 255.

19. Patrick Hanan, "Foreword" to Hayden's *Crime and Punishment in Medieval Chinese Drama: Three Judge Pao Plays.*

20. Cottle, "Mediatized rituals: Beyond manufacturing consent," p. 412.

21. Ibid., p. 411.

Chapter 4 Global Imaginary, Local Desire: Chinese Transnational Serial Drama in the 1990s

1. This serial was adapted from Cao Guilin's 1991 novel of the same name, which was published in the *Beijing Evening News* (Beijing wanbao) in October 1991. The English translation, *Beijinger in New York,* was published in 1994 (San Francisco: Cypress).

2. The popularity of this kind of television serial continues into the twenty-first century. *Farewell, Vancouver* (*Biele, wengehua,* 2004), *New York Beauty* (*Niuyue liren,* 2004), and *Dangerous Journey* (*Tou du,* 2003) are examples. My focus is the serials in the 1990s; thus only those produced in that period are included in this chapter.

3. Basically, the global corporate ideology refers to belief in free trade, no

unnecessary government intervention and regulation, and privatization. For a detailed discussion of global corporate ideology, see Edward S. Herman and Robert McChesney, "The rise of the global media," in Lisa Parks and Shanti Kumar (eds.), *Planet TV* (New York: New York University Press, 2003).

4.   For this approach, see Armand Mattelart, *Multinational Corporations and the Control of Culture* (Brighton: Harvest Press, 1979); Herbert I. Schiller, "Transnational media and national development," in K. Nordenstreng and H .I. Schiller (eds.), *National Sovereignty and International Communication* (Westport, CN: Ablex, 1979); Rohan Samarajiwa, "Third-World entry to the world market in news: Problems and possible solutions," *Media, Culture and Society* (1984) 6 (2): 119–136.

5.   Her empirical work suggests that the notion of exposure to an imperialist text producing an immediate ideological effect is naïve and improper, and that our understanding of global media should take into consideration of the critical sophistication of the ordinary viewer/reader. She highlights room for negation and possibility of local resistance.

6.   See Homi K. Bhabha, *The Location of Culture* (London: Routledge, 1994).

7.   Geremie Barmé, *In the Red: On Contemporary Chinese Culture* (New York: Columbia University Press, 1999).

8.   See James Lull, *China Turned On: Television, Reform, and Resistance* (London: Routledge, 1991), p. 172.

9.   Lydia H. Liu, *What's Happened to Ideology? Transnationalism, Postsocialism, and the Study of Global Media Culture* (Durham, NC: Asian/Pacific Studies Institute, Duke University, 1998), p. 39.

10.   Arjun Appadurai, *Modernity at Large: Cultural Dimensions of Globalization* (Minneapolis: University of Minnesota Press, 1996), p. 35.

11.   Michael Keane, "Television and moral development in China," *Asian Studies Review* (1998) 22 (4): 497.

12.   "White Babe in Beijing," available: http://goldsea.com/Features2/Dewoskin/dewoskin.html [accessed October 10, 2005].

13.   Sheldon H. Lu, *China, Transnational Visuality, Global Postmodernity* (Stanford, · CA: Stanford University Press, 2001), p. 230.

14.   For a discussion of gender representation in this television serial, see Zhong Yong, "Duokui Wang Qiming shi zai Niu Yue" (Luckily Wang Qiming is in New York), *Dushu* (Readings) (1995) 7: 85–87.

15.   Laura Mulvey, "Visual pleasure and narrative cinema," *Screen* (1975) 16 (3): 6–18.

16.   Elisabeth Croll, *Changing Identities of Chinese Women: Rhetoric, Experience and Self-perception in Twentieth-century China* (Hong Kong: Hong Kong University Press, 1995), p. 152 (emphasis added).

17.   I am not offering any judgment on socialist discourse of gender and the new reconceptualization of femininity. Although I hold the same opinion as many feminist critics that socialist ideology of gender masculinizes women

by depriving them of choices, I do not completely negate the role of socialist ideology in enhancing women's awareness of equality. Similarly, although I emphasize the agency of women in constructing their body identity, I do not embrace the new femininity without restraint. In this chapter, I am mainly describing the new phenomenon of women's increasing awareness of their body and physical appearance.

18. *Broken Blossoms* (dir. G.W. Griffith, 1919) is a film about the love of a Chinese man, whose name is Cheng Hung, for a white woman. He is presented as a feminized character, feeble and fragile. He walks slowly like a woman, holding a lady's fan. He is played by a Caucasian actor, Richard Barthelmess, whose performance was praised as "very convincing" by a *New York Times* film review in 1919. Exotic and erotic image of Chinese women are very common on Hollywood screen. Anna May Wong, the first Chinese-American movie star, appeared in over thirty films and TV shows. Her name was synonymous with exotic, Asian-themed productions. For more detailed study of Chinese women in Hollywood films, see Dorothy B. Jones, *The Portrayal of China and India on the American Screen, 1896–1955: The Evolution of Chinese and Indian Themes, Locales, and Characters as Portrayed on the American Screen* (Cambridge, MA: Center for International Studies, Massachusetts Institute of Technology, 1955); and Gina Marchetti, *Romance and the 'Yellow Peril': Race, Sex, and Discursive Strategies in Hollywood Fiction* (Berkeley: University of California Press, 1993).

19. Rey Chow, *Primitive Passions: Visuality, Sexuality, Ethnography, and Contemporary Chinese Cinema* (New York: Columbia University Press, 1995), p. 171. There are voluminous articles that criticize the fifth-generation directors' films for repackaging Chinese customs and rituals for the gaze of the West. For example, see Dai Qing, "Raise eyebrows for *Raise the Red Lantern*," *Public Culture* (1993) 5 (2): 333–336; Zhang Yiwu, "Quanqiuxing houzhimin yujing zhong de Zhang Yimou" (Zhang Yimou in the global postcolonial context), *Dangdai dianying* (Contemporary Film) (1993) 54 (3): 18–25.

20. Sheldon H. Lu, "National cinema, cultural critique, transnational capital: The films of Zhang Yimou," in Sheldon H. Lu (ed.), *Transnational Chinese Cinemas: Identity, Nationhood, Gender* (Honolulu: University of Hawai'i Press, 1997), p. 133.

21. David Morley and Kevin Robins, *Spaces of Identity: Global Media, Electronic Landscapes and Cultural Boundaries* (London: Routledge, 1995), p. 10.

22. See Lisa Rofel, "The melodrama of national identity in post-Tiananmen in China," in Robert C. Allen (ed.), *To Be Continued . . . : Soap Operas Around the World* (London: Routledge, 1995), pp. 301–320.

23. For more details on the production of *Beijingers in New York* , see Lu, *China, Transnational Visuality, Global Postmodernity*, pp. 222–223.

24. Barmé, *In the Red*. Particularly, see Chapter 10, "To screw foreigners is patriotic."

25. For example, see Pamela Yatsko, "Inside looking out: Books and TV dramas about life overseas reflect existing Chinese biases," *Far Eastern Economic Review* (1996) 159 (15): 58.

26. Michael Keane, " 'By the Way, FUCK YOU!': Feng Xiaogang's disturbing television dramas," *Continuum* (2001) 15 (1): 62.

27. Lisa B. Rofel, " 'Yearnings': Televisual love and melodramatic politics in contemporary China," *American Ethnologist*, (1994) 21 (4): 704.

28. Benedict Anderson, *Imagined Communities: Reflections on the Origin and Spread of Nationalism* (London: Verso, 1983).

29. Critique of nationalism and embrace of the separation between identity and territory has been one of the most addressed issues in cultural studies, particularly in diaspora study. For a recent discussion, see Ien Ang, *On Not Speaking Chinese: Living Between Asia and the West* (London: Routledge, 2001).

30. Dai Jinhua, "Behind global spectacle and national image making," *Positions: East Asia Cultures Critique* (2001) 9 (1): 174.

31. Dai, "Behind global spectacle and national image making," p. 175.

Chapter 5　Family Matters: Reconstructing the Family on the Chinese Television Screen

1. BTAC's production of *Yearning* serves as a good example of how Chinese scriptwriters and directors, in the early stages of making family dramas, searched for the keys to success from imported TV soaps, including Latin American telenovelas, and East Asian family dramas. See Jianying Zha, *China Pop: How Soap Operas, Tabloids, and Bestsellers Are Transforming a Culture* (New York: The New Press, 1995), pp. 35–38.

2. Lisa B. Rofel, " 'Yearnings': Televisual love and melodramatic politics in Contemporary China," *American Ethnologist* (1994) 21 (4): 706.

3. The genre classifications of Chinese TV drama are still unstable and controversial, with different critics and industry analysts offering quite different categorizations. While I follow the major categories identified in *China TV Drama Market Report 2003–04,* an authoritative industrial report by CSM, a joint venture of CCTV's audience research department with the French company SOFRES, I do have certain reservations and have modified some of the categories in my own list here. For example, there is considerable overlap between CSM's two categories of Urban Life and Common Folk, and other important trends, such as family values drama, can obviously cut across both those categories. I have therefore modified the overbroad subgenre of Urban Life to Urban Romances, as many of the examples deal with love and marriage issues. I also treat Common Folk drama and Family Values drama together since they are similar in style and content.

4. *Zhongguo dianshiju shichang baogao 2003–04* (Beijing: Huaxia chubanshe,

2004), p. 45. Broadcast ratings (*bochu bizhong*) means the percentage of each subgenre as a proportion of all TV dramas broadcast each year; reception ratings (*shoushi bizhong*) means the proportion of viewers watching each subgenre. Statistics on the market share of family dramas support this observation. In 2002, the market share of Ordinary Folk and Urban Life dramas was 12.5 percent and 11.6 percent respectively, ranking 2 and 3, just after Crime drama. See *Zhongguo dianshiju shichang baogao 2003–04*, p. 52.

5. Yin Hong, "Zhongguo dianshiju yishu chuantong" (The artistic tradition of Chinese television drama), in Qu Chunjing and Zhu Ying (eds.), *Zhongmei dianshiju bijiao yanjiu* (Comparative research on television drama in China and America) (Shanghai: Sanlian chubanshe, 2004).

6. Much research has been done on the changes and crises facing urban families in contemporary China, and my description is based on both literary works devoted to this subject, as well as academic research such as Ding Wen and Xu Tailing's *Dangdai zhongguo jiating jubian* (The great change in the contemporary Chinese family) (Jinan: Shandong daxue chubanshe, 2001). Various other statistics and surveys also support this general picture of "family crisis." According to statistics from the Ministry of Civil Affairs, the divorce rate more than doubled from 1985 to 1995, and by 2005, the rate had more than tripled, to 1.37 divorces per 1,000 people. In 2005 alone, 1.79 million couples divorced. See Wu Zhong, "Divorce, Chinese style," *Asia Times* online, July 18, 2007, available: http://www.atimes.com/atimes/China/IG18Ad01.html.

7. In China, TV drama has built up a close relationship with literature both in terms of sharing creative resources and in its narrative tradition. Since the Chinese TV industry is a relatively new media industry and its exponential growth has led to a serious shortage of competent screenwriters, the potential for lucrative rewards and mass media exposure has attracted serious literary writers to venture into the film and TV industry in the 1990s. Many of them have subsequently become successful TV drama scriptwriters and even producers. On top of this, the scarcity of good scripts has also led to a trend of adapting literary works, especially bestsellers, into TV dramas. See Shuyu Kong's discussion of "Television/film literature" in *Consuming Literature: Bestsellers and the Commercialization of Literary Production in Contemporary China* (Stanford: Stanford University Press, 2005), pp. 172–176.

8. For the promotion of urban romances by Chunfeng Publishing House, see Chapter 4 in Shuyu Kong, *Consuming Literature*.

9. For example, in 2000, Chi Li, a popular writer who is famous for depicting romantic and family relationships set in the local surroundings of Wuhan City, wrote the screenplay for the TV serial *Lipstick* (*Kouhong*) on commission after her novel *Coming and Going* was successfully adapted for television in 1999. Similarly, Wan Fang, a Beijing writer, has frequently shifted between literary writing and screenwriting. The TV drama, *Mirror*, was adapted by

herself based on her novel of the same title. She also wrote the screenplay for another series, *Empty House*, specially for television.

10. Besides the high broadcast and reception ratings reported in the industry survey in *China TV Drama Market Report 2003–04*, cited in n. 4, the reception ratings of TV dramas such as *Elder Sister, Mother-in-Law* and *Romantic Affairs*, which were all broadcast in prime time on CCTV Channel One, have all been very high, respectively 8.54%, 8.37% and 7.35%.

11. For example, *Yearning* juxtaposed the lives of a poor working family with a rich intellectual family, obviously aiming to appeal to a broad range of viewers from different social classes.

12. See the section on TV drama audience analysis in *China TV Drama Market Report 2003–04*, pp. 41–43.

13. The recent official discourse of building a "harmonious society" explicitly articulated by the Hu Jintao regime can, however, be traced as far back as the Deng Xiaoping era with its discourse of "social stability." In fact, for a long while, the state has admitted that China's economic reforms have led to social stratification, and has therefore encouraged cultural producers to make sense of this issue "correctly." Despite the potential criticism represented by the existence of urban poor such as Zhang Damin depicted in many TV dramas and fictional works about urban ordinary folk, the cultural officials consciously supervise and "guide" these kinds of works instead of simply banning or disregarding them completely. This "invisible guiding hand" works increasingly through regulatory and administrative means as well as through self-censorship and "social obligations" of creative personnel, and thus creates a kind of self-correcting mechanism through which socialist spiritual civilization is "voluntarily" built. I find the exchange between the creative personnel of this drama and its viewers to be particularly revealing in understanding the coalition between artists and the state in constructing a harmonious society. See "Interview with the *Happy Life* Crew," from *People's Daily* online edition, available: http://www.people.com.cn/wsrmlt/jbft/2000/juzu.html. For an overview of the new methods of propaganda control in the media and television industries in contemporary China, see Eric Kit-wai Ma, "Rethinking media studies: The case of China," in James Curran and Myung-jin Park (eds.), *De-westernizing Media Studies* (London; New York: Routledge, 2000), pp. 21–34, and Yuezhi Zhao, "The state, the market and media control in China," in Pradip Thomas and Zahoram Nain (eds.), *Who Owns the Media: Global Trends and Local Resistance* (London; New York: Zed Books, 2004), pp. 179–212.

14. In April of 2004, the State Administration of Radio, Film and Television issued a special notice on regulating the adaptation of Red Classics, and then another notice on tightening the approval for broadcasting Crime Dramas, especially during prime-time. Recently, the government has often used such "industrial regulation" to "guide" cultural production.

15. As early as *Yearning*, cultural officials, the state-controlled mass media and state-sponsored artists had come out in force to extol the serial as representing a positive model of social relationships. They reinterpreted the family melodrama as a work of pure socialist morality. See a collection of media coverage and reader's response on *Yearning*, Yang Wenyong and Xie Yuzhang (eds.), *Kewang chongjibo* (The shock waves of *Yearning*) (Beijing: Guangming ribao chubanshe, 1991).

16. Because of its political importance, BTAC spent over a year producing *Year after Year*. One of the directors, Li Xiaolong, recalled that before the actual shooting started, the creative team spent a long time discussing how to insert the social and political messages into its plot while still retaining its "ordinary family" appeal. The solution was to produce "a chronicle of ordinary people, instead of a chronicle of political events." See Li Xiaolong, "Biaoxian lao baixing shenghuo de bianqian: 'Yinian you yinian' daoyan tan" (Representing the changes in ordinary people's lives: Director's notes on *Year after Year*), *Dianying yishu*, 2000 (01): 81–83.

17. Li Xiaoming, "Zuotian yu geshi: 'Yinian you yinian' chuangzuo suixiang" (Yesterday and another world: Notes on the creation of *Year after Year*), *Zhongguo dianshi*, 1999 (12): 19–21.

Chapter 6   Maids in the Televisual City: Competing Tales of Post-Socialist Modernity

1. The *hukou* system (household or residential registration), since its introduction in the 1950s, has effectively differentiated the Chinese population along urban-rural lines and regional differences. Reforms in the *hukou* system in recent decades have made it easier for rural residents to enter the cities in search of work. However, they have by no means eliminated the discrimination against rural population. The large number of migrant domestic workers in the Chinese cities is closely related to the urban-rural gap and the continued salience of *hukou* that perpetuates that gap. The *hukou* system and its discriminatory impact are crucial to understanding the work and life of domestic workers. Rural *hukou* excludes rural migrants from claiming an entire range of urban entitlements, including education, housing subsidies, job opportunities, and medical care, thus effectively turning rural migrants into the city's second-class citizens. There is a growing body of literature on *hukou* system and its impact on rural migrants. See, for instance, Fei-ling Wang, *Organizing Through Division and Exclusion: China's Hukou System* (Stanford: Stanford University Press, 2005); Dorothy Solinger, *Contesting Citizenship in Urban China: Peasant Migration, the State, and the Logic of the Market* (Berkeley, CA: University of California Press, 1999), and Aihwa Ong, *Flexible Citizenship: The Cultural Logics of Transnationality* (Durham: Duke University Press, 1999).

2. See untitled news item from http://www.cctv.com/news/financial/20020612/274.html [accessed February 2004].

3. "Beijing baomu shichang duandang" (Beijing Baomu market supply too low). Available: http://www.cctv.com/news.society/20031126/100610.shtml [accessed February 2004).

4. Personal communication with Dr Li Tianguo, senior research fellow of the Institute for Labor, Ministry of Labor and Social Security, China, February 2004.

5. This estimation comes from unnamed experts, quoted in Yang Jie, "Jiazheng ye chengwei Zhongguo xina laodongli de zhongyao qudao" (Domestic work is becoming an important means of absorbing labour). Available: http://www.cctv.com/news/financial/20020612/274.html [accessed May 2005].

6. This figure is provided by Li Dajing, the deputy director of Beijing Domestic Service Association. See Gao Youxin and Wu Wenjie, "Jiazheng fuwu zhiyehua zhi lu haiyou duo yuan" (How far is the road to the professionalisation of domestic work?), *Jingji Ribao* (Economic Daily), May, 2, 2005, p. A11.

7. At the time of writing, one US dollar was equivalent to approximately eight yuan.

8. Wanning Sun, "The invisible entrepreneur: The case of Anhui Women," *Provincial China* (2002) 7 (2): 178–195.

9. Haiyan Lee, "Nannies for foreigners: The enchantment of Chinese womanhood in the age of millennial capitalism," *Public Culture* (2006) 18 (3): 507–529.

10. James Donald, *Imagining the Modern City* (London: Athlone Press, 1999).

11. See Michael Keane, "TV drama in China," in Tim Craig and Richard King (eds.), *Global Goes Local: Popular Culture in Asia* (Vancouver: University of British Columbia Press, 2002), pp. 176–202. Also see Sheldon Lu, "Soap opera in China: The transnational politics of visuality, sexuality, and masculinity," *Cinema Journal* (2000), 40 (1): 25–47.

12. Wanning Sun, "Semiotic over-determination or indoctri-tainment: Television, citizenship, and the Olympic Games," in Stephanie Donald, Michael Keane and Yin Hong (eds.), *Media in China: Consumption, Content and Crisis* (London: RoutledgeCurzon, 2002), p. 116.

13. See Lee Chin-Chuan (ed.), *Power, Money and Media: Communication Patterns and Bureaucratic Control in Cultural China* (Evanston, IL: Northwestern University Press, 2000); Yuezhi Zhao, "From commercialization to conglomeration: The transformation of the Chinese press within the orbit of the party state," *Journal of Communication* (2000) Spring: 3–25; *Media, Market, and Democracy in China* (Urbana, IL: University of Illinois Press, 1997). Also see Zhao Bin, "Mouthpiece or money-spinner? The double life of Chinese television in the late 1990s," *International Journal of Cultural Studies* (1999) 2 (3): 291–306, and Zhao Bin, "Popular family television and party ideology: The Spring Festival Eve Happy Gathering," *Media Culture and Society* (1998) 20: 43–58.

14. Yin Hong, "Meaning, production, consumption: The history and reality of television drama in China," in Donald, Keane, and Hong, *Media in China*, p. 33.
15. Yin, "Meaning, production, consumption," p. 33.

Chapter 7   Pink Dramas: Reconciling Consumer Modernity and Confucian Womanhood

1. Translation by author.
2. See Sarah Chaplin, "Interiority and the modern women in Japan," and S. Munshi, "Marvellous me: The beauty industry and the construction of the 'modern' Indian woman," in Shoma Munshi (ed.), *Images of the "Modern Woman" in Asia: Global Media, Local Meanings* (London: Curzon, 2001), pp. 55–94.
3. Eric Hobsbawn and Terence Ranger, *The Invention of Tradition* (Cambridge: University of Cambridge, 1983).
4. Beverly Hooper, *Inside Peking: A Personal Report* (London: MacDonald and Jane's, 1979); Jane Barrett, "Women hold up half the sky," in Marilyn B. Young (ed.), *Women in China: Studies in Social Changes and Feminism* (Ann Arbor: Centre for Chinese Studies, The University of Michigan, 1973), pp. 34–67; Mayfair Yang, "From gender erasure to gender difference: State feminism, consumer sexuality, and women's public sphere in China," in *Spaces of Their Own: Women's Public Sphere in Transnational China* (Minneapolis: Minnesota University Press, 1999), pp. 35–68.
5. The Mandarin version of *ELLE*, World Fashion Institute *ELLE* (*Shijie shizhuang zhiyuan ELLE*) entered the Chinese market in 1988, followed by *Cosmopolitan* in 1998, *Harper's Bazzar* in 2001, *Marie Claire* in 2002, and *Vogue* in 2005. More discussion on contemporary women's fashion magazine in China can be found in "Vogue cruises into China," *China Economic Net*, available: http://en.ce.cn/Life/entertainment/fashion&beauty/EFBn/200509/10/t20050910_4645651.shtml [accessed September 10, 2005].
6. Kara Chan and Fanny Chan, "Information content of television advertising in China: An update," *Asian Journal of Communication,* (2005) 15 (1): 1–15; and Conghua Li, *China: The Consumer Revolution* (New York: John Wiley and Son Inc., 1998).
7. The term "pink collar" was first used by Kapp Howe in his book, *Pink Collar Workers* (1978). Contrary to how the term is used in the Chinese context, in the Western literatures, "pink collar" is often linked to women with lower education or single mothers who take on secondary jobs such as administrative, caring and lower educational positions.
8. Yin Hong, "Meaning, production, consumption: The history and reality of television drama in China," in Stephanie Hemelryk Donald, Michael Keane,

and Yin Hong (eds.), *Media in China: Consumption, Content and Crisis* (London: RoutledgeCurzon, 2002), pp. 28–40.

9. Thomas Gold, "Go with your feelings: Hong Kong and Taiwan popular culture in Greater China," in David Shambaugh (ed.), *Greater China: The Next Superpower?* (Oxford: Oxford University Press, 1995), pp. 255–274.

10. Thomas Gold, "Go with your feelings: Hong Kong and Taiwan popular culture in Greater China," pp. 255–274.

11. Michael Keane, "Send in the clones: Television formats and content creation in the People's Republic of China," in S. H. Donald, M. Keane, and Yin Hong (eds.), *Media in China: Consumption, Content and Crisis* (London: RoutledgeCurzon, 2002), pp. 80–90.

12. John Sinclair, Elizabeth Jacka, and Stuart Cunningham, "Global and regional dynamics of international television flows," in Daya K. Thussu (ed.), *Electronic Empires: Global Media and Local Resistance* (London: Arnold, 1998), pp. 179–192; Indrajit Banerjee, "The locals strike back? Media globalization and localization in the new Asian television landscape," *The International Journal for Communication Studies* (2002) 64 (6): 517–535.

13. Silvio Waisbord, "Mc TV: Understanding the global popularity of television formats," *Television and New Media* (2004) 5 (4): 359–381.

14. Michael Keane, Anthony W. H. Fung, and Albert Moran (eds.), *New Television, Globalization and the East Asian Cultural Imagination* (Hong Kong: Hong Kong University Press, 2007).

15. Michael Keane, "Send in the clones," pp. 80–90.

16. Michael Keane, "Television drama in China: Remaking the Market," *Media International Australia* (2005) (115): 82–93.

17. Ibid.

18. For more discussions on conceptualizing an East Asian popular culture, see Beng Huat Chua, "Conceptualizing an East Asian popular culture," *Inter-Asia Cultural Studies* (2004) 5 (2): 200–221.

19. Amy Sohn, *Sex and the City: Kiss and Tell* (New York: Pocket Books, 2002).

20. Broadcast in 2003, a Taiwanese series titled *Mature Women's Diary* (*Shounü yuwang riji*), and a Hong Kong series, *Male and Female Dictionary* (*Nannü zidian*), were highly advertised in the media as "local versions of *Sex and the City*." There was also another Hong Kong series titled *Women on the Run* broadcast on pay television in 2005.

21. Perry Johansson, "Selling the 'modern woman': Consumer culture and Chinese gender politics," in S. Munshi (ed.), *Images of the "Modern Woman" in Asia: Global Media, Local Meanings* (London: Curzon, 2001), pp. 94–122.

22. Jane Arthurs, "*Sex and the City* and Consumer Culture: Remediating postfeminist drama," *Feminist Media Studies* (2003) 3 (1): 83–97.

23. Wei Hui, *Shanghai Baby* (London: Robinson, 2001).

24. Canyin Luo, "Competing discourses on gender model: Discourse analysis

on reports of adult film event in the newspaper," *Taiwan Social Studies Quarterly* (1997) 25: 169–208.

25. You Kou, "Shi haoxiang tanlianai haishi haoxiang jiaren?" (Is it falling in love or falling for marriage?). Available: http://life.people.com.cn/BIG5/8223/50801/50802/3671255.html [accessed September 2, 2005].

26. Ying Jiang, "Nüren xing de fengfan, bie guanyi Yuwang Chengshi de ming" (Capitalize on women and sex, do not use the name of *Sex and the City*). Available: http://ent.tom.com/1030/1587/2003821-52458.html [accessed August 22, 2003].

27. See Fabienne Darling-Wolf, "Finding a place in the capitalist world order: Japanese women and the losses (or gains) of Western capitalism," *Asian Journal of Women's Studies* (2003) 9 (3): 46–77; Yachien Huang, "Thinking of Manhattan, living in Taipei: Female pleasure in watching *Sex and the City*," paper presented in the Third MARG Conference: Media and Identity in Asia. Miri: Curtin University of Technology Sarawak Malaysia, February 2006; Youna Kim, "Experiencing globalization: Global TV, reflexivity and the lives of young Korean women," *International Journal of Cultural Studies* (2005) 8 (4): 446–463.

28. See Angela McRobbie, "Postfeminism and popular culture," *Feminist Media Studies* (2004) 4 (3): 255–263, and Kristyn Gorton, "(Un)fashionable feminists: The media and *Ally McBeal*," in Stacy Gillis, and Gill Howie (eds.), *Third Wave Feminism* (New York: Palgrave Macmillan, 2004), pp. 154–164.

Chapter 8   A Brief History of Chinese Situation Comedies

1. John Hartley, "Comedy, domestic settings," in Horace Newcomb (ed.), *Encyclopedia of Television*, second edition (New York: Dearborn, 2004), pp. 556–559.

2. For a discussion, see Michael Keane, "Television drama in China: Engineering souls for the market," in Timothy J. Craig and Richard King (eds.), *Global Goes Local: Popular Culture in Asia* (Vancouver: University of Columbia Press, 2002), pp. 120–137.

3. Chen Yanni, *Meiguo zhihou: 50 wei lumei renshi de guiguo zhi lu* (After the US: Return Journeys of 50 Chinese Expatriates in the US) (Beijing: Writers' Publishing House, 2000), p. 367.

4. This figure was mentioned by Wang Xiaojing, general manager of the Ying Co. See *21st Century Economic Herald*, September 28, 2003.

5. Zhang Jianzhen, "Yingxiang xianshi: meijie shidai de qingjing xiju" (Cinematic reality: Situation comedy in an age of media), *Xinwen yu chuanbo yanjiu* (Journalism and Communications Research) (2002) 2: 58.

6. *Beijing yule xinbao* (Beijing Entertainment Messenger), March 19, 2004.

7. See *ershiyi shiji jingji daobao* (21st Century Economic Herald), September 28, 2003.

8. The statistics and information cited above were not publicly reported; they were obtained from the author's personal contacts with production team members, such as Ying Da, Liang Zuo, Xiao Feng (chief of the literature department of The Ying Co.), and Fu Si (chief of the Economic Television Program Center of CCTV).

9. "Ying Da: dianshi gaibian le 300 nian xinshang xiju de fangshi" (Television changes the 300-Year Tradition of Comedy), *Nanfang zhoumo* (Southern Weekends), December 19, 2002.

10. See *Beijing qingnian bao* (Beijing Youth Daily), November 5, 2002.

11. Personal interview with Xiao Feng, chief of the literature department of The Ying Co., a creator of the show.

12. *Jianghu* refers to an imaginary world in novels, films and dramas about knights errant. Inhabited by martial arts masters, this world is characterized by a blurred boundary between the good and the evil, and is governed by its own distinct set of rules.

13. See relevant reports in *Zhongguo guangbo ying shi* (Chinese Radio, Film and Television) in the first half of April 2006.

14. See "Ting daoyan Shang Jing jiangshu 'wulin waizhuan' chenggong de mijue" (Listen to how Director Shang Jing tells the secret weapons of *Tales of Jianghu*), available: http://ent.sina.com.cn [accessed January 25, 2006].

15. See relevant reports in *Zhongguo guangbo ying shi* (Chinese Radio, Broadcast and Television) in the first half of April 2006.

16. See *ershiyi shiji jingji daobao* (21st Century Economic Herald), January 10, 2004, p. C4.

Chapter 9 Carnivalesque Pleasure: The Audio-visual Market and the Consumption of Television Drama

1. By video in this chapter, I refer to video disks, not videotapes.

2. The WTO Secretariat's 1998 Background Note on Audiovisual Services notes difficulty in determining exactly the boundary between "services classified under telecommunications and those classified under audiovisual services." The document is accessible at http://www.wto.org/english/tratop_e/serv_e/w40.doc.

3. "Regulations on the Administration of Audio-visual Products" (No. 341 Order of the State Council of the People's Republic of China), promulgated on December 25, 2001, available at http://newmedia.gapp.gov.cn/Main/Articlex.aspx?cateid=H0102&artid=0000000374. An English version can be found in Jesse T. H. Chang, Isabelle I. H. Wan, and Philip Qu (eds.), *China's Media and Entertainment Law (Vol. 1)* (Hong Kong: TransAsia Publishing, 2003).

4. China began to produce audio cassettes in 1979 and video tapes in 1980.

See Wang Ju, "Zhongguo yinxiangye de chanye guimo yu jiegou" (The scope and structure of China's audio-visual industry), in *Zhongguo wenhua chanye fazhan baogao, 2003* (Report on development of China's cultural industry, 2003) (Beijing: Shehui kexue wenxian chubanshe, 2003), p. 157.

5. "2003 nian quanguo yinxiang chubanye jiben qingkuang" (An overview of the national audio-visual industry in 2003). The article is published by the General Administration of Press and Publication on its official website, available at http://newmedia.gapp.gov.cn. A different source puts the number of publishing companies at 302. See *Zhongguo hangye fazhan baogao, 2004: Chuanmeiye* (China industry development report, 2004: Media) (Beijing: Zhongguo jingji chubanshe, 2004), p. 67.

6. "Profile of the audio and video market of China," available: http://www.chinaembassy.org.pl/pol/wh/Nw/t129222.htm [accessed February 26, 2006]. Another source puts the number of audio-visual reproduction companies at 169. See *Zhongguo hangye fazhan baogao: Chuanmeiye* (China industry development report: Publishing), p. 67. See also "China to curtail audio-visual Market," available: http://english.people.com.cn/english/200103/15/print20010315_65055.html [February 26, 2006].

7. Wang Ju, "Zhongguo yinxiangye de fazhan xianzhuang" (Current status of the development of China's audio-visual industry), in *Zhongguo wenhua chanye fazhan baogao: 2005* (Report on development of China's cultural industry: 2005), pp. 151–152.

8. Bruce C. Klopfenstein, "The diffusion of the VCR in the United States," in Mark R. Levy (ed.), *The VCR Age: Home Video and Mass Communication* (Thousand Oaks, CA: Sage, 1989), pp. 22–26.

9. Wang Ju, "Zhongguo yinxiangye jingzhengli fenxi" (Analysis of the competitiveness of China's recording and video industry), in Qi Shuyu (ed.), *Zhongguo wenhua chanye guoji jingzhengli baogao* (Report on international competitiveness of China's cultural industry) (Beijing: Shehui kexue wenxian chubanshe, 2004), p. 198; Wang Ju, "Zhongguo yinxiangye de fazhan xianzhuang" (Current status of the development of China's audio-visual industry), p. 154.

10. Wang Ju, "Zhongguo yinxiangye de fazhan xianzhuang," p. 154.

11. Shuren Wang, *Framing Piracy: Globalization and Film Distribution in Greater China* (New York: Rowman and Littlefield, 2003), p. 50.

12. Wang, *Framing Piracy*, p. 52.

13. Yin Hong, "Quanqiuhua beijing xia Zhongguo yinxiangye de fazhan celüe chutan" (Preliminary analysis of the development strategies of China's audio-visual industry in the age of globalization), in Liu Yuzhu (ed.) *Zhongguo wenhua shichang fazhan baogao, 2004* (Report on the development of China's cultural market, 2004), p. 236.

14. Wang Ju, "Zhongguo yinxiangye de fazhan xianzhuang," p. 155.

15. Ibid., 156.

16. Yang Lei, "DVD bofangji de zuotian, jintian he mingtian" (The history of DVD players in China: Yesterday, today, and tomorrow), available: http://tom.yesky.com/data/279/2500779.shtml [accessed August 14, 2007].

17. Video tapes were still used in some less developed areas in China.

18. Wang Ju, "Zhongguo yinxiangye de fazhan xianzhuang," pp. 155–157.

19. *Zhongguo dianshiju shichang baogao, 2003–2004* (China TV drama report, 2003–2004) (Beijing: Shanghai TV Festival and CVSC-SOFRES Media, 2003), p. 220. One could surmise that the waning interest in Japanese TV series had something to do with the mounting tensions between China and Japan since the 1990s. Anti-Japan sentiments ran high among the Chinese populace who resented Japan's unwillingness to fully accept its responsibilities toward the war crimes against China and its Asian neighbors.

20. It was reported that the award-winning American series *Desperate Housewives* did not fare well when it was debuted on CCTV-8 in December 2006. Critics reason that the reality in the series is too far removed from the lives of ordinary Chinese and that the dubbed series, with its convolute twists and turns and literary references, is too highbrow for the majority of Chinese TV viewers. See Raymond Zhou, "Why *Desperate Wives* flopped in China," available: http://www.chinadaily.com.cn/english/doc/2005-12/31/content_508261.htm.

21. Interview with an official of the General Administration of Press and Publication on June 28, 2005.

22. For an extensive study on piracy in China and Taiwan, see for example, Shuren Wang, *Framing Piracy*. But the statistics in Wang's study were only current up to 2001.

23. IIPA (International Intellectual Property Alliance) 2001 Special 301 Report: People's Republic of China (p. 25), available: http://www.iipa.com/rbc/2001/2001SPEC301CHINA.pdf.

24. IIPA 2005 Special 301Report: People's Republic of China (pp. 183–184), available: http://www.iipa.com/rbc/2005/2005SPEC310PRCrev.pdf.

25. USTR 2006 Special 301 Report, available: http://ustr.gov/assets/Document_Library/Reports_Publications/2006/2006/_Special_301_Review/asset_upload-file473-9336.pdf?ht= [accessed May 23, 2006]. According to IIPA, countries or economies on the Priority Watch List do not provide enough IPR protection or enforcement of laws protecting IPR, or market access for persons relying on intellectual property protection.

26. "DVD yasuodie chongji yinxiangye, shiyi jia faxingshang mimou duice" (Compressed DVD threatens audio-visual industry, eleven publishers strategize behind closed door), *Beijing yule xin bao* (Beijing Daily Messenger), November 5, 2004, available: http://tech.sina.com.cn/it/2004-11-05/0735454018.shtml [accessed August 23, 2005].

27. "Yasuo DVD dong le shui de nailao, xianjin jishu he bu weimin fuwu" (Whose interest did the HDVD harm, why not use advanced technology to

serve the people?), available: http://www.jrj.com.cn/NewsRead/Detail. asp?NewsID=962673 [accessed August 23, 2005].

28. "Zhengban HDVD nan zu daoban hengxing" (Legal HDVD cannot stop rampant circulation of pirated HDVD), available: http://www.morningpost. com.cn/articleview/2006-1-27/article_view_6130.htm [accessed February 15, 2006].

29. "DVD yasuodie chongji yinxiangye, shiyi jia faxingshang mimou duice" (Compressed DVD threatens audio-visual industry, eleven publishers strategize behind closed doors). See also "Yasuo DVD dong le shui de nailao, xianjin jishu he bu weimin fuwu" (Whose interest did the HDVD harm, why not use advanced technology to serve the people).

30. "DVD yasuodie xianfan banfei tixi, chubanshang jujue zuochu tuoxie" (Compressed DVDs upset copyright fees, publishers refuse to budge), *Nanfang zhoumo* (Southern Weekend) (December 23, 2004), available: http:// tech.sina.com.cn/it/2004-12-23/1204482845.shtml [accessed August 23, 2005]. "Wanneng DVD youmeiyou hefahua tujing" (Is there a way to legitimize the super DVD?), available: http://www.njnews.cn/n/ca571464.htm [accessed August 23, 2005]. See also "Yasuo DVD zhongchuang zhengban shichang, dianshiju banquanfei kuangdie yiban" (Compressed DVD ravages legitimate market, TV drama copyright fees plunge by 50 percent), *Beijing yule xin bao* (Beijing Daily Messenger), November 2, 2004, available: http:// tech.sina.com.cn/it/2004-11-02/0909452054.shtml [accessed August 23, 2005].

31. "DVD yasuodie tunshi wu cheng zhengban shichang" (Compressed DVDs gobble up 50 percent of legitimate DVD market), *Jingji cankaobao* (Economic Information Daily), November 22, 2005, available: http:// finance.sina.com.cn?review/obsere/20041122/10091170728.shtml [accessed February 15, 2006].

32. Ibid.

33. "Guangdong yinxiang jutou lianshou, chizi wubai wan qingjiao DVD yasuodie" (Audio-visual biggies in Guangdong pooling RMB 5 million to stamp out HDVD piracy), *Nanfang ribao* (Nanfang Daily), November 12, 2004, available: http://tech.sina.com.cn/it/2004-11-12/0943458185.shtml [accessed August 23, 2005].

34. "Zhanwang 2006: yinxiang hangye huhuan chunjie yundong" (Looking ahead to 2006: audio-visual industry calls for regulatory measures), available: http://newmedia.gapp.gov.cn/Main/Articlex.aspx?cateid=H22&artid =0000003571 [accessed February 15, 2006].

35. "Nanhai chahuo jinnian zui da pi feifa yinxiang zhipin" (The largest seizure of pirated audio-visual products in Nanhai this year), available: http:// newmedia.gapp.gov.cn/Main/Articlex.aspx?cateid=H06&artid=0000003416 [accessed February 15, 2006].

36. "DVD yasuodie xianfan banfei tixi, chubanshang jujue zuochu tuoxie" (Compressed DVD upsets copyright fees and publishers refuse to budge).

37. Ibid. See also Min Yunshi, " 'Boda' de dizhi daoban zhi lu" (Boda's anti-piracy strategy), in Wang Yongzhang (ed.) *Zhonguo wenhua chanye dianxing anli xuanbian* (Chinese cultural industry: Typical cases) (Bejing: Beijing daxue chubanshe, 2003), p. 120; "Shoujie Beijing yinxiangjie shiyue di juban chaodi jiawei zhanxiao zhengban yinxiang zhipin" (The first audio-visual festival will sell legitimate audio-visual products at super low prices at the end of October), available: http://newmedia.gapp.gov.cn/EJurnal/Articlex.aspx?cateid=E14&artid=0000003341 [accessed February 15, 2006].

38. "Wanneng DVD youmeiyou hefahua tujing" (Is there a way to legitimize the super DVD?).

39. Interview with an official of the General Administration of Press and Publication on June 28, 2005. See also Shuren Wang, *Framing Piracy*, p. 55.

40. According to one estimate, market demand for VCD in 2000 was 800 million discs, but the supply was only 200 million, 600 million short. See Shuren Wang, *Framing Piracy,* p. 56. The cost of a pirated HDVD is about two yuan and it sells for about seven yuan on the market. For every piece sold, the profit is about five yuan. See "DVD yasuodie tunshi wu cheng zhengban shichang" (Compressed DVDs gobble up 50 percent of legitimate DVD market).

41. *Zhongguo dianshiju shichang baogao, 2003–2004* (China TV drama report, 2003–2004), pp. 41–43.

42. "Yinxiang shichang huanjing quxiang haozhuan, dan daoban chuxian xin miaotou" (Audio-visual market environment improves, but new trend in piracy appears), available: http://newmedia.gapp.gov.cn/Audio-visual/Articlex.aspx?cateid=A14&artid=0000003240 [accessed February 15, 2006].

43. "DVD yasuodie xianfan banfei tixi, chubanshang jujue zuochu tuoxie" (Compressed DVD upsets copyright fees and publishers refuse to budge).

44. "DVD yasuodie tunshi wu cheng zhengban shichang" (Compressed DVDs gobble up 50 percent of legitimate DVD market).

45. "Zhengban HDVD nan zu daoban hengxing" (Legitimate HDVD cannot stop rampant piracy).

46. Manuel Alvarado (ed.), *Video World-Wide: An International Study* (London: UESCO, John Libbey, 1988), p. 5.

47. Laikwan Pang, *Cultural Control and Globalization in Asia: Copyright, Piracy, and Cinema* (London and New York: Routledge, 2006), pp. 80–83. The quote appears on p. 83.

48. Ibid., 3, 98–106.

49. Pang mentions that economics was also a factor in movie piracy. It in fact plays a central role, as proven by the widespread phenomenon in Western countries where there is a different relationship between the film industry and the state, though in the West movie piracy in recent years takes the more hi-tech form of illegal downloading over the internet. High movie ticket price is a major reason for continual decline of box office in China. A ticket for the film, *The Promise* (*Wuji*, 2005) directed by Chen Kaige, cost

more than RMB 70 when it was shown in Beijing. Historically movie
ticket prices moved up 300 percent since 1989. It will take more than
ideological relaxation to lure Chinese moviegoers back to theaters. Even if
more foreign films are available, it is doubtful that people will choose theater
over cheap pirated copies given the high admission fee. See Lin Qi, "Bie
rang gao piaojia dangzhu guanzhong" (Don't let high ticket price keep the
audience out of movie theaters), available: http://news.xinhuanet.com/
focus/2006-01/09/content_4028295.htm [accessed August 14, 2007].

50. "The Rules for the Administration of the Import and Broadcast of Foreign
Television Programs," promulgated by the Ministry of Radio, Film, and
Television, February 3, 1994.

51. Bi Jiangyan and Li Hongling, "Zhongguo dianshiju shoushi shichang pandian,
2004," in *Zhongguo chuanmei chanye fazhan baogao, 2004–2005* (Report on
development of China's media industry, 2004–2005), pp. 273–274; *Zhongguo
dianshiju shichang baogao, 2003–2004* (China TV drama report, 2003–2004),
pp. 215–216.

52. Yuan Fang, "Cong quan ma pao di dao jing geng xi zuo: Jinnian woguo
dianshi meiti bianhua saomiao ji zhanwang" (From territorialization to careful
cultivation: Development and trends in Chinese television industry in recent
years), in *Zhongguo chuanmei chanye fazhan baogao, 2004–2005* (Report on
development of China's media industry, 2004–2005), pp. 273–274.

53. Bernard C. Cohen, *The Press and Foreign Policy* (Princeton, NJ: Princeton
University Press, 1963), p. 13.

54. "Baogao xianshi: Neng zhuanqian de dianshiju buzu liangcheng" (Report
indicates that only twenty percent of TV drama are profitable), available:
http://www.jschina.com.cn/gb/jschina/job/node1262/userobject1ai164702.
html [accessed September 27, 2005]. According to the trade magazine *Electronics*
(Asian Sources) the 1997 sales of VCD players in China accounted for more
than 80 percent of the world's total consumption: cited in Laikwan Pang,
Cultural Control and Globalization in Asia, p. 86.

55. Laikwan Pang, 102.

56. Paddy Scannell, "Radio times: The temporal arrangements of broadcasting
in the modern world," in Philip Drummond and Richard Paterson (eds.),
Television and Its Audience (London: British Film Institute, 1988), p. 28.

57. Wang Lanzhu (ed.), *Zhongguo dianshi shoushi nianjian, 2003* (Yearbook of
TV Reception in China: 2003) (Beijing: Beijing guangbo xueyuan, 2003),
p. 73. Of course, this is not unique to China. The major national news
networks in the United States, such as ABC, CBS, NBC, CNN, and Fox,
are also where most Americans get news. The significant difference lies in
that these news media are not controlled by the US government.

58. The popularization of television in China has been spectacular since the late
1970s. By 2004 television transmission signals had reached 95.3 percent of
the population. See Sun Xianghui, Huang Wei, and Hu Zhengrong, "2004

nian Zhongguo guangdian chanye fazhan baogao," in *Zhonggo chuanmei chanye fazhan baogao, 2004–2005* (Report on development of China's media industry: 2004–2005), p. 60.

59. John Ellis, *Visible Fictions, Cinema: Television: Video* (London: Routledge and Kegan Paul, 1983), p. 137. See also David Morley's discussion of the "distracted gaze" in his *Family Television: Cultural Power and Domestic Leisure* (London: Comedia, 1986).

Chapter 10 From National Preoccupation to Overseas Aspiration

1. In 2004, the total number of broadcast hours was 1,2591,569; of this television drama occupied 5,599,022 hours (Basic Statistics on Radio and Television Programs, State Statistical Bureau 2005). The national audience of a hit drama can extend to 400 million people, particularly if broadcast on China Central Television (CCTV). See *2006 nian Zhongguo guangbo yingshi fazhan baogao* (Blue book of China's radio, film and television) (Beijing: CASS Publishing, 2006), p. 171.

2. "China's cultural trade deficit on rise", *People's Daily Online,* April 15, 2005, available: http://www1.cei.gov.cn/ce/doc/cenzq/200504151806.htm.

3. See Michael Keane, *Created in China: The Great New Leap Forward* (London: Routledge, 2007).

4. For a discussion of cultural proximity in relation to television, see Joseph Straubhaar, "Beyond media imperialism: Asymmetrical interdependence of television programming in the Dominican Republic," *Journal of Communication,* (1991) 41 (5): 53–69.

5. Translation costs, such as subtitling and dubbing, are usually undertaken by the buyer. In China, dubbing is the dominant model for broadcast TV; this process has the advantage of screening out ideological differences. In Korea, however, dubbing is seldom allowed for imports. For a discussion of transborder video economics see Benjamin J. Bates, "The economics of transborder video," in Anura Goonasekera and Paul S. N. Lee (eds.), *TV Without Borders: Asia Speaks Out* (Singapore: AMIC, 1998), pp. 224–258.

6. Jorge González, "Understanding telenovelas as a cultural front: A complex analysis of a complex reality," *Media International Australia* (2003) 106: 89.

7. Speech at the Second International Cultural Industries Conference, September 12–16, 2004, Taiyuan, Shanxi Province, China.

8. *People's Daily,* August 22, 2005, available at *Peoples' Daily Online,* http://english.com.cn/200504/15/print20050415_181119.html [accessed October 10, 2006].

9. Bruno Wu, head of Sun Media, Australia China Business Council, Stamford Plaza Hotel, Brisbane, August 4–5, 2006.

10. *People's Daily Online*, "China's TV series fair seeks cooperation between producers, broadcasters," August 22, 2007; available at http://english.people.com.cn/90001/90778/6245416.html.

11. Indeed, these constraints also impact upon the sale of TV drama within national boundaries.

12. The number of TV stations in China varies according to sources. According to the most authoritative sources, the *Blue Books* series published by the Chinese Academy of Social Sciences, the number of stations that originate content is between 314 and 347; see *Blue Book of China's Radio, Film and Television*, p. 171.

13. Colin Hoskins and Rolf Mirus, "Reasons for the US dominance of the international trade in television programmes," *Media, Culture and Society* (1988) 10: 499–515.

14. These include *Expectations* (*Kewang*), *Live Life to the Limit* (*Guo ba yin*) and *I Love You Absolutely* (*Ai ni mei shangliang*). For a discussion see Michael Keane, "Television drama in China: Engineering souls for the market," in Timothy J. Craig and Richard King (eds.), *Global Goes Local: Popular Culture in Asia* (Vancouver: UBC Press, 2002), pp. 176–202.

15. For a discussion see Junhao Hong, *The Internationalization of Television in China: The Evolution of Ideology, Society and Media Since the Reform* (Westport: Praeger, 1998).

16. The literal translation of *shimin* is "resident of a city."

17. While Wang Shuo is often celebrated as the inspiration for several popular TV dramas produced by the Beijing Television Arts Center, other contributors included Li Xiaoming and Feng Xiaogang.

18. My own Ph.D. research "Television, the market and the state development of culture in Urban China" (Griffith University, 1999) examined readings of *Beijingers in New York* by Mainland and Diaspora audiences.

19. For a discussion of Hengdian World Studios, see Michael Keane, *Created in China: The Great New Leap Forward* (London: Routledge, 2007).

20. Also known as *Outlaws of the Marsh*.

21. For discussion of the Korean Wave, see Hae-Joang Cho, "Reading the Korean Wave as a sign of global shift," *Korea Journal* (2005) 45 (4): 147–182; Doobo Shim, "Hybridity and the rise of Korean popular culture in Asia," *Media Culture and Society* (2006) 28 (1): 25–44.

22. Yu Shu, Chen Minghui, and Li Li, "Zhongguo haiwaiju shichang bu leguan" (No optimism for China's overseas drama markets), *Yangcheng Evening News*, October 31, 2005.

23. Koichi Iwabuchi, *Recentring Globalization: Popular Culture and Japanese Transnationalism* (Durham: Duke University Press, 2002).

24. Claim made by Pu Shulin, in Song Wenjuan, "TV dramas marketing in 2007: Import and export," *Zhongguo guangbo yingshi* (China broadcasting film and TV), March 28, 2007.

25. China Media Intelligence, December 22, 2006.

26. Xinhua 2005, "China launches satellite TV service in Asian region," Xinhua News Agency online report, http://news.xinhuanet.com/english/2005-02/01/content_2536307.htm [accessed 19 May, 2008].

27. Satellite packages of Chinese channels including Hunan Satellite are purchased from TVB Jade (Hong Kong).

28. Ning Ling, "Lanmu gongsihua tuisheng da gaige: yangshi changtu chanyehua" (Professionalising programming promotes a great revolution: CCTV's attempt to make an industry from television drama), Xinhua News Agency, available at http://press.gapp.gov.cn/news/wen.php?val=news&aid=4954 [accessed May 19, 2008].

29. Lucy Montgomery and Michael Keane, "Learning to love the market: Copyright, culture and China," in Pradip Thomas and Jan Servaes (eds.), *Intellectual Property Rights and Communications in Asia: Conflicting Traditions* (Delhi: Sage, 2006), pp. 130–148.

Chapter 11 A Trip Down Memory Lane: Remaking and Rereading the Red Classics

1. See Meng Yue, "Bai Mao Nü yanbian de qishi" (Inspirations from the evolution of the White-haired Girl), in X. Tang (ed.), *Zai jiedu: Dazhong wenyi yu yishi xingtai* (Rereading: Popular art and ideology) (Hong Kong: Oxford University Press, 1993), pp. 68–89. Meng gives a fine-grained analysis of the transformation of *The White-haired Girl* (*Bai Mao Nü*) from a popular folk tale in Northern China to its varied propagandist versions as drama, film, ballet, and musical. For similar discussions on *The White-haired Girl*, also see Christopher J. Berry and Mary Ann Farquhar, "Shadow opera: Toward a new archaeology of the Chinese cinema," in S. H. Lu and E. Y. Yeh (eds.), *Chinese-Language Film: Historiography, Poetics, Politics* (Honolulu: University of Hawai'i Press, 2005), pp. 27–51.

2. Geremie Barmé, *In the Red: On Contemporary Chinese Culture* (New York: Columbia University Press, 1999), pp. 316–344.

3. For detailed discussion of the "Mao Fever," see Dai Jinhua, "Jiushu yu xiaofei" (Redemption and consumption), in Y. Wang (ed.), *Meijie Zhexue* (Media philosophy) (Kaifeng: Henan University Press, 2004), pp. 68–80.

4. Tao Dongfeng, "Hougeming shidai de geming wenhua" (Revolutionary culture in a postrevolutionary era), available: http://www.frchina.net/data/personArticle.php?id=3651 [accessed February 8, 2006].

5. In 1993, for instance, the government initiated a series of large-scale events to commemorate the centenary birthday of Mao. The Pacific Video and Audio Publishing Company, seeing the opportunity to cash in on these events, came up with the idea to publish a cassette with thirty revolutionary songs sung by popular singers and with modern electronic accompaniment.

With a next-to-nothing production budget, six million copies of the cassette were sold. Many families, all by now equipped with hi-fi CD players, bought cassette players just to listen to this tape.

6. Vanke Film and Television Co. Ltd. was formerly Vanke Cultural Communication Co. Ltd. Established in 1992, the company specializes in film and television planning and production. It has branches in Beijing and Hong Kong. See http://mt.vanke.com/.

7. Li Yan, "Xinban 'Hongse Niangzijun' gen hongse bu tiebian" (The new version of *The Red Detachment of Women* has nothing to do with "Red"), *Beijing Youth Daily*, July 3, 2006, p. B6.

8. Cai Nan, "Youjian Qionghua: Daiying 'Hongse niangzijun' beihou de gushi" (The stories behind *The Red Detachment of Women*), *China Television News,* June 12, 2006, p. 42.

9. Dai Jinhua, *Scene in the Fog: Chinese Cinema Culture: 1978–1998* (Beijing: Beijing University Press, 2000).

10. State Administration of Radio, Film and Television, *Guanyu renzhen duidai "hongse jingdian" gaibian dianshiju youguan wenti tongzhi* (A circular regarding some problems in adapting "Red Classics" into television drama), May 2004.

11. See Qiu Hongjie, "Zhongguo wenyi hanwei 'Hongse jingdian' " (Chinese art circles defend "Red Classics"). Available: http://news.xinhuanet.com/newscenter/2004-05/23/content_1485678.htm [accessed April 10, 2006]; Li Yan, "Xinban 'Hongse Niangzijun' gen hongse bu tiebian" (The new version of *The Red Detachment of Women* has nothing to do with "Red"), p. B6.

12. Anonymous, "Cehua: Dianshiju gaibian, ruhe chengshou 'Hongse jingdian' zhi zhong" (The unbearable heaviness of remaking "Red Classics"). Available: http://www.people.com.cn/GB/yule/1083/2437692.html [accessed April 9, 2004].

13. Some of the heroes and heroines in the original works were heavily revised over time to keep in line with the political and ideological requirement of the state. For more detailed discussions of the sublimation of the revolutionary hero, see Ban Wang, *The Sublime Figure of History: Aesthetics and Politics in Twentieth Century-China* (Stanford: Stanford University Press, 1997).

14. Li Yan, "Xinban 'Hongse Niangzijun' gen hongse bu tiebian," p. B6.

15. For a detailed discussion of the strategies to popularize red songs, see Andrew Jones, *Like a Knife: Ideology and Genre in Contemporary Chinese Popular Music* (New York: Cornell University, 1992).

16. Chen Yiming, "Cui Yongyuan: Zai 'Hongse jingdian' qian" (Cui Yongyuan on "Red Classics") *Southern Weekend*, May 6, 2005, p. C14, 19.

17. Zhao Yong, "Shui zai shouhu 'Hongse jingdian': Cong 'Hongse jingdian' ju gaibian kan guanzhongde 'Zhengzhi wuyishi' " (Who is guarding the "Red Classics": An analysis of the audiences' "political unconsciousness" through the "Red Classics" remakes), *Southern Cultural Forum* (2005) 6: 36–39.

18. Stuart Hall, "Encoding and decoding," in Stuart Hall (ed.), *Culture, Media, Language: Working Papers in Cultural Studies, 1972–1979* (London: Hutchinson and the Centre for Contemporary Cultural Studies, University of Birmingham, 1980), pp. 128–138.

19. Chantal Mouffe, "Hegemony and new political subjects: Toward a new concept of democracy," in Cary Nelson and Larry Grossberg (ed.), *Marxism and the Interpretation of Culture* (Urbana: University of Illinois Press, 1988), p. 94.

20. See Cheng Guangwei, "Ershi shiji liushi niandai de dianying yu wenhua shishang" (Film and cultural trends in the 1960s), *Journal of Xinyang Teachers' College* (2002), January: 96–101. Cheng discusses various readings of the Red Classics films in the 1960s divergent from or against the dominant ideological operations. For example, anti-Japanese war films such as *The Tunnel War* (*Didaozhan*) and *The Mine War* (*Dileizhan*) did not attract children with its grand narrative of revolution, but through its depiction of the magic military tactics of the guerrilla war and farcical scenes where Japanese soldiers flee helter-skelter, which happens to cater to the juveniles' need for playful games. Cheng's observations should indicate the fact that film or television texts are open and offer a variety of interpretations to the audience.

21. To protect the identities of the participants, I use pseudonyms for the names of all interviewees quoted.

22. Lisa Rofel, *Other Modernities: Gendered Yearnings in China After Socialism* (Berkeley: University of California Press, 1999), p. 97.

23. Ibid., pp. 129–131.

Chapter 12 Looking for Taiwan's Competitive Edge: The Production and Circulation of Taiwanese TV Drama

1. Changlin Ou-Yang, "The Marketing Manipulation of Princess Huangzhu," available: http://www.people.com.cn/ [accessed July 18, 2003].

2. Eric Lin, "The Stories of Prime Time," *Taiwan Panorama Magazine* (January 2000), 25 (1): 94. Available: http://www.sinorama.com.tw.

3. GIO (Government Information Office), 2005 ROC Yearbook, available: http://www.gio.gov.tw/.

4. Lai Tsung Pi, Vice President of Planning Department, Gala Television Corporation (GTV), Taipei, interviewed on April 21, 2006.

5. *China TV Drama Report 2002–2003* (Shanghai: Shanghai TV Festival and CVSC-SOFRES Media, 2003).

6. Koichi Iwabuchi, "Becoming culturally proximate: A/scent of Japanese idol dramas in Taiwan," in Brian Moeran (ed.), *Asian Media Productions* (London: Curzon Press, 2001), pp. 55–74.

7. Koichi Iwabuchi, "Localizing Japan in the booming Asian media markets,"

in *Recentering Globalization: Popular Culture and Japanese Transnationalism* (Durham, NC: Duke University Press, 2002), Chapter 3, pp. 121–157.

8. Chua Beng Huat, "Conceptualizing an East Asian popular culture," *Inter-Asia Cultural Studies* (2004) 5(2): 200–221.

9. Zhan Chang-Yu, "The Chinese audiences have to wait awhile to see *Meteor Garden,*" *United Daily News*, March 11, 2002, p. 27.

10. Editorial, "An obstacle between Taiwan and China TV communication," *Ming-Sheng Newspaper*, March 18, 2002, p. A2.

11. Chen Yixiu, "Shaping the television audience: The historic analysis of the rise of Korea drama market in Taiwan," Master thesis, Graduate Institute of Communication, Tamkang University, Taiwan, June 2004.

12. Hanes Chin, section chief of the International Channel and Program Distribution Department, Sanlih E-Television Co. (SETTV), Taipei, interviewed on April 2, 2006.

13. Youli Liu and Yixiang Chen, "Cloning, adaptation, import, and originality: Taiwan in the global television format business," in Albert Moran and Michael Keane (eds.), *Television across Asia: Television Industries, Program Formats and Globalization* (London: Routledge, 2004), pp. 67–72.

14. Robert Xue, assistant manager of Digital Contents Department, Sanlih E-Television Co. (SETTV), Taipei, interviewed on March 9, 2006.

15. J. D. Straubhaar, "Beyond media imperialism: Asymmetrical interdependence and cultural proximity," *Critical Studies in Mass Communication* (1991) 8: 39–59.

16. Xiancheng Liu, *Transborder Crossing: The Regional Competition of Chinese Media Industries* (Taipei: Asia-Pacific Press, 2004).

17. Vincent Jiang, deputy director, International Affairs and Program Department, Formosa Television (FTV), Taipei, interviewed on March 16, 2006.

18. Jessie Y. W. Shi, chief director of International Communications Planning Department, Public Television Service Foundation (PTS), Taipei, interviewed on March 29, 2006.

19. Claire Young, planning/marketing manager, Zoom Hunt International Productions Co., Taipei, interviewed on April 6, 2006.

Chapter 13 From the Margins to the Middle Kingdom: Korean TV Drama's Role in Linking Local and Transnational Production

1. The term was first coined by the Chinese mass media in 2001 in response to the rising popularity of Korean pop culture products and stars. See Suhyun Jang (ed.), *Junggukeun wae Hanliureul suyong hana* (Why China receives *hanliu*) (Seoul: Hakkojae, 2004). It has since been actively adopted by the Korean mass media to refer to their unexpected popularity throughout Asia.

2. David Waterman and Everett Rogers, "The economics of television program production and trade in Far East Asia," *Journal of Communication* (1994) 44 (3): 89–111.
3. Anura Goonasekera and Paul Lee, *TV Without Borders: Asia Speaks Out* (Singapore: AMIC, 1998).
4. Daya Kishan Thussu, *International Communication: Continuity and Change* (London: Arnold, 2000).
5. See Hyun Mee Kim, "Ilbon daejung munhwa ui sobiwa 'fandom' ui hyeongseong" (J-Pop consumption and the formation of "fandom"), *Hanguk Munhwa Inryuhak* (Korean Cultural Anthropology) (2003) 36 (1): 149–186; Jaesik Yoon and Yungyeong Jung, *Saeggye bangsongyeongsang contents yutong business* (World distribution business of broadcasting contents) (Seoul: Korean Broadcasting Institute, 2002); Jongwon Ha and Eungyeong Yang, "Dong Asia television ui jiyeokhwa wa Hanliu" (Regionalization of East Asian television and *Hanliu*), *Bangsong yeongu* (Broadcasting Studies) (2002 Winter): 67–103.
6. *Hanliu* challenges the notion of unilateral globalization, cultural imperialism, and the dichotomy of Western dominance, and peripheral dependency in the international communication system. Studies on intra-East Asian cultural traffic have shown that Western dominance through cultural products and capital is not sufficient to explain the regionalization of TV program exchanges and the dynamic relationship between global convergence and local specificity. See Koichi Iwabuchi, *Recentering Globalization: Popular Culture and Japanese Transnationalism* (Durham: Duke University Press, 2002). See also Koichi Iwabuchi (ed.), *Feeling Asian Modernities: Transnational Consumption of Japanese TV Dramas* (Hong Kong: Hong Kong University Press, 2004).
7. The introduction of new terrestrial and cable television channels in Korea in the 1990s resulted in an expanded market for foreign television programs, mostly from the United States. Total television program imports from foreign countries exceeded exports until 2001.
8. Hangjae Cho, "Oejujungchaui gonggwa" (Merits and demerits of outsourcing policy), presented at the Korean Association for Broadcasting and Telecommunication Studies seminar in 2003.
9. These do not include sitcoms and one-act dramas.
10. Yoon argues that the relationship between broadcasters and independent production companies is not equal; see Taejin Yoon, "Daejung munhwa ui saengsangujo" (Production structure of popular culture), *Bangsong munhwa yeongu* (Studies of Broadcasting Culture) (2005) 17 (2): 9–44.
11. Jaebok Park, *Hanliu, geullobal sidae ui munhwa gyungjaengryuk* (Hanliu: A cultural power in the age of globalization) (Seoul: Samsung Economic Research Institute, 2005).
12. O-Dae Kwon, a content producer in the Global Strategy Team at KBS, was interviewed on October 21, 2005.

13. Interview with Jonghak Kim, *The Hankyoreh*, December 13, 2004, p. 13.
14. "Drama funds pour in," *Korean Economic Daily*, June 15, 2006.
15. John Sinclair, "The business of international broadcasting: Cultural bridges and barriers," *Asian Journal of Communication* (1997) 7 (1): 137–155.
16. Jean-Luc Renaud and Barry L. Litman, "Changing dynamics of the overseas marketplace for TV programming," *Telecommunication Policy* (1985) 9 (4): 245–261.
17. Colin Hoskins, Stuart McFadyen, and Adam Finn, "International joint ventures in the production of Australian feature films and television programs," *Canadian Journal of Communications* (1999) 24 (1): 127–139.
18. Stuart McFadyen, Colin Hoskins, and Adam Finn, "The effect of cultural differences on the international co-production of television and feature films," *Canadian Journal of Communications* (1998) 23 (4): 523–538.
19. See "Anti-*hanliu* signs in China," *Yonhap News*, January 16, 2006; "Will *Hanliu* be blocked by the Great Wall of China?" *Munhwa Ilbo*, June 21, 2006.
20. Although it had been planned to be broadcast in two countries at the same time in May 2004 after its completion, its final editing was not completed until the scheduled airtime, and the Korean broadcaster could not delay its programming. While it was broadcast in Korea from May 10 to July 13, 2004, it was broadcast in China from June 23, 2004, one and a half months later.
21. Internationally co-produced cultural products tend to search for transcendent and universal subject matter to serve the capitalistic logic of the market and to avoid cultural discounting. In fact, the co-produced dramas usually favor universal human relations and emotions as their subject matter. For example, see Serra Tinic, "Going global: International co-productions and the disappearing domestic audience in Canada," in Lisa Parks and Shanta Kumar (eds.), *Planet TV: A Global Television Reader* (New York: New York University Press, 2003), pp. 169–186.
22. "Korea used to be China's dependency? KBS's apology," *Joongang Ilbo*, May 23, 2004.
23. It was released in China in 2005, but it was not released in Korea by 2007. It has been said that its revised version will be broadcast in 2008 in Korea.
24. Interviewed on June 19, 2006.

Chapter 14 Rescaling the Local and the National: Trans-border Production of Hong Kong TV Dramas in Mainland China

1. For example, see Amos Owen Thomas, *Imagi-nations and Borderless Television: Media, Culture and Politics across Asia* (Thousand Oaks: Sage, 2005); Anura

Goonasekera and Lee Siu Nam (eds.), *TV Without Borders: Asia Speaks Out* (Singapore: Asian Media Information and Communication Centre, 1998).

2. W. Breitung, "Transformation of a boundary regime: The Hong Kong and mainland case," *Environmental and Planning A* (2002) 34: 1749–1762.

3. Chik produced his first trans-border production, *Fight for Love (Tantanqing lianlianwu)* in 2001, but the scriptwriter is Pao Wai-chung instead of Chow.

4. For a discussion on the flexibility of the economy of space and signs, see Scott Lash and John Urry, *Economies of Signs and Space* (London: Sage, 1994).

5. Ma Kit Wai, "Complex realism," paper presented at the Hong Kong Cultural Politics Conference, the Chinese University of Hong Kong, November 2005.

6. Michael Curtin, "Media capital: Towards the study of spatial flows," *International Journal of Cultural Studies* (2003) 6 (2): 202–228.

7. Jeremy Tunstall, *Television Producers* (London: Routledge, 1993).

8. Three kinds of trans-border productions are adopted by TVB: trans-border production entirely financed by TVB (e.g *War and Beauty*); co-production by TVB and a Mainland media institution, in which TVB finances half of the total cost of production and contributes its production teams as well as actors and actresses (e.g. *Blade Heart*); and similar to the second type, but differing in that TVB contributes only the actors and actresses but not the production teams (e.g. *Twin of Brothers*, or *Da Tang Shuanglong Zhuan*). In this chapter, we focus on the first two options. The third option of providing TVB's actresses and actors for Mainland productions is not relevant to our research question of the effects of trans-border productions on Hong Kong TV producers.

9. Toby Miller et al., *Global Hollywood* (London: British Film Institute, 2001).

10. For a discussion of joint ventures in media industries, see Michael Keane, *Created in China: The Great New Leap Forward* (London: Routledge, 2007).

11. There is no official English name for this drama.

12. All trans-border productions needed to align with a Mainland broadcast station at that time.

13. Lau's popular trans-border productions such as *Plain Love (Qingnong dadi,* 1995), *Plain Love II (Cha shi guxiang nong,* 1999), *Dark Tales I & II (Liaozhaizhiyi I & II,* 1996, 1998), *Journey to the West I & II (Xiyou Ji I & II,* 1996, 1998), and *Country Spirit (Jiu shi guxiang chun,* 2001) were shot in the Guangdong and Guangxi Provinces.

14. Joseph Man Chan, "Television Development in Greater China: Structure, exports, and market formation," in John Sinclair et al. (eds.), *New Patterns in Global Television: Peripheral Vision* (Oxford: Oxford University Press, 1996), pp. 126–160; Joseph Man Chan, "Commercialization without independence: Media Development in China," in J. Cheng and M. Brosseau (eds.), *China Review 1993* (25) (Hong Kong: Chinese University Press), pp. 1–19.

15. Candice Tsang, Sandy Wong, Emily Li and Steve Pang, "CEPA and its impact on the development of the telecommunications and media industries in China and Hong Kong." Available: http://newmedia.cityu.edu.hk/cyberlaw/index24.html [accessed June 24, 2006].
16. Ibid., for a discussion of CEPA's impact on the TV industry in Hong Kong.
17. The title is expressed in Cantonese dialect instead of formal Chinese language.
18. Examples of successful productions produced by Chik and Chow include *Criminal Investigator I & II* (*O'ji shilu*, 1995, 1996), the epic drama serials *Cold Blood Warm Heart* (*Tiandi nan'er*, 1996), *Secret of the Heart* (*Tiandi haoqing*, 1998), and *At the Threshold of an Era* (*Chuang shiji*, 1999–2000).
19. John Agnew, "The dramaturgy of horizons: Geographical scale in the *Reconstruction of Italy* by the new Italian political parties, 1992–95," *Political Geography* (1997) 16 (2): 99–121.
20. Michael Billig, *Banal Nationalism* (London: Sage, 1995).
21. In this context, Allen J. Scott has provided a strong thesis on the relation between the geographic specificities of a place and the cultural products produced in that particular place in his book *The Cultural Economy of Cities: Essays on the Geography of Image-Producing Industries* (London: Sage, 2000).
22. This is similar to what Benedict Andersons contends about the effect of print journalism on the formation of national imagination in *Imagined Communities: Reflections on the Origin and Spread of Nationalism* (London: Verso, 1983).
23. Features and commentaries can be seen in Hong Kong elite papers such as the *South China Morning Post* and *Ming Pao*, and very popular Mainland weeklies such as the *Southern Weekly* (Nanfang zhoumo).

References

"2003 nian quanguo yinxiang chubanye jiben qingkuang" (An Overview of the National Audio-Visual Industry in 2003). Available: http://newmedia.gapp.gov.cn.

"2006 nian Zhongguo guangbo yingshi fazhan baogao" (Blue Book of China's Radio, Film and Television). Beijing: shehui kexue wenxian chubanshe, 2006.

Agnew, John, "The Dramaturgy of Horizons: Geographical Scale in the 'Reconstruction of Italy' by the New Italian Political Parties, 1992–95," *Political Geography*, Vol. 16, No. 2, 1997, pp. 99–121.

Allen, Robert C., *Speaking of Soap Operas*. Chapel Hill: University of North Carolina Press, 1985.

———, *To Be Continued . . . : Soap Operas around the World*. London: Routledge, 1995.

Alvarado, Manuel, ed., *Video World-Wide: An International Study*. UNESCO, London: John Libbey, 1988.

Anderson, Benedict, *Imagined Communities: Reflections on the Origin and Spread of Nationalism*. London and New York: Verso, 1983; 1991.

Ang, Ien, *Watching Dallas: Soap Opera and the Melodramatic Imagination*. London: Methuen, 1985.

———, *On Not Speaking Chinese: Living between Asia and the West*. London: Routledge, 2001.

"Anti-Hanliu Signs in China," *Yonhap News*, January 16, 2006.

Appadurai, Arjun, *Modernity at Large: Cultural Dimensions of Globalization*. Minneapolis: University of Minnesota Press, 1996.

Arthurs, Jane, "*Sex and the City* and Consumer Culture: Remediating Postfeminist Drama," *Feminist Media Studies*, Vol. 3, No. 1, 2002, pp. 83–97.

Bai, Ruoyun, "Anticorruption Television Dramas: Between Propaganda and Popular Culture in Globalizing China," Ph.D. Dissertation, University of Illinois, 2007.

Banerjee, Indrajit, "The Locals Strike Back? Media Globalization and Localization in the New Asian Television Landscape," *The International Journal for Communication Studies*, Vol. 64, No. 6, 2002, pp. 517–535.

"Baogao xianshi: neng zhuanqian de dianshiju buzu liangcheng" (Report Indicates That Only Twenty Percent of TV Drama Are Profitable). Available: www.jschina.com.cn/gb/jschina/job/node1262/userobject1ai164702.html [accessed September 27, 2005].

Barmé, Geremie, "The Graying of Chinese Culture," in Kuan Hsin-chi and Maurice Brosseau, eds., *China Review 1992*. Hong Kong: Chinese University Press, 1992.

————, *In the Red: On Contemporary Chinese Culture*. New York: Columbia University Press, 1999.

Barrett, Jane, "Women Hold up Half the Sky," in Marilyn B. Young, ed., *Women in China: Studies in Social Changes and Feminism*. Ann Arbor: Centre for Chinese Studies, The University of Michigan, 1973, pp. 34–67.

Bates, Benjamin J., "The Economics of Transborder Video," in Anura Goonasekera and Paul S. N. Lee, eds., *TV without Borders: Asia Speaks Out*. Singapore: AMIC, 1998, pp. 224–258.

"Beijing baomu shichang duandang" (Beijing Baomu Market Supply Too Low). Available: http://www.cctv.com/news.society/20031126/100610.shtml [accessed February 2004].

Chris, Berry, Review of Kam Louie's *Theorising Chinese Masculinity: Society and Gender in China*. Cambridge: Cambridge University Press, 2002. Also in *Intersections: Gender, History and Culture in the Asian Context*, No. 8, October 2002. Available: http://intersections.anu.edu.au/issue8/berry_review.html [accessed May 22, 2006].

Berry, Christopher J. and Mary Ann Farquhar, "Shadow Opera: Toward a New Archaeology of the Chinese Cinema," in Sheldon H. Lu and Emilie Y. Yeh, eds., *Chinese-Language Film: Historiography, Poetics, Politics*. Honolulu: University of Hawai'i Press, 2005, pp. 27–51.

Bhabha, Homi K., *The Location of Culture*. London: Routledge, 1994.

Bi Jiangyan and Li Hongling, "Zhongguo dianshiju shoushi shichang pandian, 2004," in *Zhongguo chuanmei chanye fazhan baogao, 2004–2005* (Report on Development of China's Media Industry, 2004–2005), pp. 273–274.

Billig, Michael, *Banal Nationalism*. London: Sage, 1995.

Breitung, W. "Transformation of a Boundary Regime: The Hong Kong and Mainland Case," *Environmental and Planning A*, Vol. 34, 2002, pp. 1749–1762.

Cai Nan, "Youjian Qionghua: Daiying 'Hongse niangzijun' beihou de gushi" (The Stories behind *The Red Detachment of Women*), *Zhongguo dianshibao,* June 12, 2006.

Cai Xiang, "1982–1992: Woguo tongsu dianshiju de huigu yu qianzhan," (1982–1992: Chinese Television Drama – Looking back and to the Future), *Dianshi yishu*, No. 4, 1993, p. 7.

Cao Guilin, *Beijing ren zai niuyue* (Beijinger in New York). Beijing: Zhongguo wenlian chuban gongsi, 1991.

"Cehua: Dianshiju gaibian, ruh chengshou 'hongse jingdian' zhizhong" (The Unbearable Heaviness of Remaking "Red Classics"). Available: http://www.people.com.cn/GB/yule/1083/2437692.html [accessed April 9, 2004].

Chan, Kara and Fanny Chan, "Information Content of Television Advertising in China: An Update," *Asian Journal of Communication*, Vol. 15, No. 1, 2005, pp. 1–15.

Chan, Joseph Man, "Commercialization without Independence: Media Development in China," in J. Cheng and M. Brosseau, eds., *China Review 1993*. Hong Kong: Chinese University Press, pp. 25: 1–19.

———, "Television Development in Greater China: Structure, Exports, and Market Formation," in John Sinclair et al., eds., *New Patterns in Global Television: Peripheral Vision*. Oxford: Oxford University Press, 1996, pp. 126–160.

Chaplin, Sarah, "Interiority and the 'Modern Woman' in Japan," in Shoma Munshi, ed., *Images of the "Modern Woman" in Asia: Global Media, Local Meanings*. London: Curzon, 2001, pp. 55–77.

Cheng Guangwei, "Ershi shiji liushi niandai de dianying yu wenhua shishang," (Film and Cultural Trends in the 1960s), *Xinyang shiyuan xuanbao,* January, 2002, pp. 96–101.

Chen Yanni, *Meiguo zhihou: 50 wei lümei renshi de guiguo zhi lu* (After the US: Return Journeys of 50 Chinese Expatriates in the US). Beijing: Zuojia chubanshe, 2000.

Chen Yiming, "Cui Yongyuan: Zai 'Hongse jingdian' qian" (Cui Yongyuan on "Red Classics"), *Nanfang zhoumo*, May 6, 2005.

Chen, Yixiu, "Dazao dianshi guanzhong: Taiwan hanju shichang xingqi zhi licheng fenxi" (Shaping the Television Audience: The Historic Analysis of the Rise of Korea Drama Market in Taiwan), Master Thesis, Graduate Institute of Communication, Tamkang University, Taiwan, June 2004.

"China Launches Satellite TV Service in Asian Region," Xinhua News Agency online report. Available: http://news.xinhuanet.com/english/2005-02/01/content_2536307.htm [accessed May 19, 2008].

"China to Curtail Audio-Visual Market." Available: http://english.people.com.cn/english/200103/15/print20010315_65055.html [accessed February 26, 2006].

"China's Cultural Trade Deficit on Rise," *People's Daily Online* (English), April 15, 2005. Available: http://www1.cei.gov.cn/ce/doc/cenzq/200504151806.htm.

"China's TV Series Fair Seeks Cooperation between Producers, Broadcasters," *People's Daily Online*, August 22, 2007. Available: http://english.people.com. cn/90001/90778/6245416.html.

Cho, Hae-Joang, "Reading the Korean Wave as a Sign of Global Shift," *Korea Journal*, Vol. 45, No. 4, 2005, pp. 147–182.

Cho, Hangjae, "Oejujungchaui gonggwa" (Merits and Demerits of Outsourcing Policy), presented at Korean Association for Broadcasting and Telecommunication Studies seminar in 2003.

Chow, Rey, *Primitive Passions: Visuality, Sexuality, Ethnography, and Contemporary Chinese Cinema*. New York: Columbia University Press, 1995.

Chua, Beng Huat, "Conceptualizing an East Asian Popular Culture," *Inter-Asia Cultural Studies*, Vol. 5, No. 2, 2004, pp. 200–221.

Cohen, Bernard C., *The Press and Foreign Policy*. Princeton, NJ: Princeton University Press, 1963.

Corner, John, "Framing the New," in Su Holmes and Deborah Jermyn, eds., *Understanding Reality Television*. London: Routledge, 2004.

Cottle, Simon, "Mediatized Rituals: Beyond Manufacturing Consent," *Media, Culture and Society*, Vol. 48, No. 3, 2006, pp. 411–432.

Croll, Elisabeth, *Changing Identities of Chinese Women: Rhetoric, Experience and Self-Perception in Twentieth-Century China*. Hong Kong: Hong Kong University Press, 1995.

Curtin, Michael, "Media Capital: Towards the Study of Spatial Flows," *International Journal of Cultural Studies,* Vol. 6, No. 2, 2003, pp. 202–228.

Dai Jinhua, *Wuzhong fengjing: 1978–1998 zhongguo dianying wenhua* (Scene in the Fog: Chinese Cinema Culture: 1978–1998). Beijing: Beijing daxue chubanshe, 2000.

———, "Behind Global Spectacle and National Image Making," *Positions: East Asia Cultures Critique*, Vol. 9, No. 1, 2001, pp. 161–186.

———, "Jiushu yu xiaofei" (Redemption and Consumption), in Wang Yuechuan, ed., *Meijie Zhexue*. Kaifeng: Henan daxue chubanshe, 2004, pp. 68–80.

Dai Qing, "Raise Eyebrows for *Raise the Red Lantern*," *Public Culture*, Vol. 5, No. 2, 1993, pp. 333–336.

Darling-Wolf, Fabienne, "Finding a Place in the Capitalist World Order: Japanese Women and the Losses (or Gains) of Western Capitalism," *Asian Journal of Women's Studies*, Vol. 9, No. 3, 2003, pp. 46–77.

Ding Wen and Xu Taling, *Dangdai Zhongguo jiating jubian* (The Great Change in the Contemporary Chinese Family). Jinan: Shanghai daxue chubanshe, 2001.

Ding, Xueliang, "The Illicit Asset Stripping of Chinese State Firms," *The China Journal,* No. 43, 2000, pp. 1–28.

Ding Zhaoqin, *Suwenxue zhong de Baogong* (Lord Bao in Popular Culture). Taipei: Weijin chubanshe, 2000.

Donald, James, *Imagining the Modern City*. London: Athlone Press, 1999.

Dovey, Jon, "Confession and the Unbearable Lightness of Factual," *Media International Australia*, No. 104, 2002, pp. 101–119.

"Drama Funds Pour In," *Korean Economic Daily*, June 15, 2006.

"DVD yasuodie chongji yinxiangye, shiyi jia faxingshang mimou duice" (Compressed DVD Threatens Audio-Visual Industry, Eleven Publishers Strategize behind Closed Door), *Beijing yule xin bao*, November 5, 2004. Available: http://tech.sina.com.cn/it/2004-11-05/0735454018.shtml [accessed August 23, 2005].

"DVD yasuodie tunshi wu cheng zhengban shichang' (Compressed DVDs Gobble up 50 Percent of Legitimate DVD Market), *Jingji cankaobao*, November 22, 2005. Available: http://finance.sina.com.cn?review/obsere/20041122/10091170728.shtml [accessed February 15, 2006].

"DVD yasuodie xianfan banfei tixi, chubanshang jujue zuochu tuoxie" (Compressed DVDs Upset Copyright Fees, Publishers Refuse to Budge), *Nanfang zhoumo*, December 23, 2004). Available: http://tech.sina.com.cn/it/2004-12-23/1204482845.shtml [accessed August 23, 2005].

Ellis, John, *Visible Fictions: Cinema, Television, Video*. London: Routledge and Kegan Paul, 1983.

Feng Yingbing, "Li Ruihuan deng lingdao tongzhi yu *Kewang* juzu tan fanrong wenyi zhi lu (Li Ruihuan and Other Leaders Talk with the Cast and Crew of *Kewang* about How to Revive Literature and Art), *Renmin Ribao*, overseas edition, January 9, 1991, p. 1.

Fewsmith, Joseph, "The Emergence of Neo-Conservatism," in *China since Tiananmen: The Politics of Transition*. Cambridge: Cambridge University Press, 2001.

Fiske, John, *Television Culture*. London: Routledge, 1987.

Fiske, John and John Hartley, *Reading Television*. London: Methuen, 1978.

Gao Jianmin, "Guanyu guochan dianshiju zhizuo de jige wenti" (Several Issues Concerning Domestic Television Drama Production), *Zhongguo guangbo yingshi*, No. 24, 2000, pp. 62–65.

Gao Youxin and Wu Wenjie, "Jiazheng fuwu zhiyehua zhu lu haiyou duo yuan" (How Far Is the Road to the Professionalisation of Domestic Work?), *Jingji ribao*, May 2, 2005.

Gitlin, Todd, "Prime-time Ideology: The Hegemonic Process in Television Entertainment," *Social Problems*, Vol. 26, 1979, pp. 251–266.

Gold, Thomas B., "Go with Your Feelings: Hong Kong and Taiwan Popular Culture in Greater China," in David Shambaugh, ed., *Greater China: The Next Superpower?* Oxford: Oxford University Press, 1995, pp. 255–274.

Gong, Ting, "Dangerous Collusion: Corruption as a Collective Venture in Contemporary China," *Communist and Post-Communist Studies*, Vol. 35, No. 1, 2002, pp. 85–103.

González, Jorge, "Understanding Telenovelas as a Cultural Front: A Complex

Analysis of a Complex Reality," *Media International Australia*, No. 106, 2003, pp. 84–93.

Goonasekera, Anura and Paul Lee, *TV without Borders: Asia Speaks Out*. Singapore: AMIC, 1998.

Gorton, Kristyn, "(Un)fashionable Feminists: The Media and *Ally McBeal*," in Stacy Gillis and Gill Howie, eds., *Third Wave Feminism*. New York: Palgrave Macmillan, 2004, pp. 154–164.

Grossberg, Lawrence, *We Gotta Get out of This Place: Popular Conservatism and Postmodern Culture*. New York: Routledge, 1992.

Guan Lianhai, "Yingping zaire fanfu xi, daxue wuhen huo haoping" (Anticorruption Dramas Made Hits; Pure as Snow Won Critical Acclaim), *Beijing wanbao*, February 20, 2001.

"Guangdong yinxiang jutou lianshou, chizi wubai wan qingjiao DVD yasuodie" (Audio-Visual Biggies in Guangdong Pooling RMB 5 Million to Stamp out HDVD Piracy), *Nanfang ribao*, November 12, 2004. Available: http://tech. sina.com.cn/it/2004-11-12/0943458185.shtml [accessed August 23, 2005].

Ha, Jongwon and Eungyeong Yang, "Dong asia television ui jiyeokhwa wa Hanliu" (Regionalization of East Asian Television and Hanliu), *Bangsong yeongu* (Broadcasting Studies), Winter, 2002, pp. 67–103.

Hall, Stuart, "Culture, Media, and the 'Ideological Effect'," in James Curran, Michael Gurevitch and Janet Woollacott, eds., *Mass Communication and Society*. London: Edward Arnold, 1977.

———, "Encoding and Decoding," in Stuart Hall, ed., *Culture, Media, Language: Working Papers in Cultural Studies, 1972–1979*. London: Hutchinson and the Centre for Contemporary Cultural Studies, University of Birmingham, 1980.

Hartley, John, "Comedy, Domestic Settings," in Horace Newcomb, ed., *Encyclopedia of Television*, second edition. New York: Dearborn, 2004, pp. 556–559.

Hayden, George A., *Crime and Punishment in Medieval Chinese Drama: Three Judge Pao Plays*. Cambridge, MA: Harvard University Press, 1978.

Herman, Edward S. and Robert McChesney, "The Rise of the Global Media," in Lisa Parks and Shanti Kumar, eds., *Planet TV*. New York: New York University Press, 2003.

Hobsbawm, Eric and Terence Ranger, *The Invention of Tradition*. Cambridge: University of Cambridge, 1983.

Hong, Junhao, *The Internationalization of Television in China: The Evolution of Ideology, Society and Media since the Reform*. Westport: Praeger, 1998.

Hooper, Beverley, *Inside Peking: A Personal Report*. London: MacDonald and Jane's, 1979.

Hoskins, Colin and Rolf Mirus, "Reasons for the US Dominance of the International Trade in Television Programmes," *Media, Culture and Society*, Vol. 10, 1988, pp. 499–515.

Hoskins, Colin, Stuart McFadyen, and Adam Finn, "International Joint Ventures in the Production of Australian Feature Films and Television Programs," *Canadian Journal of Communications*, Vol. 24, No. 1, 1999, pp. 127–139.

Hu Mei, "Yige minzu de shengsheng sisi" (Life and Death of a Nation), *Dianying dianshi yishu yianjiu*, No. 3, 1999, pp. 83–86.

Huang, Yachien, "Thinking of Manhattan, Living in Taipei: Female Pleasure in Watching *Sex and the City*," paper presented in the Third MARG Conference: Media and Identity in Asia, Miri: Curtin University of Technology Sarawak Malaysia, February 2006.

IIPA (International Intellectual Property Alliance) 2001 Special 301 Report: People's Republic of China. Available: http://www.iipa.com/rbc/2001/2001SPEC301CHINA/pdf.

IIPA 2005 Special 301 Report: People's Republic of China. Available: http://www.iipa.com/rbc/2005/2005SPEC310PRCrev.pdf.

Iwabuchi, Koichi, "Becoming Culturally Proximate: A/Scent of Japanese Idol Dramas in Taiwan," in Brian Moeran, ed., *Asian Media Productions*. London: Curzon Press, 2001, pp. 55–74.

———, *Recentring Globalization: Popular Culture and Japanese Transnationalism*. Durham, NC: Duke University Press, 2002.

———, ed., *Feeling Asian Modernities: Transnational Consumption of Japanese TV Dramas*. Hong Kong: Hong Kong University Press, 2004.

Jang, Suhyun, ed., *Junggukeun wae Hanliureul suyong hana* (Why China Receives Hanliu). Seoul: Hakkojae, 2004.

Johansson, Perry, "Selling the 'Modern Woman': Consumer Culture and Chinese Gender Politics," in Shoma Munshi, ed., *Images of the "Modern Woman" in Asia: Global Media, Local Meanings*. London: Curzon, 2001, pp. 94–122.

Jones, Andrew, *Like a Knife: Ideology and Genre in Contemporary Chinese Popular Music*. Ithaca, NY: Cornell University East Asia Program, 1992.

Jones, Dorothy B., *The Portrayal of China and India on the American Screen, 1896–1955: The Evolution of Chinese and Indian Themes, Locales, and Characters as Portrayed on the American Screen*. Cambridge, MA: Center for International Studies, Massachusetts Institute of Technology, 1955.

Keane, Michael, "Television and Moral Development in China," *Asian Studies Review*, Vol. 22, No. 4, 1998, pp. 475–504.

———, "Television, the Market and the State Development of Culture in Urban China," Ph.D. Dissertation, Griffith University, 1999.

———, "'By the Way, FUCK YOU!': Feng Xiaogang's Disturbing Television Dramas," *Continuum*, Vol. 15, No. 1, 2001, pp. 57–66.

———, "Send in the Clones: Television Formats and Content Creation in the People's Republic of China," in Stephanie H. Donald, Michael Keane and Yin Hong, eds., *Media in China: Consumption, Content and Crisis*. London: RoutledgeCurzon, 2002, pp. 80–90.

———, "Facing off on the Final Frontier: China, the WTO and National Sovereignty," *Media International Australia*, No. 105, 2002, pp. 130–146.

————, "Television Drama in China: Engineering Souls for the Market," in Timothy J. Craig and Richard King, eds., *Global Goes Local: Popular Culture in Asia*. Vancouver: UBC Press, 2002.

————, "Television Drama in China: Remaking the Market," *Media International Australia*, No. 115, 2005, pp. 82–93.

————, *Created in China: The Great New Leap Forward*. London: Routledge, 2007.

Keane, Michael, Anthony Fung, and Albert Moran, eds., *New Television, Globalization and the East Asian Cultural Imagination*. Hong Kong: Hong Kong University Press, 2007.

Kim, Hyun Mee, "Ilbon daejung munhwa ui sobiwa 'fandom' ui hyeongseong" (J-Pop Consumption and the Formation of "Fandom"), *Hanguk Munhwa Inryuhak*, Vol. 36, No. 1, 2003, pp. 149–186.

Kim, Youna, "Experiencing Globalization: Global TV, Reflexivity and the Lives of Young Korean Women," *International Journal of Cultural Studies*, Vol. 8, No. 4, 2005, pp. 446–463.

Klopfenstein, Bruce C., "The Diffusion of the VCR in the United States," in Mark R. Levy, ed., *The VCR Age: Home Video and Mass Communication*. Thousand Oaks, CA: Sage, 1989.

Kong, Shuyu, *Consuming Literature: Bestsellers and the Commercialization of Literary Production in Contemporary China*. Stanford: Stanford University Press, 2005.

"Korea Used to be China's Dependency? KBS's Apology," *Joongang Ilbo*, May 23, 2004.

"Lack of Savvy Behind Cultural Trade Deficit," *China Daily*, April 19, 2005.

Lash, Scott and John Urry, *Economies of Signs and Space*. London: Sage, 1994.

Lee, Chin-Chuan, ed., *Power, Money and Media: Communication Patterns and Bureaucratic Control in Cultural China*. Evanston, IL: Northwestern University Press, 2000.

Lee, Haiyan, "Nannies for Foreigners: The Enchantment of Chinese Womanhood in the Age of Millennial Capitalism," *Public Culture*, Vol. 18, No. 3, pp. 507–529.

Li, Conghua, *China: The Consumer Revolution*. New York: John Wiley and Son Inc., 1998.

Li Xiaolong, "Biaoxian laobaixing shenghuo de bianqian: 'Yinian you yinian' daoyan tan" (Representing the Changes in Ordinary People's Lives: Director's Notes on *Year after Year*), *Dianying yishu*, No. 1, 2000, pp. 81–83.

Li Xiaoming, "Zuotian yu geshi: 'Yinian you yinian' chuangzuo suixiang" (Yesterday and Another World: Notes on the Creation of *Year after Year*), *Zhongguo dianshi*, No. 12, 1999, pp. 19–21.

Li Yan, "Xinban 'Hongse Niangzijun' gen hongse bu tiebian" (The New Version of *The Red Detachment of Women* Has Nothing to Do with "Red"), *Beijing qingnian bao*, July 3, 2006.

"Liangan dianshi jiaoliu de bozhe" (An Obstacle between Taiwan and China TV Communication," *Mingsheng ribao*, March 18, 2002.

Lin, Eric, "Badiandang lianxuju xiaozhuan" (The Stories of Prime Time), *Taiwan Panorama Magazine*, Vol. 25, No. 1, January 2000. Available: http://www. sinorama.com.tw.

Lin Qi, "Bie rang gao piaojia dangzhu guanzhong" (Don't Let High Ticket Price Keep the Audience out of Movie Theaters). Available: http://news. xinhuanet.com/focus/2006-01/09/content_4028295.htm [accessed August 14, 2007].

Lin Yutang, *Moment in Peking: A Novel of Contemporary Chinese Life*. New York: The John Day Company, 1939.

Liu Jianghua, "Zhang Henshui's Descendent Comment on the Story of a Nobel Family: Idol Actors Hard to Make Either Side Happy." Jin Yang Net. Available: http://ent.sina.com.cn/m/2003-04-11/1239144362.html [accessed July 24, 2007].

Liu, Lydia H., *What's Happened to Ideology? Transnationalism, Postsocialism, and the Study of Global Media Culture*. Durham, NC: Asian/Pacific Studies Institute, Duke University, 1998.

Liu, Xiancheng, *Transborder Crossing: The Regional Competition of Chinese Media Industries*. Taipei: *Asia-Pacific Press*, 2004.

Liu, Youli and Yixiang Chen, "Cloning, Adaptation, Import, and Originality: Taiwan in the Global Television Format Business," in Albert Moran and Michael Keane, eds., *Television across Asia: Television Industries, Program Formats and Globalization*. London: Routledge, 2004, pp. 67–72.

Lopez, Ana, "The Melodrama in Latin America," in Marcia Landy, ed., *Imitations of Life: A Reader on Film and Television Drama*. Detroit, MC: Wayne State University Press, 1991.

Lu, Sheldon H., "Postmodernity, Popular Culture, and the Intellectual: A Report on Post-Tiananmen China," *Boundary 2*, 23, No. 2, summer 1996, pp. 139–169.

———, "National Cinema, Cultural Critique, Transnational Capital: The Films of Zhang Yimou," in Sheldon H. Lu, ed., *Transnational Chinese Cinemas: Identity, Nationhood, Gender*. Honolulu: University of Hawai'i Press, 1997.

———, "Soap Opera in China: The Transnational Politics of Visuality, Sexuality, and Masculinity," *Cinema Journal*, Vol. 40, No. 1, 2000, pp. 25–47.

———, *China, Transnational Visuality, Global Postmodernity*. Stanford, CA: Stanford University Press, 2001.

Lull, James, *China Turned On: Television, Reform and Resistance*. London: Routledge, 1991.

———, *Media, Communication, and Culture: A Global Approach*. New York: Columbia University Press, 1995.

Luo, Canyin, "Competing Discourses on Gender Model: Discourse Analysis on

Reports of Adult Film Event in the Newspaper," *Taiwan Social Studies Quarterly*, No. 25, 1997, pp. 169–208.

Luo Yuanyuan, "Yangshi daxi shoushilü Liangjian duokui" (*Draw Your Sword Drew the Highest Ratings of All CCTV Television Dramas*), *Huashang bao*, December 5, 2005.

Ma, Eric Kit-wai, "Rethinking Media Studies: The Case of China," in James Curran and Myung-jin Park, eds., *De-Westernizing Media Studies*. London and New York: Routledge, 2000, pp. 21–34.

———, "Complex Realism", paper presented in the *Hong Kong Cultural Politics Conference*, Chinese University of Hong Kong, November, 2005.

Marchetti, Gina, *Romance and the "Yellow Peril": Race, Sex, and Discursive Strategies in Hollywood Fiction*. Berkeley: University of California Press, 1993.

Mattelart, Armand, *Multinational Corporations and the Control of Culture*. Brighton: Harvest Press, 1979.

McFadyen, Stuart, Colin Hoskins, and Adam Finn, "The Effect of Cultural Differences on the International Co-Production of Television and Feature Films," *Canadian Journal of Communications*, Vol. 23, No. 4, 1998, pp. 523–538.

McLaren, Anne E., "Chinese Cultural Revivalism: Changing Gender Constructions in the Yangtze River Delta," in Krishna Sen and Maila Stivens, eds., *Gender and Power in Affluent Asia*. London and New York: Routledge, 1998, pp. 195–221.

McRobbie, Angela, "Postfeminism and Popular Culture," *Feminist Media Studies*, Vol. 4, No. 3, 2004, pp. 255–263.

Meng, Yue, "Bai Mao Nü yanbian de qishi" (Inspirations from the Evolution of the White-Haired Girl), in Xiaobing Tang, ed., *Zai Jiedu: Dazhong wenyi yu yishi xingtai*. Hong Kong: Oxford University Press, 1993, pp. 68–89.

Miller, Toby, et al., *Global Hollywood*. London: British Film Institute, 2001.

Min Yunshi, "'Boda' de dizhi daoban zhi lu" (Boda's Anti-Piracy Strategy), in Wang Yongzhang, ed., *Zhongguo wenhua chanye dianxing anli xuanbian* (Chinese Cultural Industry: Typical Cases). Beijing: Beijing daxue chubanshe, 2003.

Mishra, Pankaj, "China's New Leftist," *New York Times*, December 15, 2006. Available: http://www.nytimes.com/2006/10/15/magazine/15leftist.html [accessed April 15, 2007].

Montgomery, Lucy and Michael Keane, "Learning to Love the Market: Copyright, Culture and China," in Pradip Thomas and Jan Servaes, eds., *Intellectual Property Rights and Communications in Asia: Conflicting Traditions*. Delhi: Sage, 2006, pp. 130–148.

Morley, David, *Family Television: Cultural Power and Domestic Leisure*. London: Comedia, 1986.

Morley, David and Kevin Robins, *Spaces of Identity: Global Media, Electronic Landscapes and Cultural Boundaries*. London: Routledge, 1995.

Mouffe, Chantal, "Hegemony and New Political Subjects: Toward a New Concept of Democracy," in Cary Nelson and Lawrence Grossberg, eds., *Marxism and the Interpretation of Culture*. Urbana: University of Illinois Press, 1988, pp. 89–101.

Mulvey, Laura, "Visual Pleasure and Narrative Cinema," *Screen*, Vol. 16, No. 3, 1975, pp. 6–18.

Munshi, Shoma, "Marvellous Me: The Beauty Industry and the Construction of the 'Modern' Indian Woman," in Shoma Munshi, ed., *Images of the 'Modern Woman' in Asia: Global Media, Local Meanings*. London: Curzon, 2001, pp. 78–94.

"Nanhai chahuo jinnian zui da pi feifa yinxiang zhipin" (The Largest Seizure of Pirated Audio-Visual Products in Nanhai This Year). Available: http://newmedia.gapp.gov.cn/Main/Articlex.aspx?cateid=H06&artid=0000003416 [accessed February 15, 2006].

Newcomb, Horace, " 'This Is Not Al Dente': *Sopranos* and the New Meaning of 'Television'," in Horace Newcomb, ed., *Television: The Critical View*, seventh edition. New York: Oxford University Press, 2006, pp. 561–578.

Newcomb, Horace and Paul Hirsch, "Television as a Cultural Forum," in Horace Newcomb, ed., *Television: The Critical View*. New York: Oxford University Press, 2000.

Ning Ling, "Lanmu gongsihua tuisheng da gaige: yangshi dianshiju changtu chanyehua" (Professionalizing Programming Promotes a Great Revolution: CCTV's Attempt to Make an Industry from Television Drama), Xinhua News Agency. Available: http://news.xinhuanet.com/newsmedia/2004-02/02/content_1294465.htm [accessed May 19, 2008].

Ong, Aihwa, *Flexible Citizenship: The Cultural Logics of Transnationality*. Durham, DC: Duke University Press, 1999.

Ou-Yang Changlin, "Dianshiju 'Huanzhu gege' shichanghua yunzuo shimo" (The Marketing Manipulation of "Princess Huangzhu"). Available: http://www.people.com.cn/ [accessed July 18, 2003].

Ownby, David, "Approximations of Chinese Bandits: Perverse Rebels, Romantic Heroes, or Frustrated Bachelors?", in Susan Brownell and Jeffery N. Wasserstrom, eds., *Chinese Feminities, Chinese Masculinities: A Reader*. Berkeley/Los Angeles: University of California Press, 2002, pp. 226–250.

Pang, Laikwan, *Cultural Control and Globalization in Asia: Copyright, Piracy, and Cinema*. London and New York: Routledge, 2006.

Park, Jaebok, *Hanliu, geullobal sidae ui munhwa gyungjaengryuk* (Hanliu: A Cultural Power in the Age of Globalization). Seoul: Samsung Economic Research Institute, 2005.

"'Pinzui zhang damin de xingfu shenghuo' juzu yu wangyou jiaoliu lu" (Interview with the *Happy Life* Crew), *People's Daily Online*. Available: http://www.people.com.cn/ wsrmlt/jbft/2000/juzu.html.

"Profile of the Audio and Video Market of China." Available: http://www.chinaembassy.org.pl/pol/wh/Nw/t129222.htm [accessed February 26, 2006].

Qiu Hongjie, "Zhongguo wenyi hanwei 'Hongse jingdian' " (Chinese Art Circles Defend "Red Classics"). Available: http://news.xinhuanet.com/newscenter/ 2004-05/23/content_1485678.htm [accessed April 10, 2006].

Qu Chunjin and Ying Zhu, *Zhongmei dianshi bijiao yanjiu* (A Comparative Anthology of Chinese and US Television Research). Shanghai: Sanlian chubanshe, 2005.

Rajagopal, Arvind, "Mediating Modernity: Theorizing Reception in a Non-Western Society," in James Curran and Myung-Jin Park, eds., *De-Westernizing Media Studies*. New York: Taylor and Francis, Inc., 2000, pp. 293–304.

"Regulations on the Administration of Audio-Visual Products" (No. 341 Order of the State Council of the People's Republic of China), in Jesse T. H. Chang, Isabelle I. H. Wan and Philip Qu, eds., *China's Media and Entertainment Law*, Vol. 1. Hong Kong: TransAsia Publishing, 2003.

Ren Yan, "Moment in Peking Is On: Comparison of New and Old Versions Causes Controversies," *Beijing yule xinbao*. Available: http://ent.sina.com.cn/ v/m/2005-10-31/0144880460.html [accessed July 24, 2007].

Renaud, Jean-Luc and Barry L. Litman, "Changing Dynamics of the Overseas Marketplace for TV Programming," *Telecommunication Policy*, Vol. 9, No. 4, 1985, pp. 245–61.

Rofel, Lisa, "'Yearnings': Televisual Love and Melodramatic Politics in Contemporary China," *American Ethnologist*, Vol. 21, No. 4 (1994), pp. 700–722.

————, "The Melodrama of National Identity in Post-Tiananmen in China," in Robert C. Allen, ed., *To Be Continued . . . : Soap Operas around the World*. London: Routledge, 1995, pp. 301–320.

————, *Other Modernities: Gendered Yearnings in China after Socialism*. Berkeley: University of California Press, 1999.

Root, Hilton, "Corruption in China: Has It Become Systemic?" *Asian Survey*, Vol. 36, No. 8, 1996, pp. 741–757.

Samarajiwa, Rohan, "Third-World Entry to the World Market in News: Problems and Possible Solutions," *Media, Culture and Society*, Vol. 6, No. 2, 1984, pp. 119–136.

Scannell, Paddy, "Radio Times: The Temporal Arrangements of Broadcasting in the Modern World," in Philip Drummond and Richard Paterson, eds., *Television and Its Audience*. London: British Film Institute, 1988.

Schiller, Herbert I., "Transnational Media and National Development," in Kaarle Nordenstreng and Herbert I. Schiller, eds., *National Sovereignty and International Communication*. Westport, CN: Ablex, 1979.

Shim, Doobo, "Hybridity and the Rise of Korean Popular Culture in Asia," *Media, Culture and Society*, Vol. 28, No. 1, 2006, pp. 25–44.

"Shoujie Beijing yinxiangjie shiyue di juban chaodi jiawei zhanxiao zhengban yinxiang zhipin" (The First Audio-Visual Festival Will Sell Legitimate Audio-Visual Products at Super Low Prices at the End of October). Available: http://newmedia.gapp.gov.cn/EJurnal/Articlex.aspx?cateid=E14&artid =0000003341 [accessed February 15, 2006].

Schudson, Michael, "Culture and the Integration of National Societies," *International Social Science Journal*, No. 46, 1994, pp. 63–81.

Seno, Alexandra A., "High-Ranking Hit," *Asiaweek* Online. Available: www.asiaweek.com/asiaweek/99/0226/feat8.html [accessed February 26, 1999].

Sinclair, John, "Mexico, Brazil and the Latin World," in John Sinclair, Elizabeth Jacka and Stuart Cunningham, eds., *New Patterns in Global Television: Peripheral Vision*. Oxford: Oxford University Press, 1996.

———, "The Business of International Broadcasting: Cultural Bridges and Barriers," *Asian Journal of Communication*, Vol. 7, No. 1, 1997, pp. 137–155.

Sinclair, John, Audrey Yue, Gay Hawkins, Kee Pookong, and Josephin Fox, "Chinese Cosmopolitanism and Media Use," in Stuart Cunningham and John Sinclair, eds., *Floating Lives: The Media and Asian Diasporas*. Lanham: Rowman and Littlefield, 1997.

Sinclair, John, Elizabeth Jacka and Stuart Cunningham, "Global and Regional Dynamics of International Television Flows," in Daya Kishan Thussu, ed., *Electronic Empires: Global Media and Local Resistance*. London: Arnold, 1998, pp. 179–192.

Sohn, Amy, *Sex and the City: Kiss and Tell*. New York: Pocket Books, 2002.

Solinger, Dorothy, *Contesting Citizenship in Urban China: Peasant Migration, the State, and the Logic of the Market*. Berkeley, CA: University of California Press, 1999.

Song Wenjuan, "2007 nian Zhongguo dianshiju shichang: yin jinlai zou chuqu" (TV Dramas Marketing in 2007: Import and Export), *Zhongguo guangbo yingshi*, March 28, 2007.

Spence, Jonathan, *The Search for Modern China*. New York: W.W. Norton and Co., 1990.

Straubhaar, Joseph, "Beyond Media Imperialism: Asymmetrical Interdependence of Television Programming in the Dominican Republic," *Journal of Communication*, Vol. 41, No. 5, 1991, pp. 53–69.

Sun, Wanning, "A Chinese in the New World: Television Dramas, Global Cities and Travels to Modernity," *Inter-Asia Cultural Studies*, Vol. 2, No. 1, 2001, pp. 81–94.

———, "The Invisible Entrepreneur: The Case of Anhui Women," *Provincial China*, Vol. 7, No. 2, 2002, pp. 178–195.

———, "Semiotic Over-Determination or Indoctri-tainment: Television, Citizenship, and the Olympic Games," in Stephanie Donald, Michael Keane and Yin Hong, eds., *Media in China: Consumption, Content and Crisis*. London: RoutledgeCurzon, 2002, pp. 116–127.

Sun Xianghui, Huang Wei, and Hu Zhengrong, "2004 nian Zhongguo guangdian chanye fazhan baogao," in Cui Baoguo, ed., *Zhonggo chuanmei chanye fazhan baogao, 2004–2005* (Report on Development of China's Media Industry: 2004–2005). Beijing: Zhongguo sheke wenxian chubanshe, 2005.

Sun, Yan, *Corruption and Market in Contemporary China.* Ithaca, NY: Cornell University Press, 2004.

Tao Dongfeng, "Hougeming shidai de geming wenhua" (Revolutionary Culture in a Post-revolutionary Era). Available: http://www.frchina.net/data/personArticle.php?id=3651 [accessed February 8, 2006].

Thomas, Amos Owen, *Imagi-nations and Borderless Television: Media, Culture and Politics across Asia.* New Delhi; Thousand Oaks, CA: Sage Publications, 2005.

Thorburn, David, "Television Melodrama," in Horace Newcomb, ed., *Television: The Critical View,* seventh edition. New York: Oxford University Press, 2006, pp. 438–450.

Thussu, Daya Kishan, *International Communication: Continuity and Change.* London: Arnold, 2000.

"Ting daoyan shang jing jiangshu 'wulin waizhuan' chenggong de mijue" (Listen to How Director Shang Jing Tells the Secret Weapons of Tales of Jianghu). Available: http://ent.sina.com.cn [accessed January 25, 2006].

Tinic, Serra, "Going Global: International Co-productions and the Disappearing Domestic Audience in Canada," in Lisa Parks and S. Kumar, eds., *Planet TV: A Global Television Reader.* New York: New York University Press, 2003, pp. 169–186.

Tsang, Candice, Sandy Wong, Emily Li and Steve Pang, "CEPA and Its Impact on the Development of the Telecommunications and Media Industries in China and Hong Kong." Available: http://newmedia.cityu.edu.hk/cyberlaw/index24.html [accessed on June 24, 2006].

Tunstall, Jeremy, *Television Producers.* London: Routledge, 1993.

USTR 2006 Special 301 Report. Available: http://ustr.gov/assets/Document_Library/Reports_Publications/2006/2006/_Special_301_Review/asset_upload-file473-9336.pdf?ht= [accessed May 23, 2006].

Vink, Nico, *The Telenovela and Emancipation: A Study of Television and Social Change in Brazil.* Amsterdam: Royal Tropical Institute, 1988.

"Vogue Cruises into China," China Economic Net. Available: http://en.ce.cn/Life/entertainment/fashion&beauty/EFBn/200509/10/t20050910_4645651.shtml.

Waisbord, Silvio, "Mc TV: Understanding the Global Popularity of Television Formats," *Television and New Media,* Vol. 5, No. 4, 2004, pp. 359–381.

Wang, Ban, *The Sublime Figure of History: Aesthetics and Politics in Twentieth Century China.* Stanford: Stanford University Press, 1997.

Wang, Chaohua, *One China, Many Paths.* London: Verso, 2003.

Wang, Fei-ling, *Organizing Through Division and Exclusion: China's Hukou System.* Stanford: Stanford University Press, 2005.

Wang, Hui, "Dangdai zhongguo de sixiang zhuangkuang yu xiandaixing" (The Circumstance of Contemporary Chinese Thought and the Problem of Modernity), *Wenyi zhengming,* No. 11, 1998, p. 20.

————, "The 1989 Social Movement and the Historical Roots of China's Neoliberalism," in Hui Wang, Theodore Huters and R. Karl, eds., *China's New Order: Society, Politics, and Economy in Transition.* Cambridge, MA: Harvard University, 2003.

Wang Ju, "Zhongguo yinxiangye de chanye guimo yu jiegou" (The Scope and Structure of China's Audio-Visual Industry), in *Zhongguo wenhua chenye fazhan baogao, 2003* (Report on Development of China's Cultural Industry, 2003). Beijing: Shehui kexue wenxian chubanshe, 2003.

————, "Zhongguo yinxiangye jingzhengli fenxi" (Analysis of the Competitiveness of China's Recording and Video Industry), in Qi Shuyu, ed., *Zhongguo wenhua chanye guoji jingzhengli baogao* (Report on International Competitiveness of China's Cultural Industry). Beijing: Shehui kexue wenxian chubanshe, 2004.

Wang Lanzhu, ed., *Zhongguo dianshi shoushi nianjian, 2003* (Yearbook of TV Reception in China: 2003). Beijing: Beijing guangbo xueyuan, 2003.

Wang Lijuan, "Guanyu lishiju zouhong de sikao" (Thoughts on the Popularity of Historical Dramas), *Zhongguo dianshi*, No. 10, 2002, pp. 18–24.

Wang, Shuren, *Framing Piracy: Globalization and Film Distribution in Greater China.* New York: Rowman and Littlefield, 2003.

Wang Yi, "Mingdai tongsu xiaoshuo zhong qingguan gushi de xingsheng jiqi wenhua yiyi" (Clean-Official Stories in Popular Novels of the Ming Period and Their Cultural Meanings), *Wenxue yichan*, No. 5, 2000, pp. 67–80.

"Wanneng DVD youmeiyou hefahua tujing" (Is There a Way to Legitimize the Super DVD?). Available: http://www.njnews.cn/n/ca571464.htm [accessed August 23, 2005].

Waterman, David and Everett Rogers, "The Economics of Television Program Production and Trade in Far East Asia," *Journal of Communication*, Vol. 44, No. 3, pp. 89–111.

Wedeman, Andrew, "The Intensification of Corruption in China," *The China Quarterly*, No. 180, 2004, pp. 895–921.

Wei Hui, *Shanghai Baby*. London: Robinson, 2001.

"White Babe in Beijing." Available: http://www.goldsea.com/Features2/ Dewoskin/dewoskin.html [accessed October 10, 2005].

"Will Hanliu Be Blocked by the Great Wall of China?" *Munhwa Ilbo*, June 21, 2006.

Williams, Raymond, *The Long Revolution*. London: Chatto and Windus, 1961.

World Trade Organization, "Audiovisual Services: Background Notes by the Secretariat," June 15, 1998. Available: http://www.wto.org/english/tratop_e/ serv_e/w40.doc.

Wu Zhong, "Divorce, Chinese Style," *Asia Times Online*, July 18, 2007. Available: http://www.atimes.com/atimes/China/IG18Ad01.html.

Yang Jie, "Jiazheng ye chengwei zhongguo xina laodongli de zhongyao qudao" (Domestic Work Is Becoming an Important Means of Absorbing Labour).

Available: http://www.cctv.com/news/financial/20020612/274.html [accessed May 2005].

Yang Lei, "DVD bofangji de zuotian, jintian he mingtian" (The History of DVD Players in China: Yesterday, Today and Tomorrow). Available: http://tom.yesky.com/data/279/2500779.shtml [accessed August 14, 2007].

Yang, Mayfair, "From Gender Erasure to Gender Difference: State Feminism, Consumer Sexuality, and Women's Public Sphere in China," in *Spaces of Their Own: Women's Public Sphere in Transnational China*. Minneapolis: Minnesota University Press, 1999, pp. 35–68.

Yang Wenyong and Xie Xizhang, eds., *Kewang chongjibo* (The Shockwave of Kewang). Beijing: Guangming ribao chubanshe, 1991.

"Yasuo DVD dong le shui de nailao, xinjin jishu he bu weimin fuwu" (Whose Interest Did the HDVD Harm, Why Not Use Advanced Technology to Serve the People?). Available: http://www.jrj.com.cn/NewsRead/Detail.asp?NewsID=962673 [accessed August 23, 2005].

"Yasuo DVD zhongchuang zhengban shichang, dianshiju banquanfei kuangdie yiban" (Compressed DVD Ravages Legitimate Market, TV Drama Copyright Fees Plunge by 50 Percent), *Beijing yule xin bao*, November 2, 2004. Available: http://tech.sina.com.cn/it/2004-11-02/0909452054.shtml [accessed August 23, 2005].

Yatsko, Pamela, "Inside Looking Out: Books and TV Dramas about Life Overseas Reflect Existing Chinese Biases," *Far Eastern Economic Review*, Vol. 159, No. 15, 1996, p. 58.

Yin Hong, "Meaning, Production, Consumption: The History and Reality of Television Drama in China," in Stephanie Hemelryk Donald, Michael Keane and Yin Hong, eds., *Media in China: Consumption, Content and Crisis*. London: RoutledgeCurzon, 2002.

———, "Zhongguo dianshiju yishu chuantong," (The Artistic Tradition of Chinese Television Drama), in Qu Chunjing and Ying Zhu, eds., *Zhongmei dianshiju bijiao yanjiu* (Comparative Research on Television Drama in China and America). Shanghai: Sanlian chubanshe, 2004.

———, "Quanqiuhua beijing xia Zhongguo yinxiangye de fazhan celue chutan" (Preliminary Analysis of the Development Strategies of China's Audio-Visual Industry in the Age of Globalization), in Liu Yuzhu, ed., *Zhongguo wenhua shichang fazhan baogao, 2004* (Report on the Development of China's Cultural Market, 2004). Beijing: Xinhua chubanshe, 2004.

"Ying Da: dianshi gaibian le 300 nian xinshang xiju de fangshi" (Television Changes the 300-Year Tradition of Comedy), *Nanfang zhoumo*, December 19, 2002.

Ying Jiang, "Nuren xing de fengfan: bieguanyi yuwangchengshi de ming" (Capitalize on Women and Sex, Do Not Use the Name of *Sex and the City*). Available: http://ent.tom.com/1030/1587/2003821-52458.html [accessed August 22, 2003].

"Yinxiang shichang huanjing quxiang haozhuan, dan daoban chuxian xin miaotou" (Audio-Visual Market Environment Improves, But New Trend in Piracy Appears). Available: http://newmedia.gapp.gov.cn/Audio-visual/Articlex.aspx?cateid=A14&artid=0000003240 [accessed February 15, 2006].

Yoon, Jaesik and Yungyeong Jung, *Saeggye bangsongyeongsang contents yutong business* (World Distribution Business of Broadcasting Contents). Seoul: Korean Broadcasting Institute, 2002.

Yoon, Taejin, "Daejung munhwa ui saengsangujo" (Production Structure of Popular Culture), *Bangsong munhwa yeongu* (Studies of Broadcasting Culture), Vol. 17, No. 2, 2005, pp. 9–44.

You Kou, "Shi hoaxing tanlianai haishi hoaxing jiaren?" (Is It Falling in Love or Falling for Marriage?). Available: http://life.people.com.cn/BIG5/8223/50801/50802 /3671255.html [accessed September 2, 2005].

Yu Jiao'Ao, "Yifenwei'er kan Dazhaimen" (Objectively Evaluate Grand Mansion Gate). Available: http://www.people.com.cn/GB/wenyu/64/130/20010519/468831.html [accessed June 16, 2006].

Yu Jinglu, "The Structure and Function of Chinese Television 1978–89," in Chin-Chuan Lee, ed., *Voices of China: The Interplay of Politics and Journalism.* New York: Guildford Press, 1990.

Yu Shu, Chen Minghui, and Li Li, "Zhongguo haiwaiju shichang bu leguan" (No Optimism for China's Overseas Drama Markets), *Yangcheng wanbo,* October 31, 2005.

Yuan Fang, "Cong quan ma pao di dao jing geng xi zuo: jinnian woguo dianshi meiti bianhua saomiao ji zhanwang" (From Territorialization to Careful Cultivation: Development and Trends in Chinese Television Industry in Recent Years), in *Zhongguo chuanmei chanye fazhan baogao, 2004–2005* (Report on Development of China's Media Industry, 2004–2005), pp. 273–274.

Zha, Jianying, *China Pop: How Soap Operas, Tabloids, and Bestsellers Are Transforming a Culture.* New York: New Press, 1995.

Zhan, Chang-Yu, "Xiangkan 'liuxing huayuan', dalu guanzhong ke dei dengyixia" (The China Audiences Have to Wait Awhile to See Meteor Garden), *Lianhe ribao,* March 11, 2002.

Zhang Jiabing, "Zou xiang shidai zui qiangyin – qianyi zhuxuanlü yu dianshiju" (Strike up the Music of the Times: On the Main Melody and Television Drama), *Zhongguo dianshi,* No. 9, 1994, pp. 2–5.

Zhang Jianzhen, "Yingxiang xianshi: meijie shidai de qingjing xiju" (Cinematic Reality: Situation Comedy in an Age of Media), *Xiinwen yu chuanbo yanjiu,* No. 2, 2002, p. 58.

Zhang Yiwu, "Quanqiuxing houzhimin yujing zhong de Zhang Yimou" (Zhang Yimou in the Global Postcolonial Context), *Dangdai dianying,* Vol. 54, No. 3, 1993, pp. 18–25.

"Zhanwang 2006: yinxiang hangye huhuan chunjie yundong' (Looking Ahead to 2006: Audio-Visual Industry Calls for Regulatory Measures). Available:

http://newmedia.gapp.gov.cn/Main/Articlex.aspx?cateid=H22&artid= 0000003571 [accessed February 15, 2006].

Zhao, Bin, "Popular Family Television and Party Ideology: The Spring Festival Eve Happy Gathering," *Media, Culture and Society*, Vol. 20, No. 1, pp. 43–58.

———, "Mouthpiece or Money-Spinner? The Double Life of Chinese Television in the Late 1990s," *International Journal of Cultural Studies*, Vol. 2, No. 3, 1999, pp. 291–306.

Zhao Yong, "Shui Zai Shouhu 'Hongse jingdian': Cong "Hongse jingdian" ju gaibian kan guanzhongde "zhengzhi wuyishi'" (Who Is Guarding the "Red Classics": An Analysis of the Audiences' "Political Consciousness" through the "Red Classics" Remakes), *Nanfang wentan*, No. 6, 2005, pp. 36–39.

Zhao, Yuezhi, "From Commercialization to Conglomeration: The Transformation of the Chinese Press within the Orbit of the Party State," *Journal of Communication*, Vol. 50, No. 2, pp. 3–25.

———, "The State, the Market and Media Control in China," in Pradip Thomas and Zahoram Nain, eds., *Who Owns the Media: Global Trends and Local Resistance*. London and New York: Zed Books, 2004, pp. 179–212.

"Zhengban HDVD nan zu daobao hengxing" (Legal HDVD Cannot Stop Rampant Circulation of Pirated HDVD). Available: http://www.morningpost.com.cn/ articleview/2006-1-27/article_view_6130.htm [accessed February 15, 2006].

Zhong Yibin and Huang Wangnan, *Zhongguo dianshi yishu fazhanshi* (The History of Chinese Television Arts). Zhejiang: Zhejiang renmin chubanshe, 1994.

Zhong Yong, "Duokui wang qiming shi zai niuyue" (Luckily Wang Qiming Is in New York), *Dushu*, No. 5, 1995, pp. 85–87.

Zhongguo dianshiju baogao 2002–2003 (China Television Drama Report, 2002–2003). Beijing: Shanghai dianshijie zuweihui; yangshi suofurui, 2003.

Zhongguo dianshiju shichang baogao 2003–04 (Report on Chinese Television Drama Market, 2003–04). Beijing: Huaxia chubanshe, 2004.

Zhongguo hangye fazhan baogao, 2004: chuanmeiye (China Industry Development Report, 2004: Media). Beijing: Zhongguo jingji chubanshe, 2004.

"Zhonggong zhongyang jueding dui chen liangyu tongzhi yanzhong weiji wenti li'an jiancha" (The Chinese Communist Party Center Starts to Investigate into the Serious Discipline Violation of Comrade Chen Liangyu), *Renmin ribao*, September 25, 2006.

Zhou, Raymond, "Why Desperate Housewives Flopped in China." Available: http://www.chinadaily.com.cn/english/doc/2005-12/31/content_508261. htm, December 31, 2005.

Zhu, Ying, "*Yongzheng Dynasty* and Chinese Primetime Television Drama," *Cinema Journal*, Vol. 44, No. 4, 2005, pp. 3–17.

———, *Television in Post-Reform China: Serial Dramas, Confucian Leadership, and Global Television Market*. London, Routledge, 2008.

Index

Cited dramas